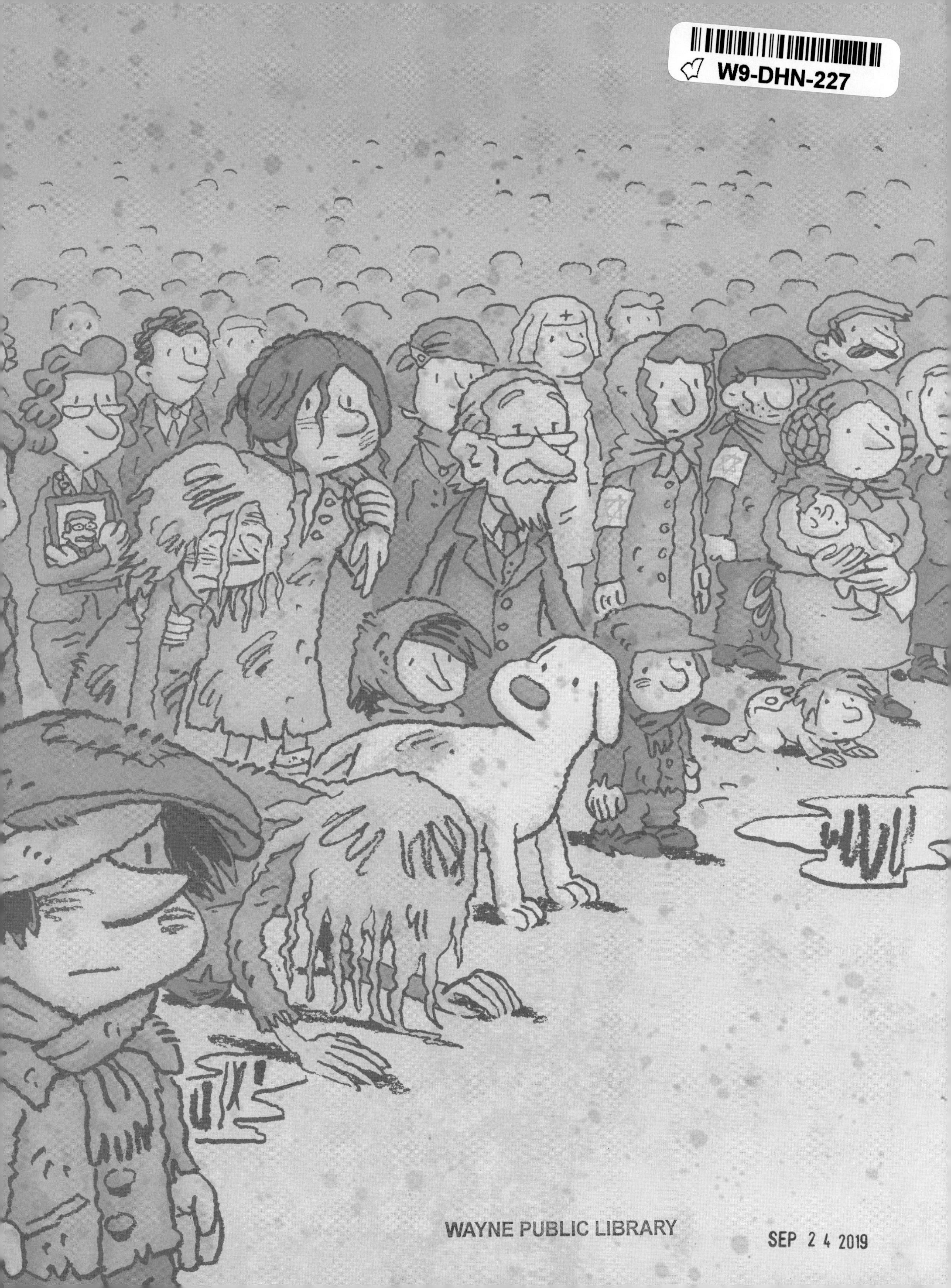

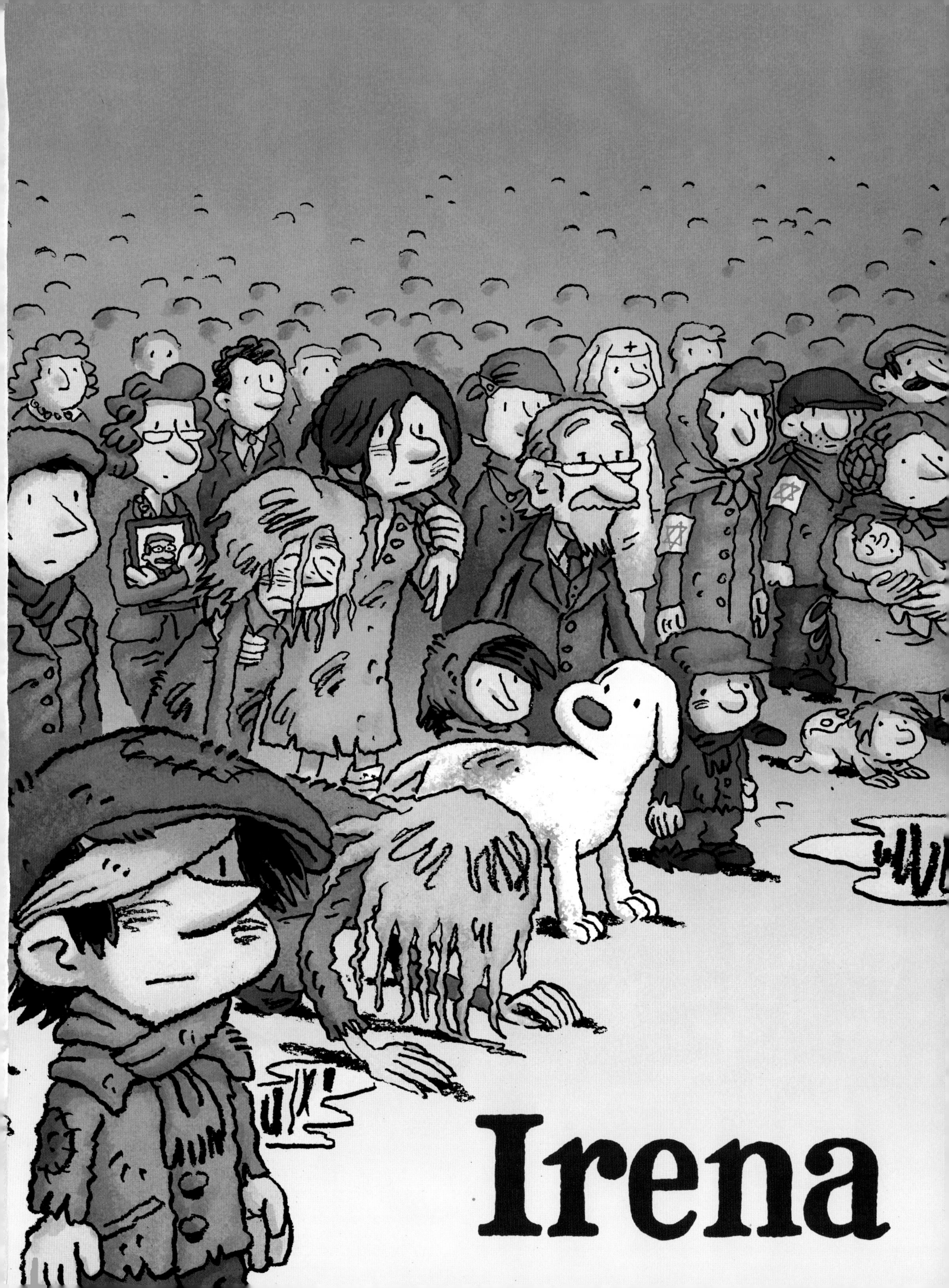

Irena

WRITTEN BY
JEAN-DAVID MORVAN AND SÉVERINE TRÉFOUËL

ILLUSTRATED BY
DAVID EVRARD

COLORED BY
WALTER

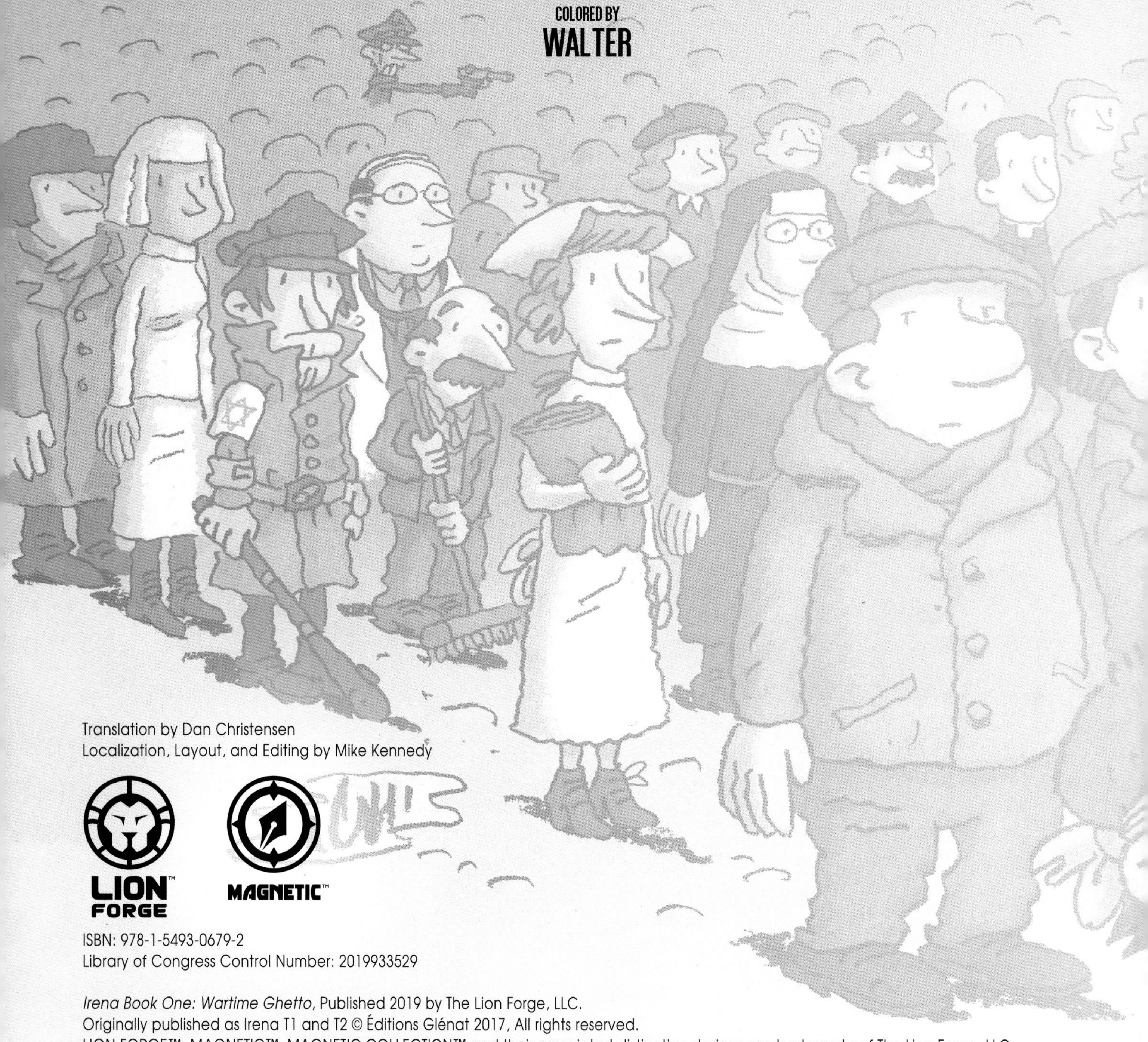

Translation by Dan Christensen
Localization, Layout, and Editing by Mike Kennedy

LION FORGE™ MAGNETIC™

ISBN: 978-1-5493-0679-2
Library of Congress Control Number: 2019933529

Irena Book One: Wartime Ghetto, Published 2019 by The Lion Forge, LLC.

Printed in China.

10 9 8 7 6 5 4 3 2 1

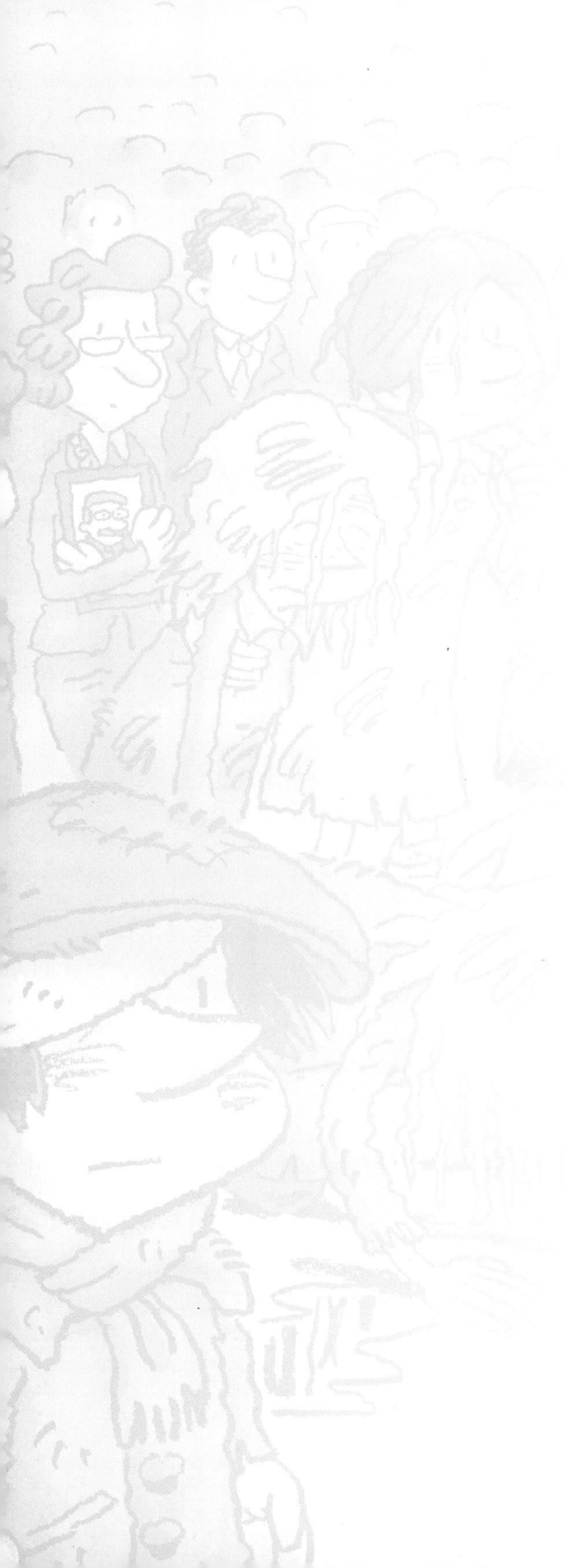

Irena Sendlerowa really existed.

Fascinated by her story, we tried to read everything that existed on her, often in a language we couldn't understand. These various sources don't always give the same information, even contradicting each other at different times with varying details.

So we decided not to present a straightforward -- and somewhat speculative -- biography, but rather to use dramatic fiction to best convey the spirit of her fight.

If you want to explore more about Irena's life, we recommend the following readings:

Irena's Children: The Extraordinary Story of the Woman who Saved 2,500 Children from the Warsaw Ghetto by Tilar J. Mazzeo

Irena's Children: Young Readers Edition; A True Story of Courage by Mary Cronk Farrell and Tilar J. Mazzeo

Life in a Jar: The Irena Sendler Project by Jack Mayer

Jars of Hope: How One Woman Helped save 2,500 Children During the Holocaust by Jennifer Roy

— The Authors

To Youyou, my little stardust...

— Séverine Tréfouël

Thanks to my parents, my wife, and my four daughters for their support, to Jean-David, my old friend of 25 years, for bringing me on board the adventure that is Irena, and to him and Séverine for their diligent coaching. To Jean-Claude Camano for his constant encouragement, to Nicolas Forsans, and to Walter for his amazing work coloring this book.

— David Evrard

To Jean-Claude Camano, my Sensei, who taught me this job, which I do largely thanks to him. Let he be warned: I do not intend to stop doing it!

— Jean-David Morvan

Irena

CHAPTER 1 – THE GHETTO

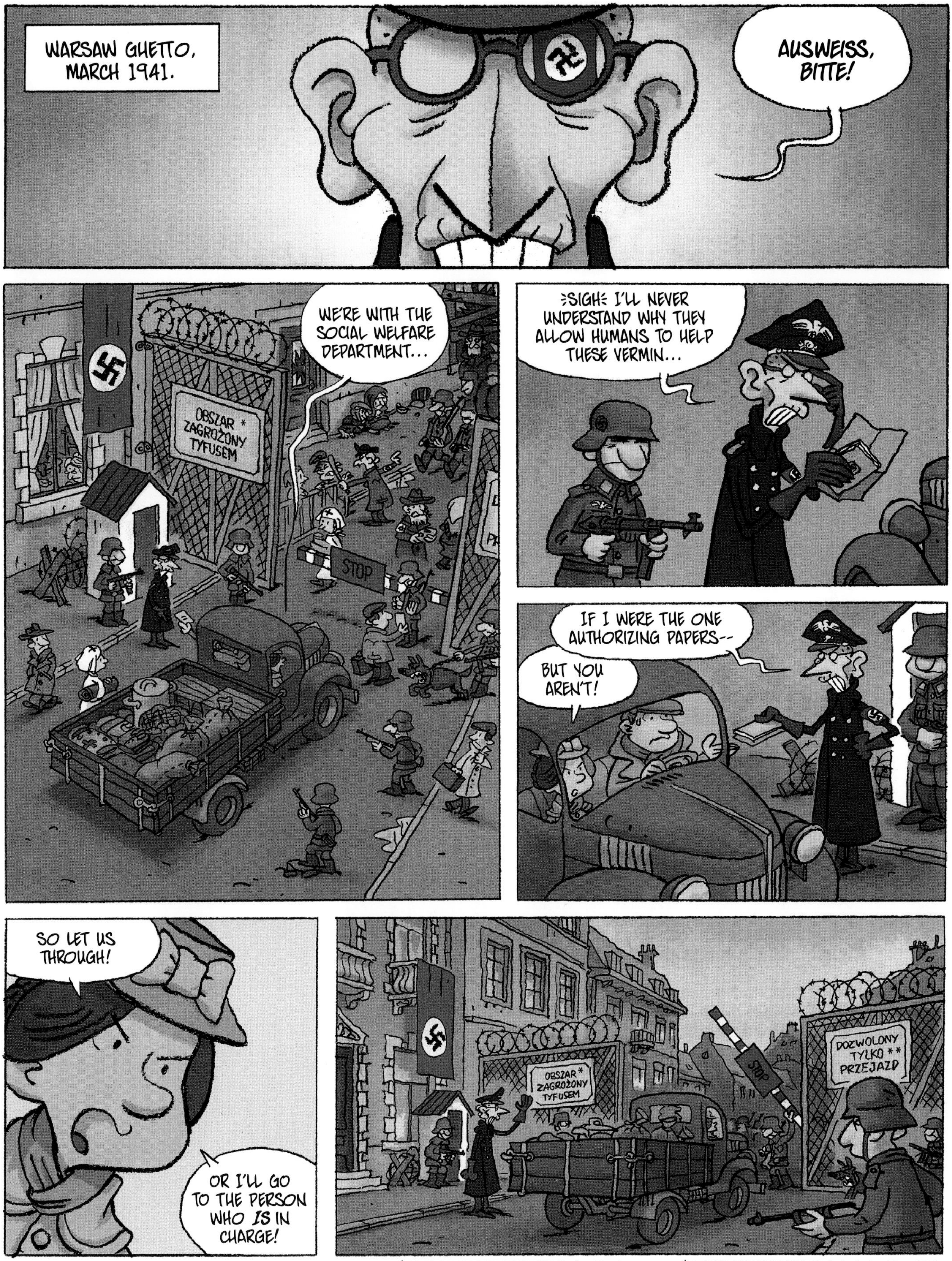
WARSAW GHETTO, MARCH 1941.
AUSWEISS, BITTE!
WE'RE WITH THE SOCIAL WELFARE DEPARTMENT...
OBSZAR * ZAGROŻONY TYFUSEM
STOP
:SIGH: I'LL NEVER UNDERSTAND WHY THEY ALLOW HUMANS TO HELP THESE VERMIN...
IF I WERE THE ONE AUTHORIZING PAPERS--
BUT YOU AREN'T!
SO LET US THROUGH!
OR I'LL GO TO THE PERSON WHO *IS* IN CHARGE!
OBSZAR* ZAGROŻONY TYFUSEM
STOP
DOZWOLONY TYLKO ** PRZEJAZD

* OBSZAR ZAGROZONY TYFUSEM: Typhus Warning

** DOZWOLONY TYLKO PRZEJAZD: Authorized Travel Only

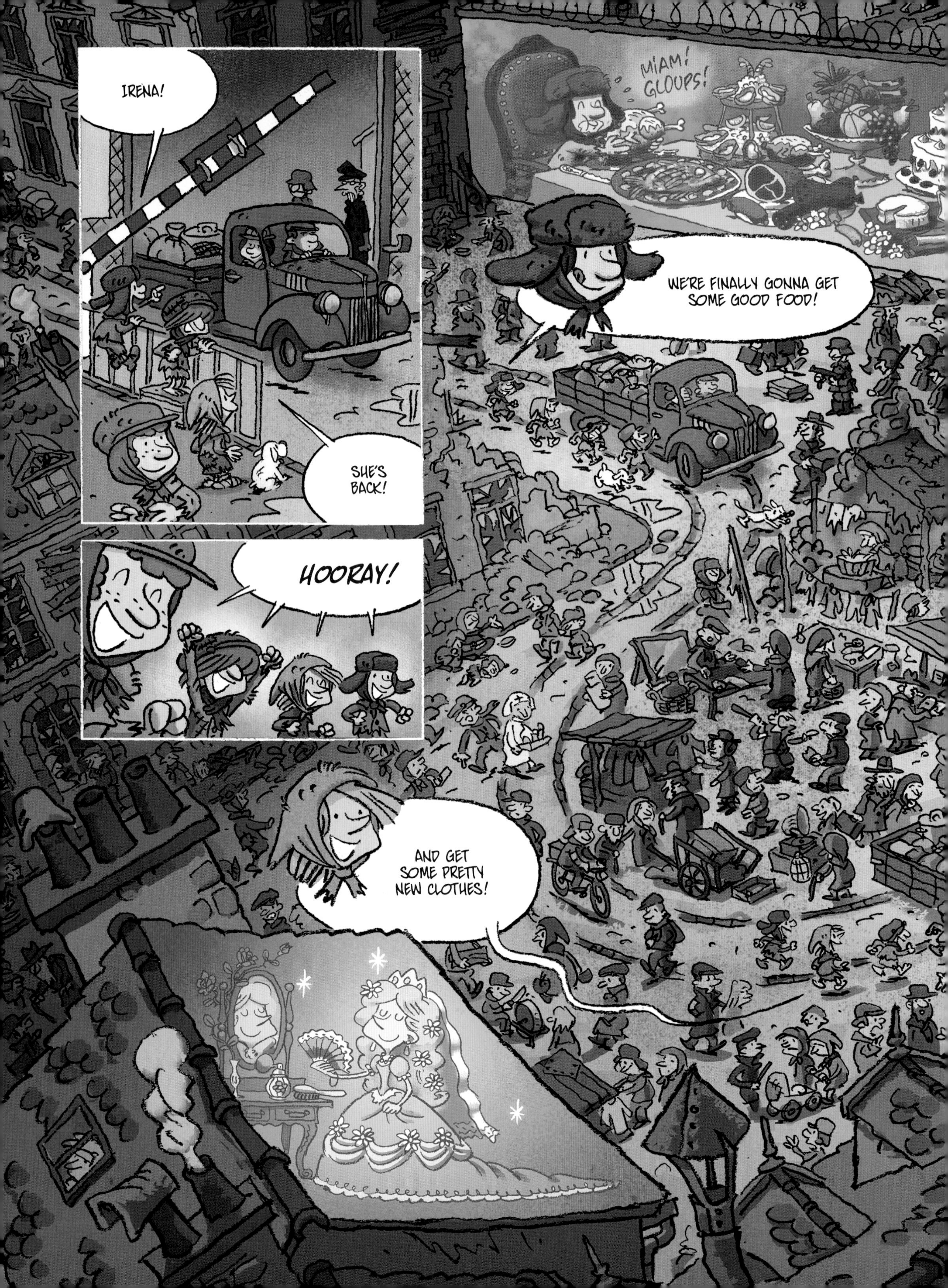
IRENA!
SHE'S BACK!
HOORAY!
MIAM! GLOUPS!
WE'RE FINALLY GONNA GET SOME GOOD FOOD!
AND GET SOME PRETTY NEW CLOTHES!

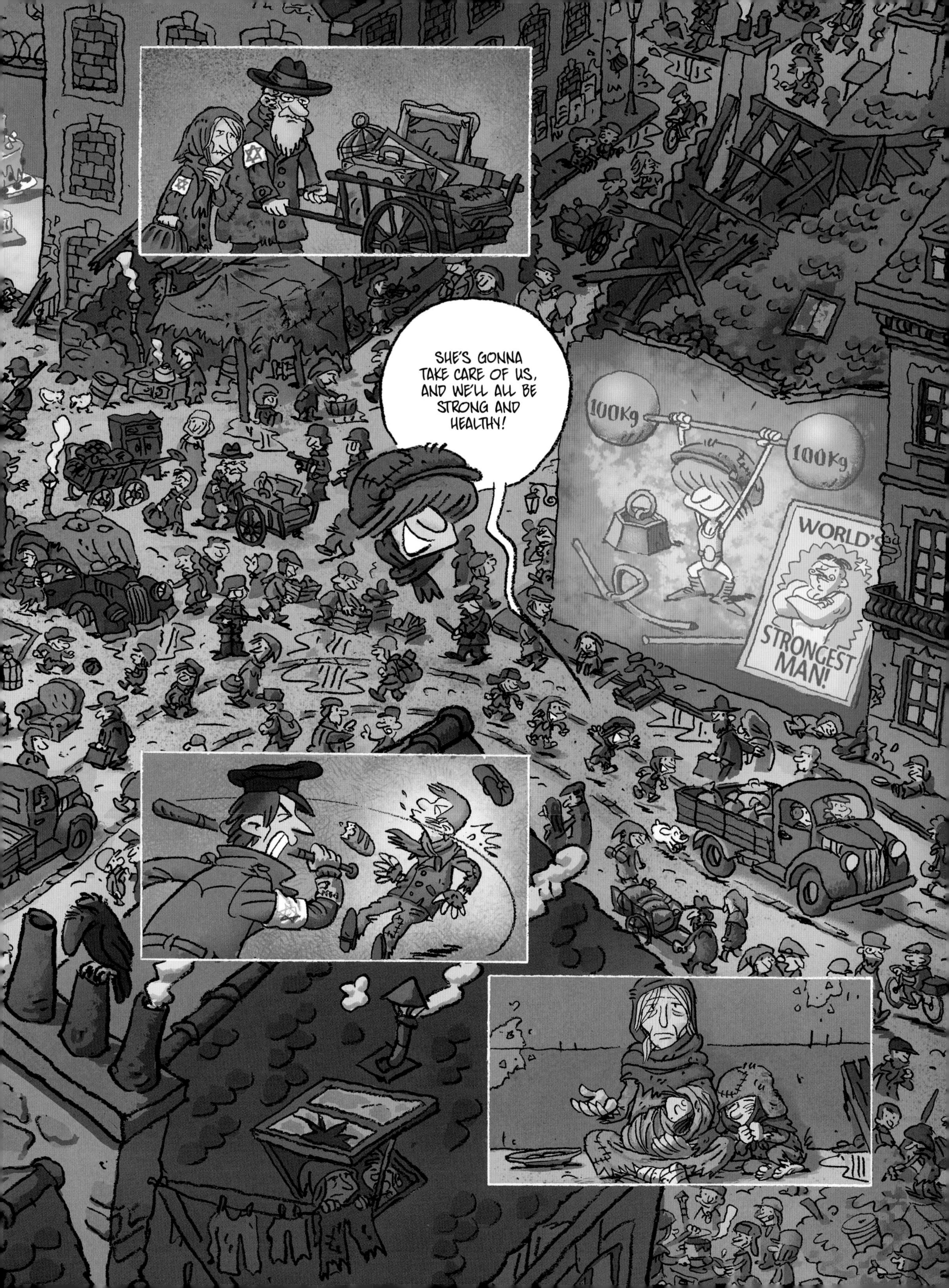
SHE'S GONNA TAKE CARE OF US, AND WE'LL ALL BE STRONG AND HEALTHY!
100Kg
100Kg
WORLD'S STRONGEST MAN!

AND MAYBE SHE'LL TURN US ALL INVISIBLE SO WE CAN GET OUT OF HERE!
NOT JUST US...
...**EVERYONE** IN THE GHETTO!
OBSZAR ZAGROŻONY TYFUSEM
DOZWOLONY TYLKO PRZEJAZD
POMOC SPOŁECZNA*

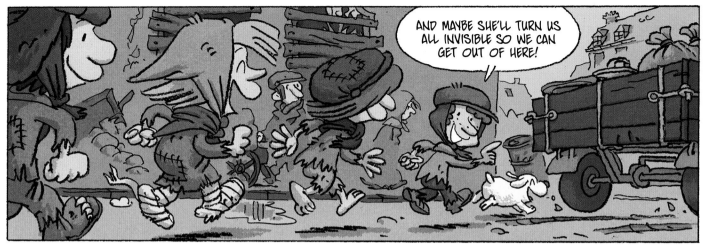

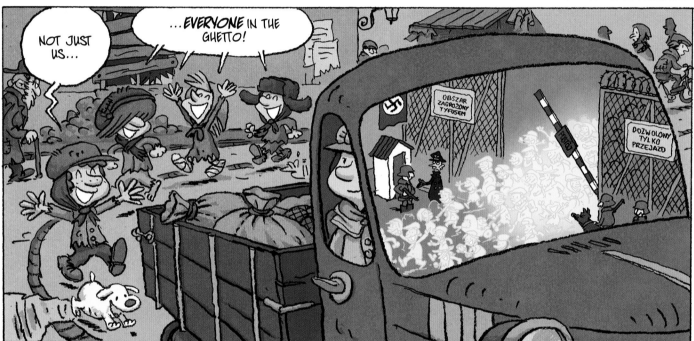

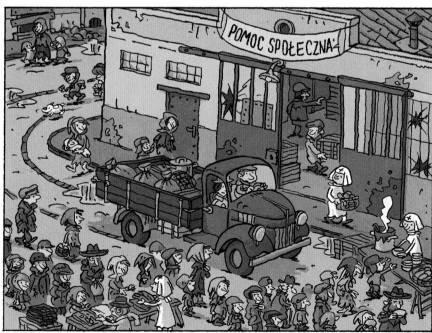

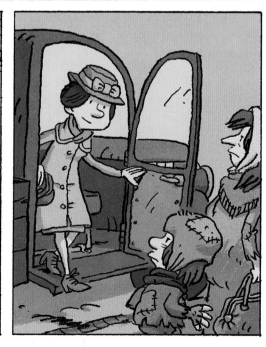

* POMOC SPOLECZNA: Social Services

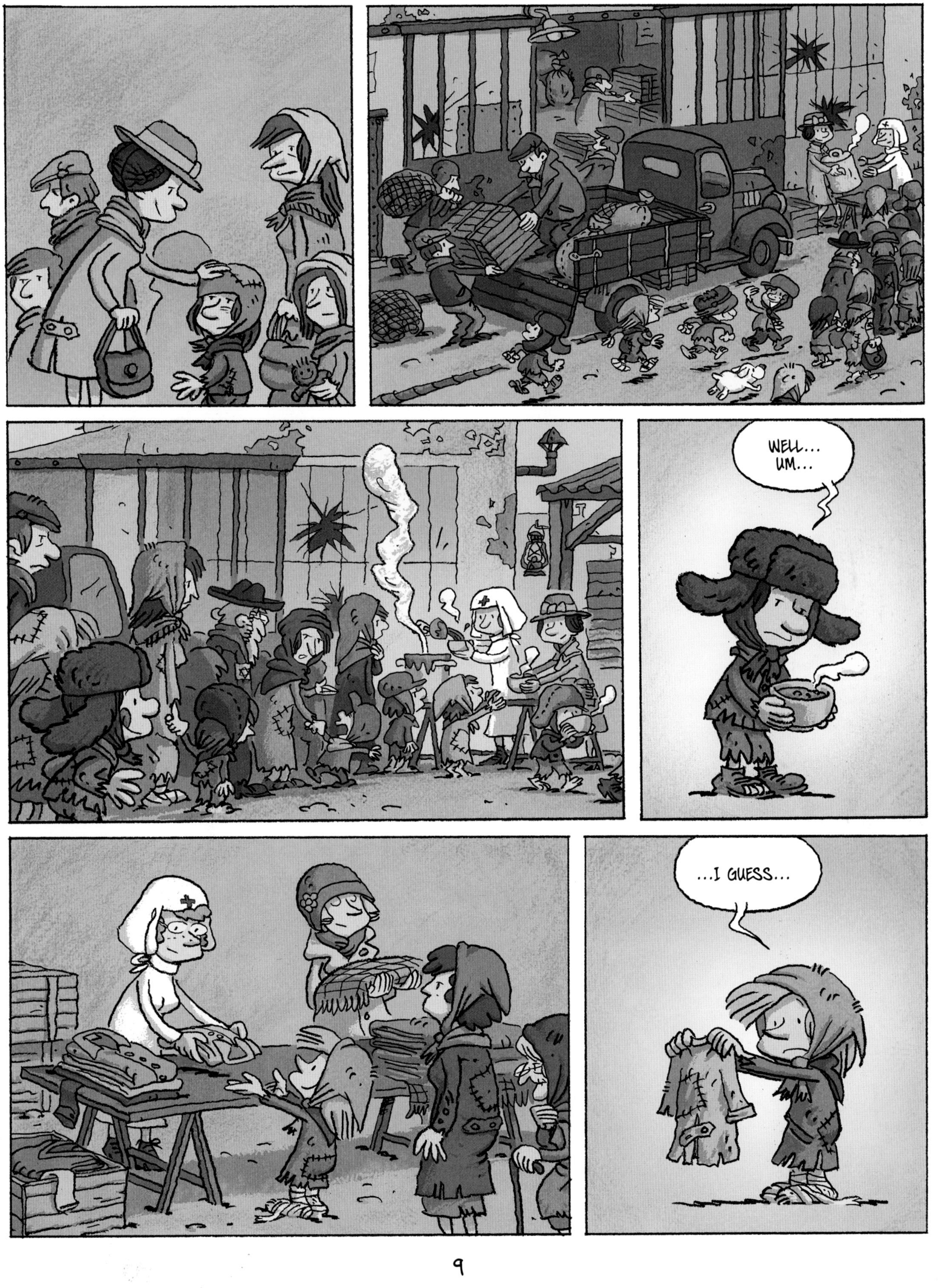
WELL... UM...
...I GUESS...

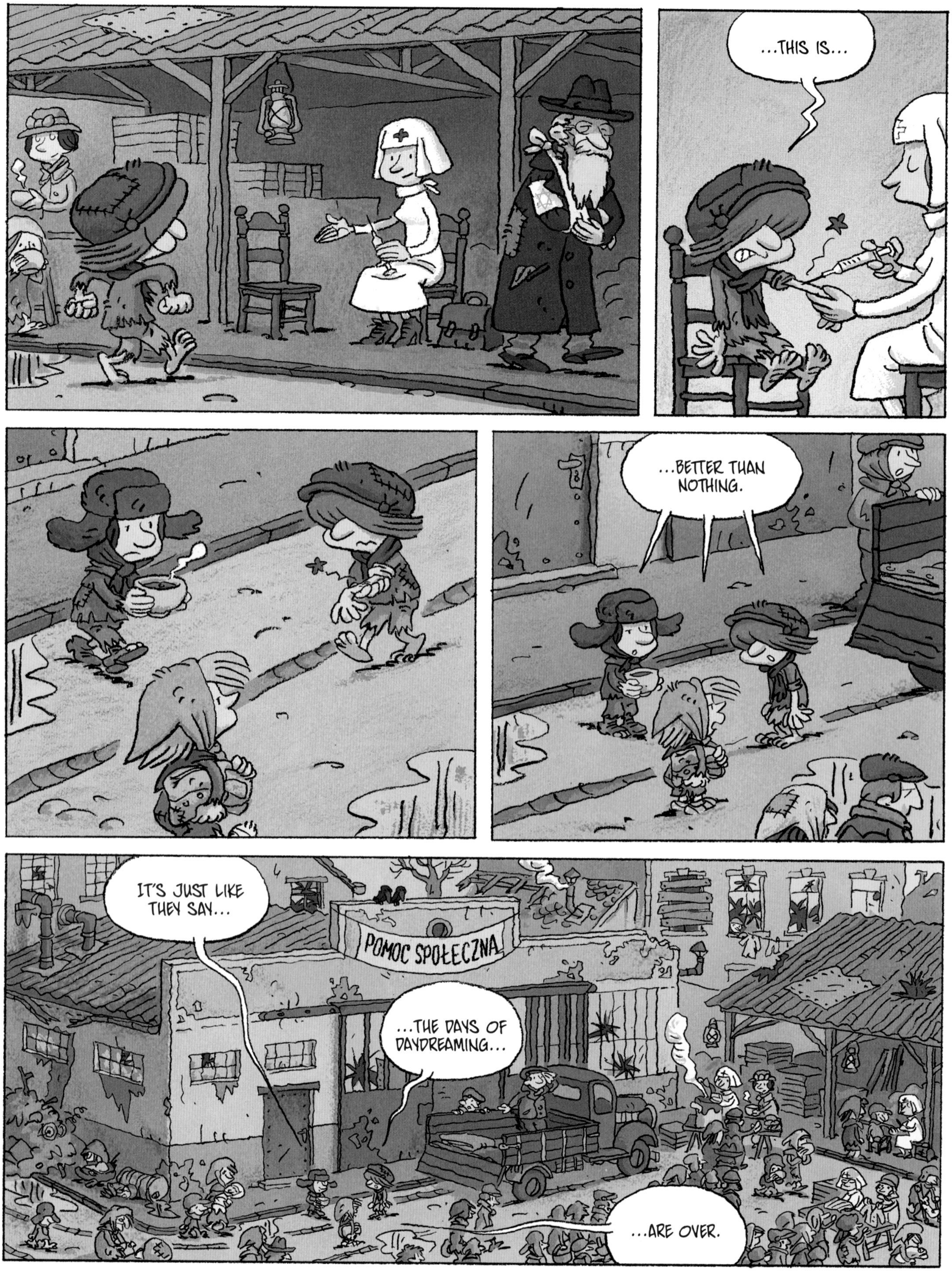
...THIS IS...
...BETTER THAN NOTHING.
IT'S JUST LIKE THEY SAY...
POMOC SPOŁECZNA
...THE DAYS OF DAYDREAMING...
...ARE OVER.

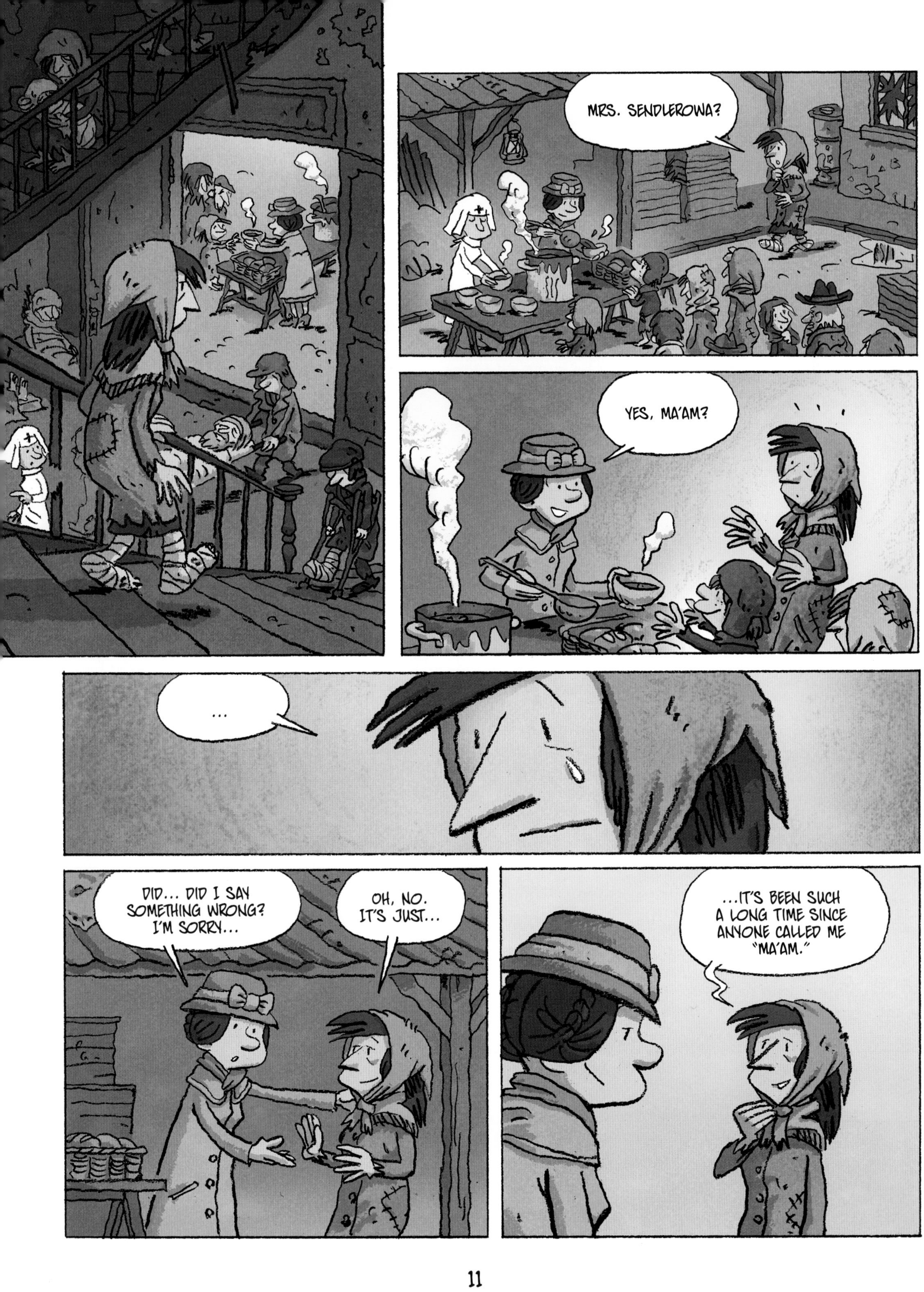
MRS. SENDLEROWA?
YES, MA'AM?
...
DID... DID I SAY SOMETHING WRONG? I'M SORRY...
OH, NO. IT'S JUST...
...IT'S BEEN SUCH A LONG TIME SINCE ANYONE CALLED ME "MA'AM."

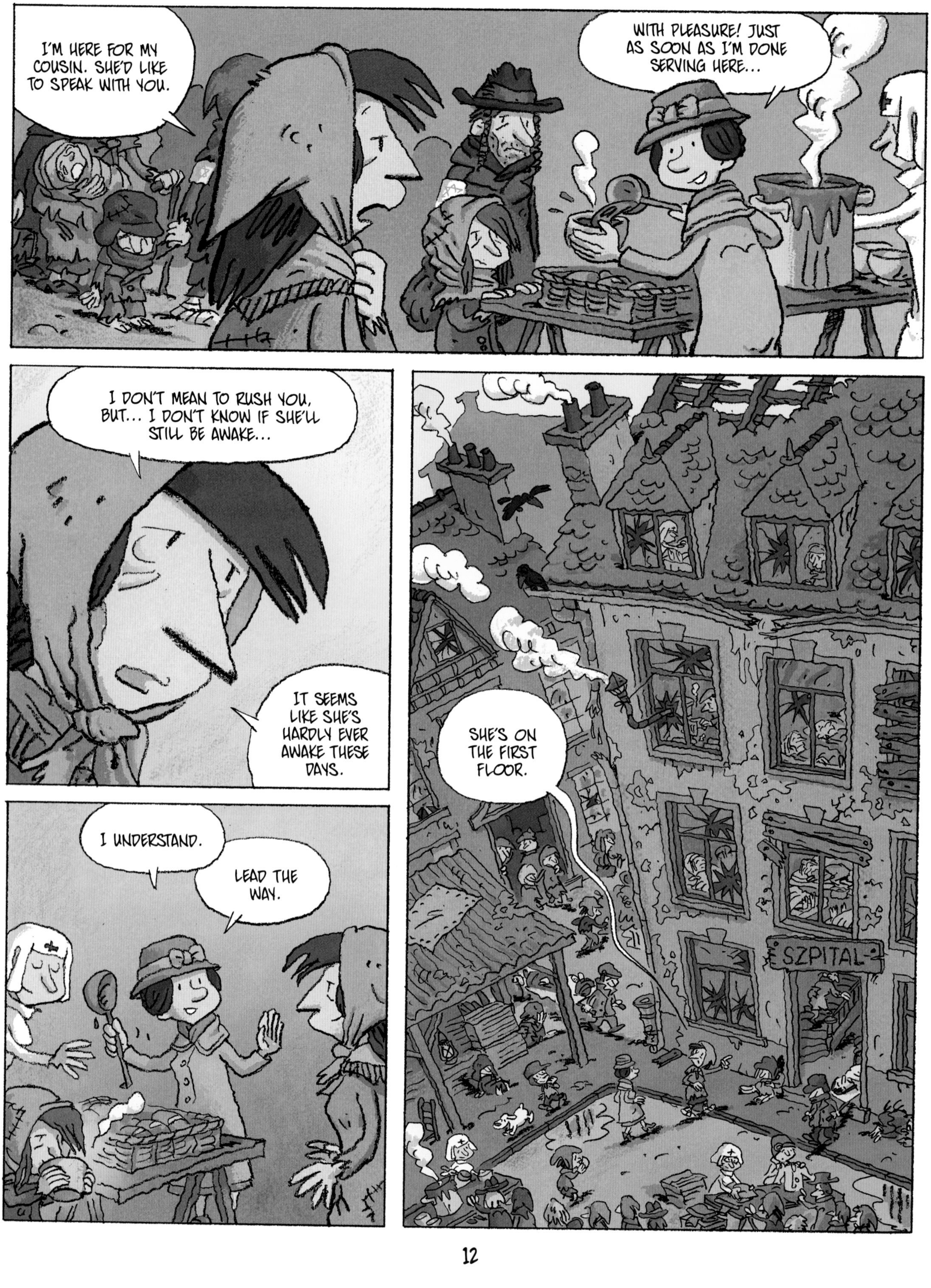
I'M HERE FOR MY COUSIN. SHE'D LIKE TO SPEAK WITH YOU.
WITH PLEASURE! JUST AS SOON AS I'M DONE SERVING HERE...
I DON'T MEAN TO RUSH YOU, BUT... I DON'T KNOW IF SHE'LL STILL BE AWAKE...
IT SEEMS LIKE SHE'S HARDLY EVER AWAKE THESE DAYS.
I UNDERSTAND.
LEAD THE WAY.
SHE'S ON THE FIRST FLOOR.
SZPITAL

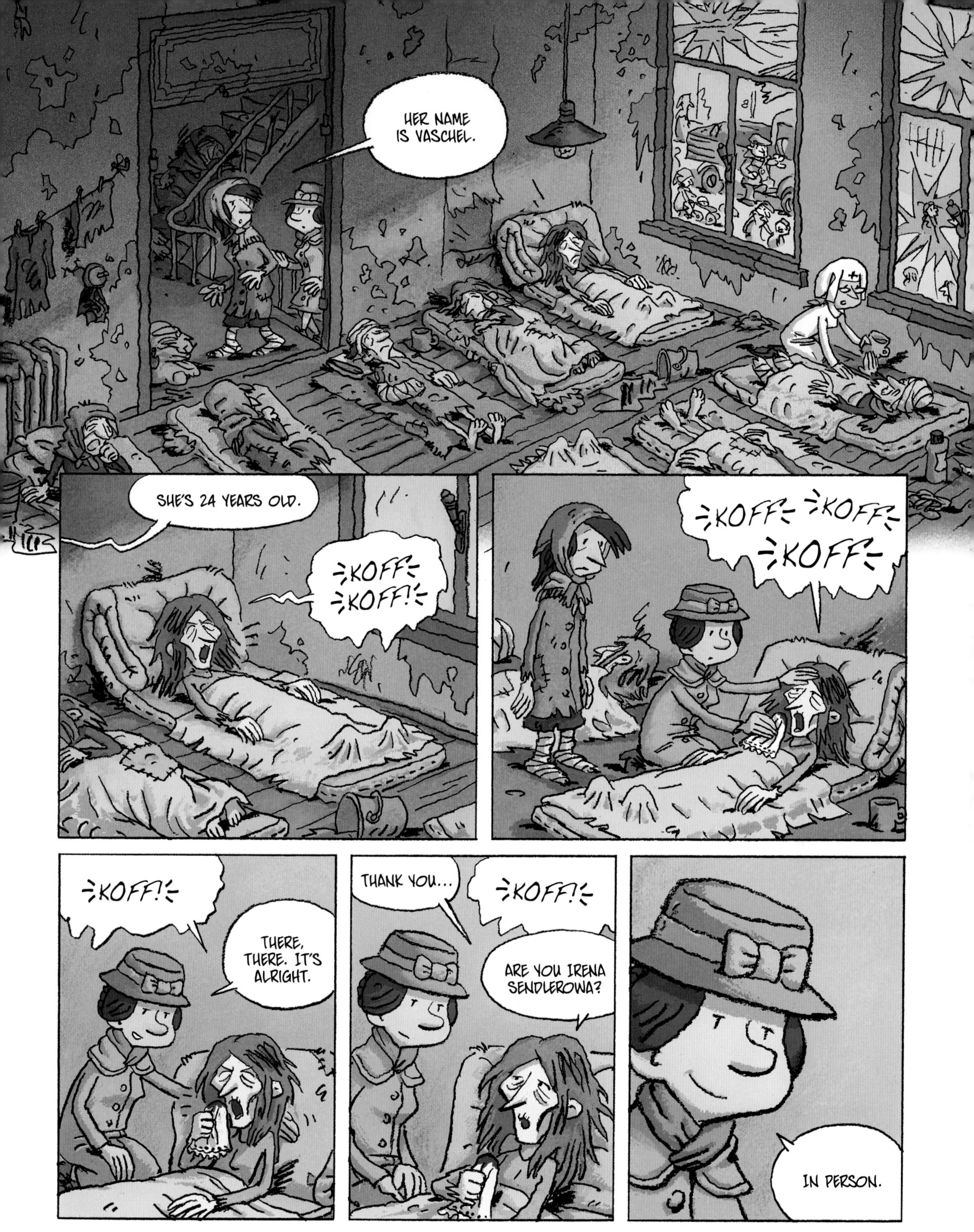

HER NAME IS VASCHEL.
SHE'S 24 YEARS OLD.
KOFF! KOFF!
KOFF! KOFF! KOFF!
KOFF!
THERE, THERE. IT'S ALRIGHT.
THANK YOU...
KOFF!
ARE YOU IRENA SENDLEROWA?
IN PERSON.

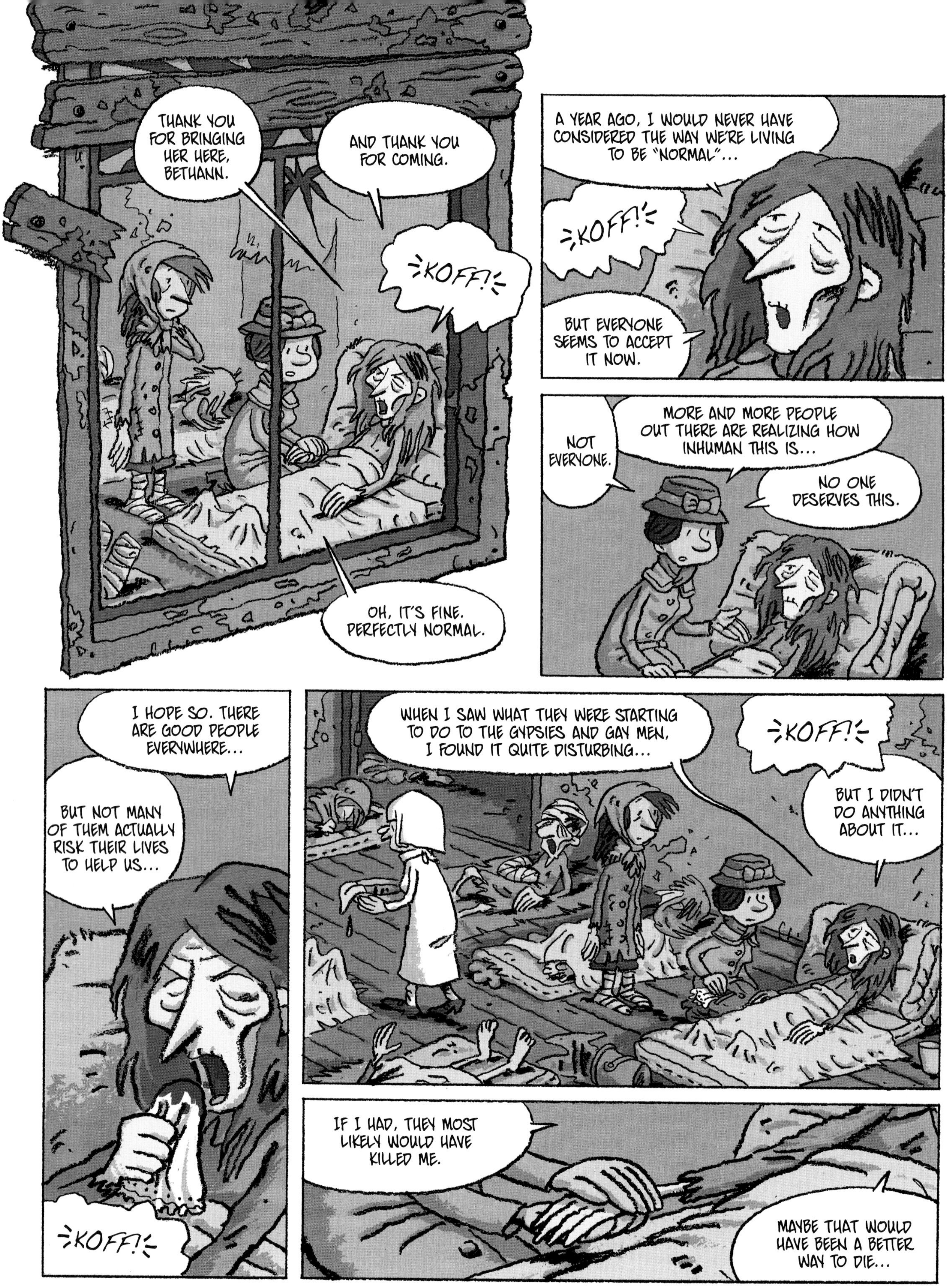
THANK YOU FOR BRINGING HER HERE, BETHANN.
AND THANK YOU FOR COMING.
KOFF!
OH, IT'S FINE. PERFECTLY NORMAL.
A YEAR AGO, I WOULD NEVER HAVE CONSIDERED THE WAY WE'RE LIVING TO BE "NORMAL"...
KOFF!
BUT EVERYONE SEEMS TO ACCEPT IT NOW.
NOT EVERYONE.
MORE AND MORE PEOPLE OUT THERE ARE REALIZING HOW INHUMAN THIS IS...
NO ONE DESERVES THIS.
I HOPE SO. THERE ARE GOOD PEOPLE EVERYWHERE...
BUT NOT MANY OF THEM ACTUALLY RISK THEIR LIVES TO HELP US...
KOFF!
WHEN I SAW WHAT THEY WERE STARTING TO DO TO THE GYPSIES AND GAY MEN, I FOUND IT QUITE DISTURBING...
KOFF!
BUT I DIDN'T DO ANYTHING ABOUT IT...
IF I HAD, THEY MOST LIKELY WOULD HAVE KILLED ME.
MAYBE THAT WOULD HAVE BEEN A BETTER WAY TO DIE...

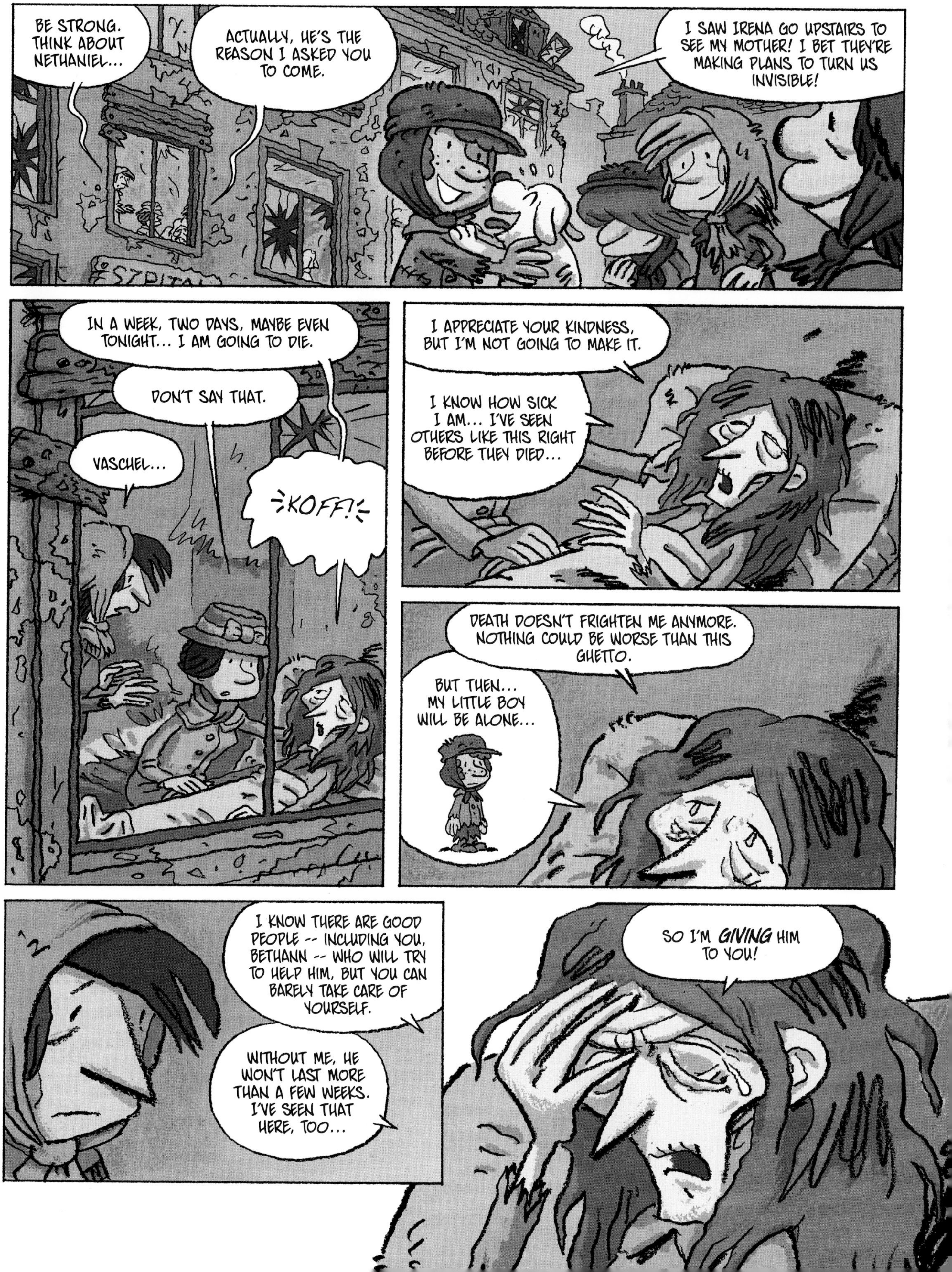
BE STRONG. THINK ABOUT NETHANIEL...
ACTUALLY, HE'S THE REASON I ASKED YOU TO COME.
I SAW IRENA GO UPSTAIRS TO SEE MY MOTHER! I BET THEY'RE MAKING PLANS TO TURN US INVISIBLE!
IN A WEEK, TWO DAYS, MAYBE EVEN TONIGHT... I AM GOING TO DIE.
DON'T SAY THAT.
VASCHEL...
KOFF!
I APPRECIATE YOUR KINDNESS, BUT I'M NOT GOING TO MAKE IT.
I KNOW HOW SICK I AM... I'VE SEEN OTHERS LIKE THIS RIGHT BEFORE THEY DIED...
DEATH DOESN'T FRIGHTEN ME ANYMORE. NOTHING COULD BE WORSE THAN THIS GHETTO.
BUT THEN... MY LITTLE BOY WILL BE ALONE...
I KNOW THERE ARE GOOD PEOPLE -- INCLUDING YOU, BETHANN -- WHO WILL TRY TO HELP HIM, BUT YOU CAN BARELY TAKE CARE OF YOURSELF.
WITHOUT ME, HE WON'T LAST MORE THAN A FEW WEEKS. I'VE SEEN THAT HERE, TOO...
SO I'M GIVING HIM TO YOU!

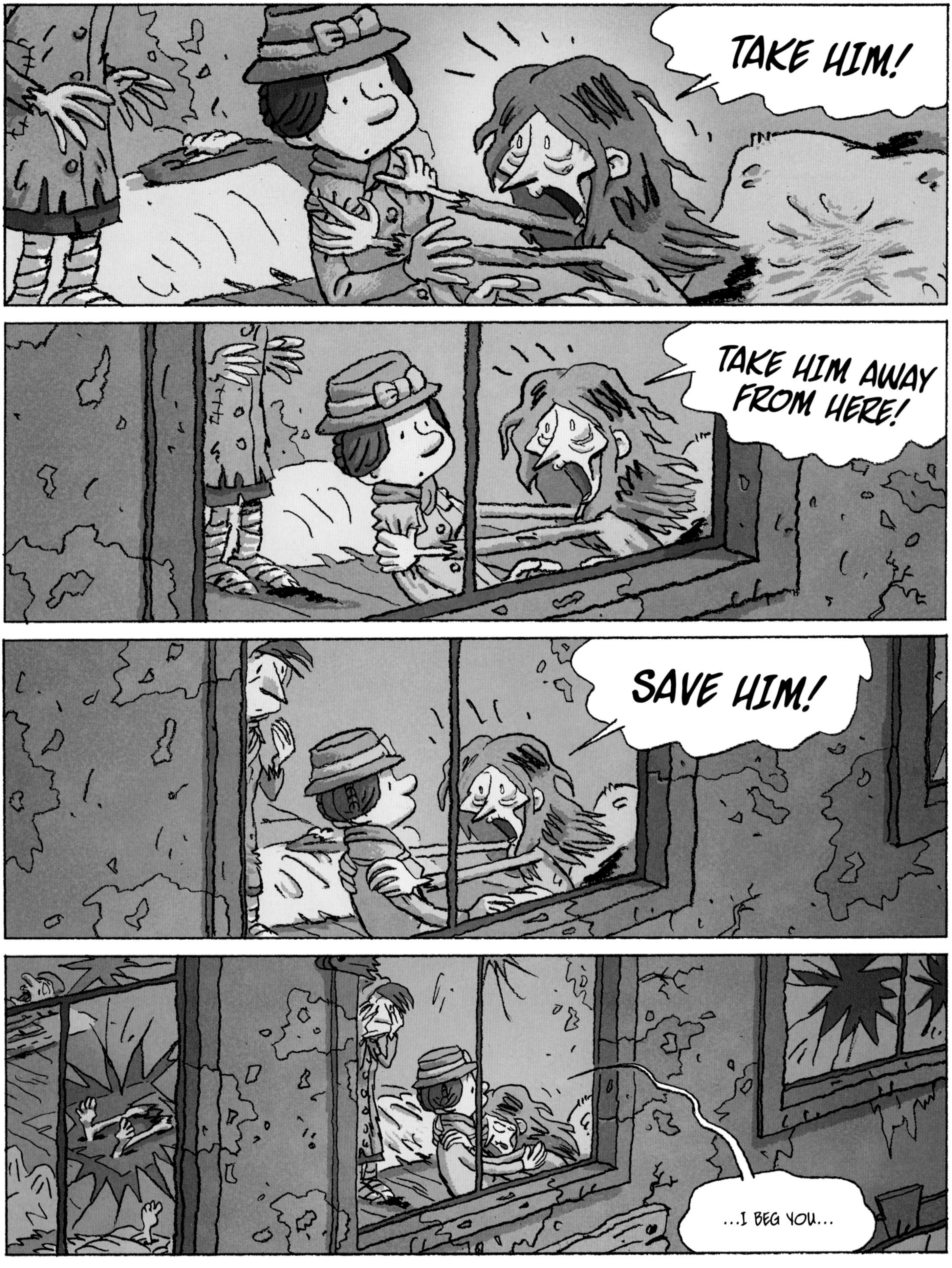
TAKE HIM!
TAKE HIM AWAY FROM HERE!
SAVE HIM!
...I BEG YOU...

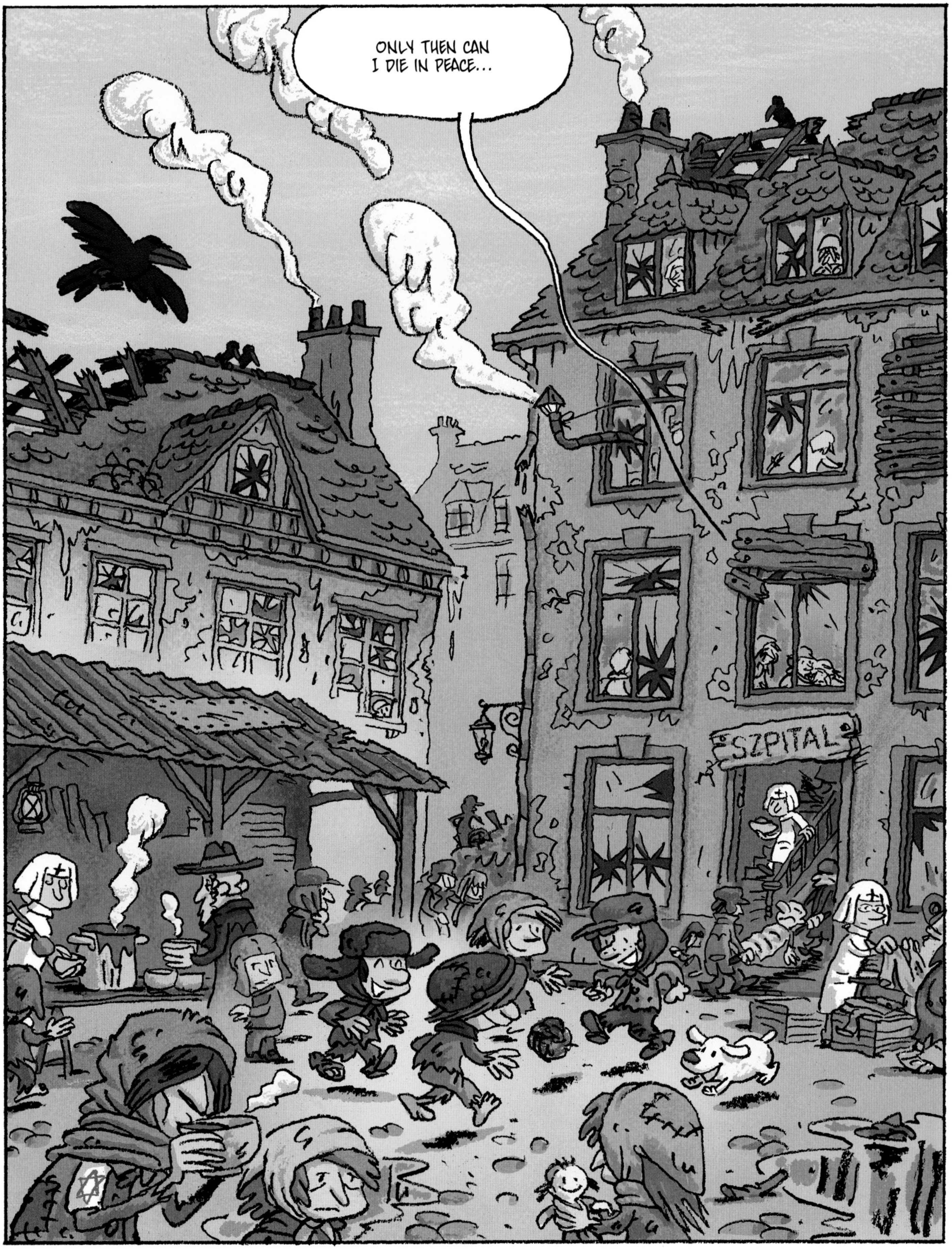
ONLY THEN CAN I DIE IN PEACE...
SZPITAL

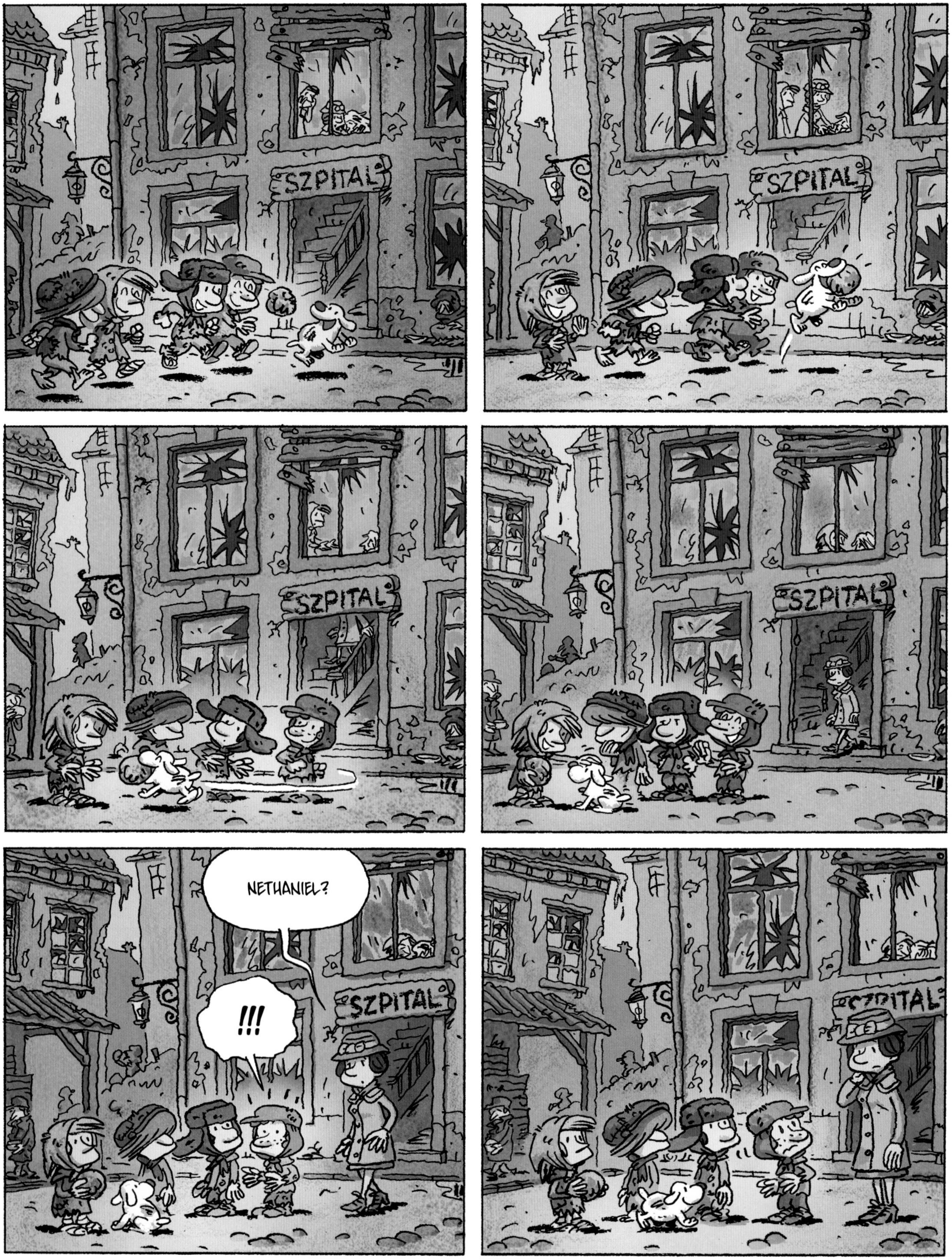
SZPITAL
SZPITAL
SZPITAL
SZPITAL
NETHANIEL?
!!!
SZPITAL
SZPITAL

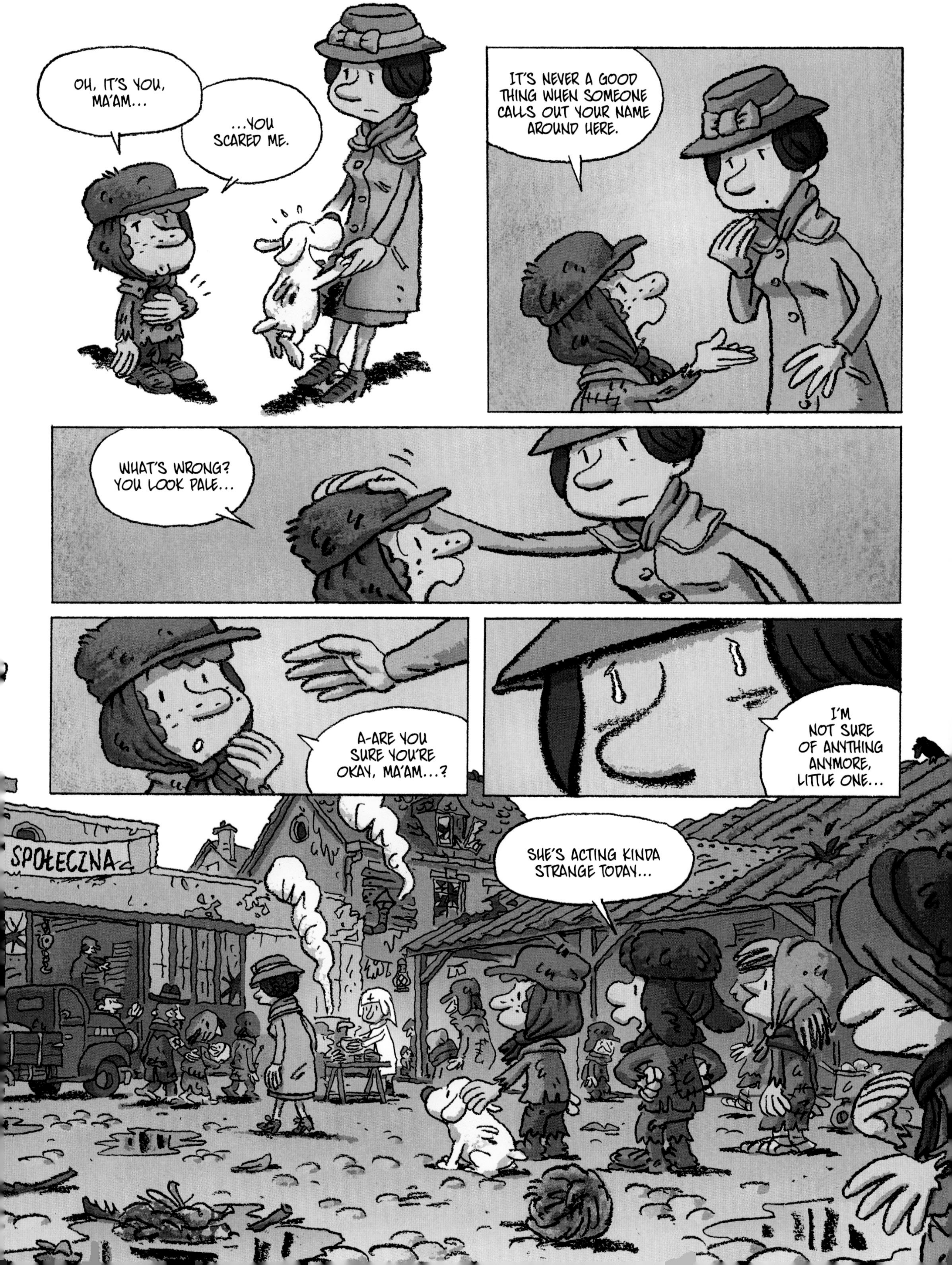
OH, IT'S YOU, MA'AM...
...YOU SCARED ME.
IT'S NEVER A GOOD THING WHEN SOMEONE CALLS OUT YOUR NAME AROUND HERE.
WHAT'S WRONG? YOU LOOK PALE...
A-ARE YOU SURE YOU'RE OKAY, MA'AM...?
I'M NOT SURE OF ANYTHING ANYMORE, LITTLE ONE...
SPOŁECZNA
SHE'S ACTING KINDA STRANGE TODAY...

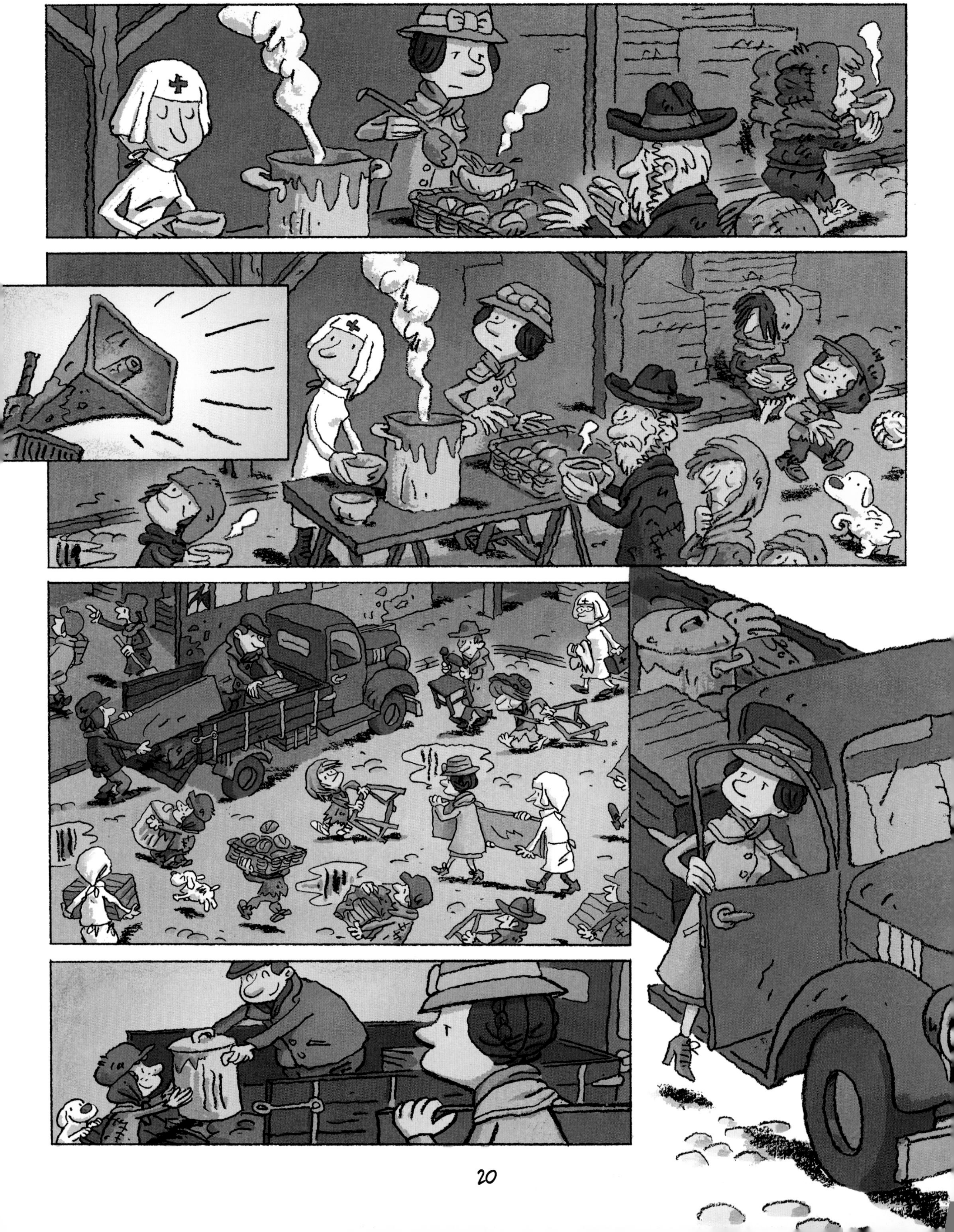

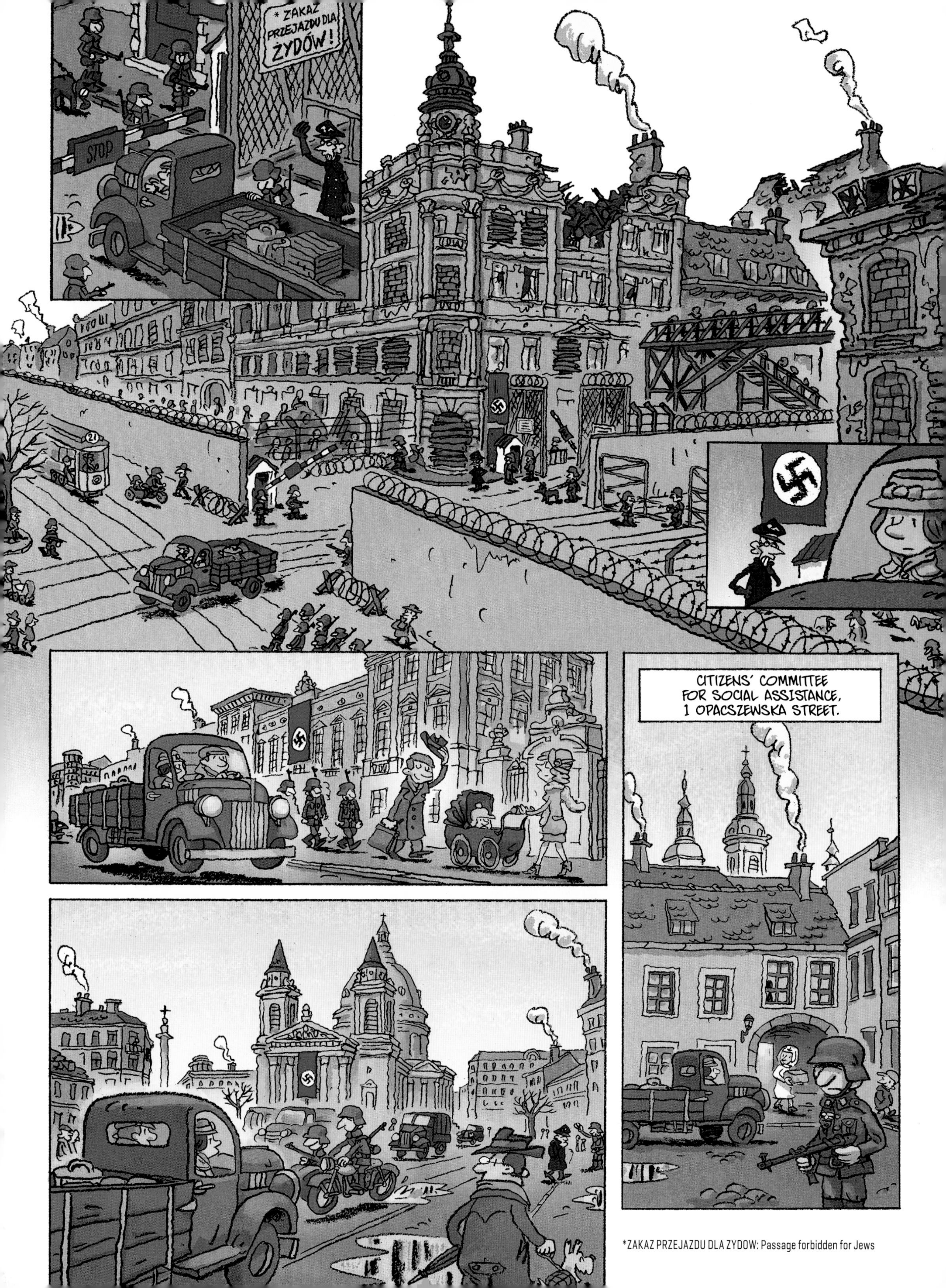
* ZAKAZ PRZEJAZDU DLA ŻYDÓW!
STOP
21
CITIZENS' COMMITTEE FOR SOCIAL ASSISTANCE, 1 OPACSZEWSKA STREET.

*ZAKAZ PRZEJAZDU DLA ZYDOW: Passage forbidden for Jews

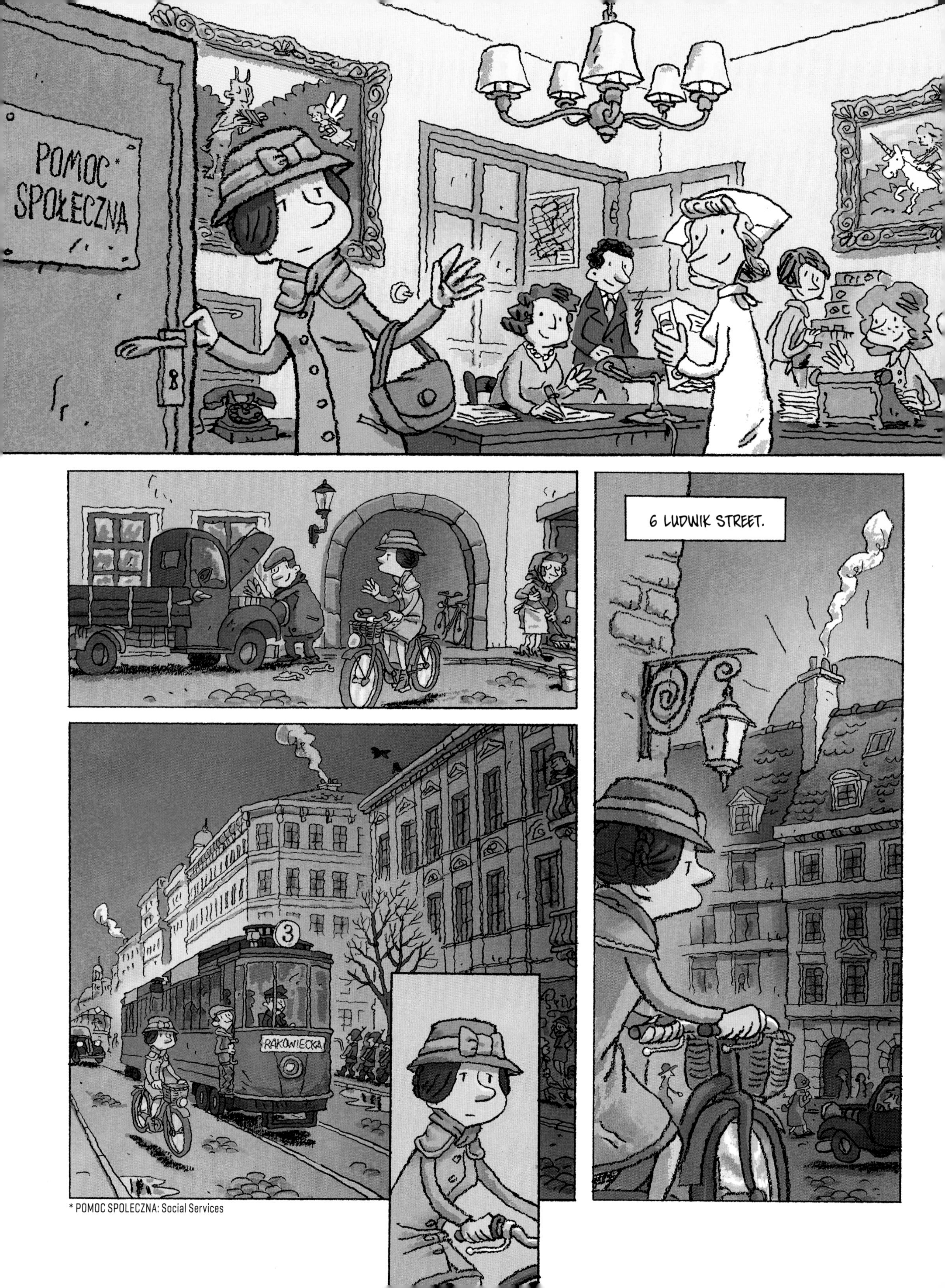
POMOC* SPOŁECZNA
6 LUDWIK STREET.
3
RAKOWIECKA

* POMOC SPOLECZNA: Social Services

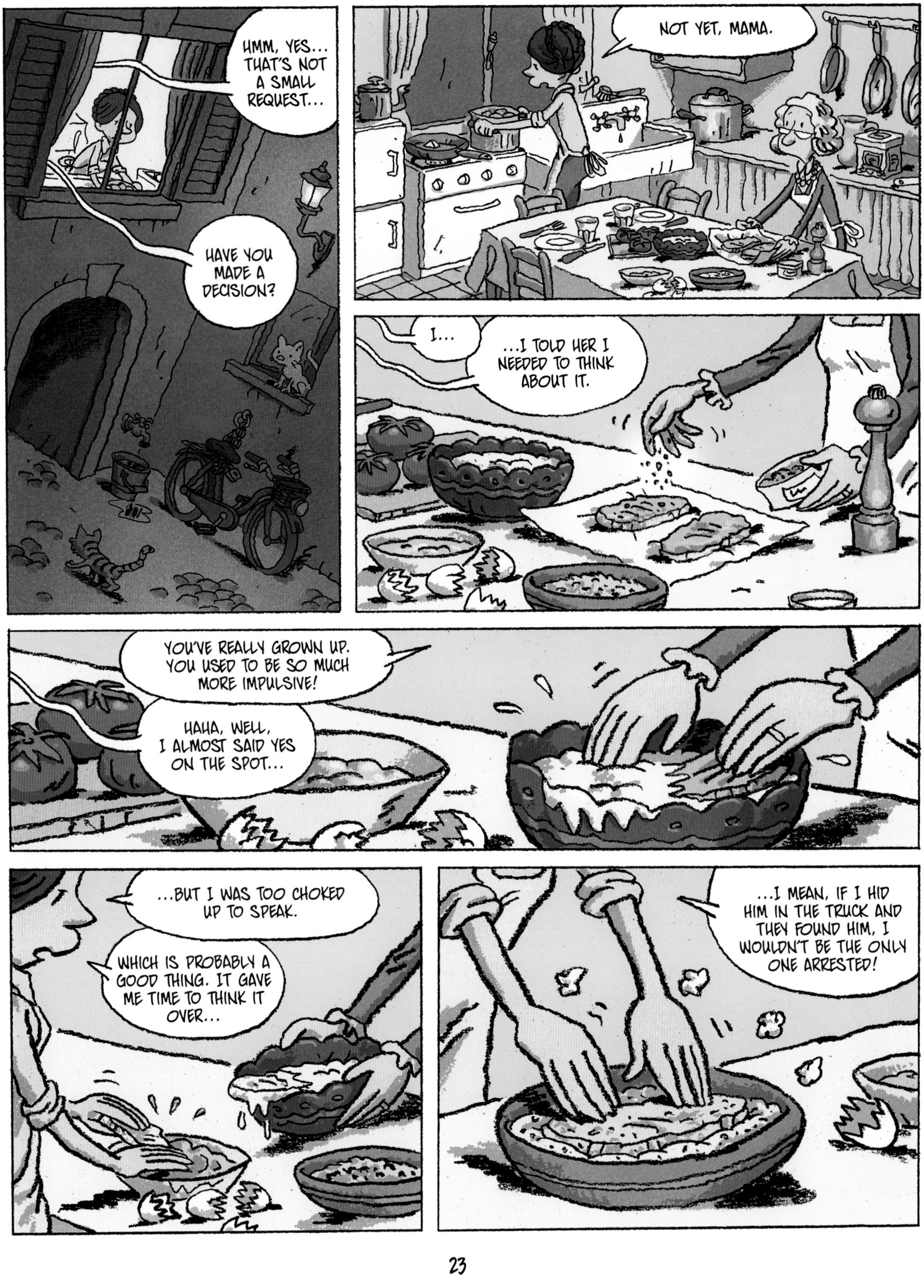
HMM, YES... THAT'S NOT A SMALL REQUEST...
HAVE YOU MADE A DECISION?
NOT YET, MAMA.
I...
...I TOLD HER I NEEDED TO THINK ABOUT IT.
YOU'VE REALLY GROWN UP. YOU USED TO BE SO MUCH MORE IMPULSIVE!
HAHA, WELL, I ALMOST SAID YES ON THE SPOT...
...BUT I WAS TOO CHOKED UP TO SPEAK.
WHICH IS PROBABLY A GOOD THING. IT GAVE ME TIME TO THINK IT OVER...
...I MEAN, IF I HID HIM IN THE TRUCK AND THEY FOUND HIM, I WOULDN'T BE THE ONLY ONE ARRESTED!

I CAN'T RISK THE LIVES OF MY COWORKERS LIKE THAT.

YOUR EMPLOYEES, YOU MEAN. YOU ARE THE HEAD OF THE DEPARTMENT, NOW.

YOU'RE RIGHT. AND THAT MAKES MY RESPONSIBILITY EVEN BIGGER....

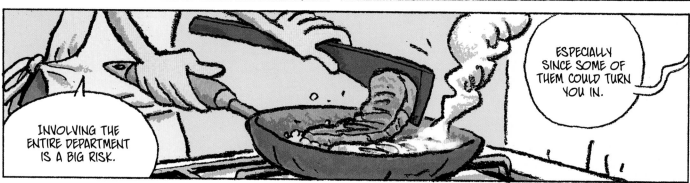

INVOLVING THE ENTIRE DEPARTMENT IS A BIG RISK.

ESPECIALLY SINCE SOME OF THEM COULD TURN YOU IN.

I DIDN'T EVEN CONSIDER THAT. DO YOU THINK ANYONE WOULD? I TRUST THEM...

IT'S THE ONES YOU TRUST THAT YOU NEED TO WATCH CLOSEST...

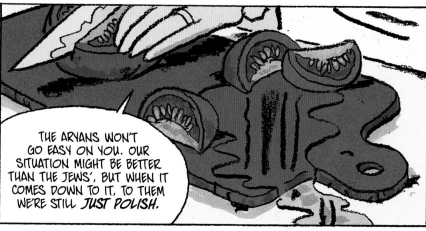

THE ARYANS WON'T GO EASY ON YOU. OUR SITUATION MIGHT BE BETTER THAN THE JEWS', BUT WHEN IT COMES DOWN TO IT, TO THEM WE'RE STILL *JUST POLISH.*

AN INFERIOR "RACE."

OUR LIVES ARE OF LITTLE VALUE TO THEM.

24

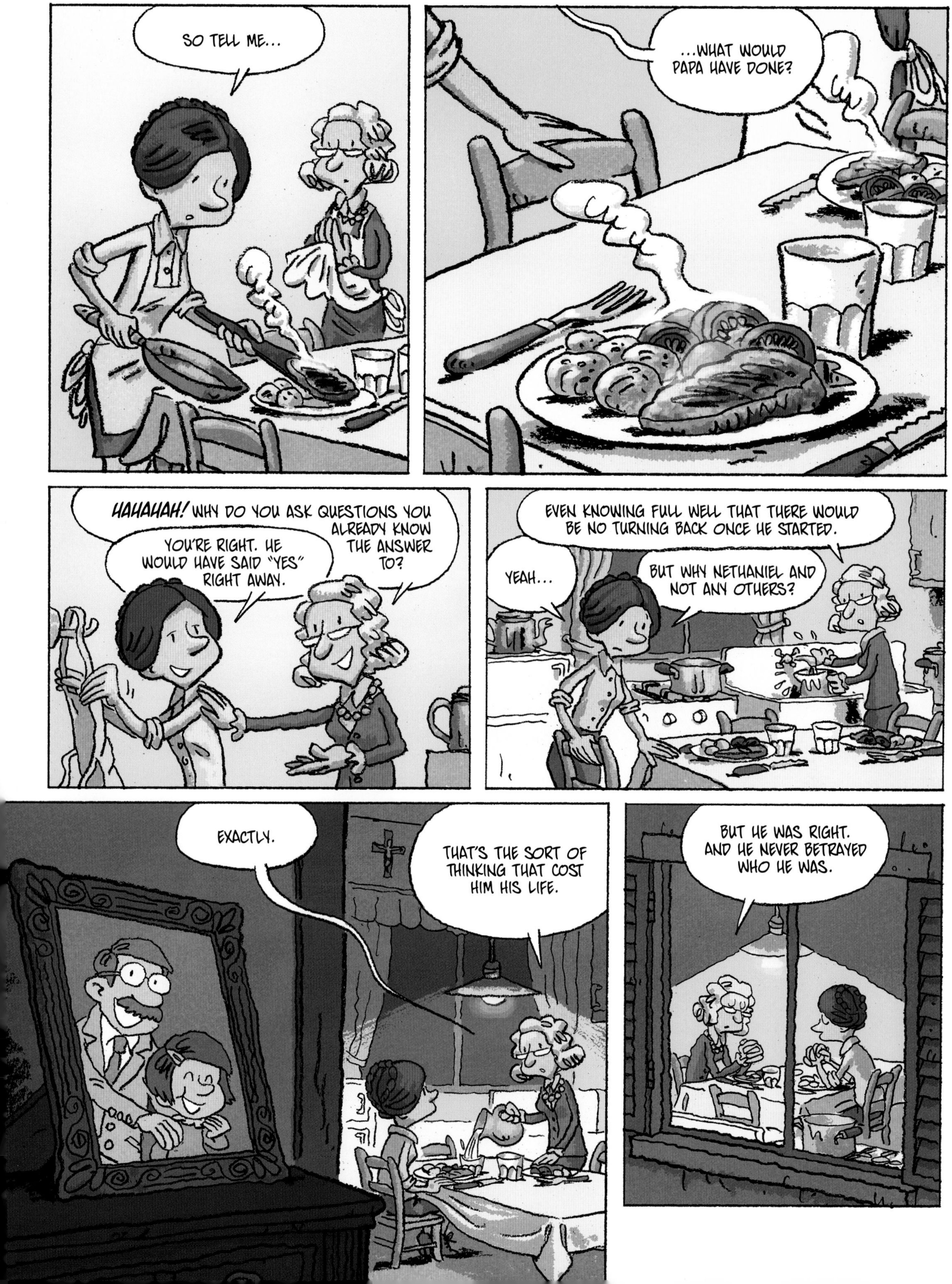
SO TELL ME...
...WHAT WOULD PAPA HAVE DONE?
HAHAHAH! WHY DO YOU ASK QUESTIONS YOU ALREADY KNOW THE ANSWER TO?
YOU'RE RIGHT. HE WOULD HAVE SAID "YES" RIGHT AWAY.
EVEN KNOWING FULL WELL THAT THERE WOULD BE NO TURNING BACK ONCE HE STARTED.
YEAH...
BUT WHY NETHANIEL AND NOT ANY OTHERS?
EXACTLY.
THAT'S THE SORT OF THINKING THAT COST HIM HIS LIFE.
BUT HE WAS RIGHT. AND HE NEVER BETRAYED WHO HE WAS.

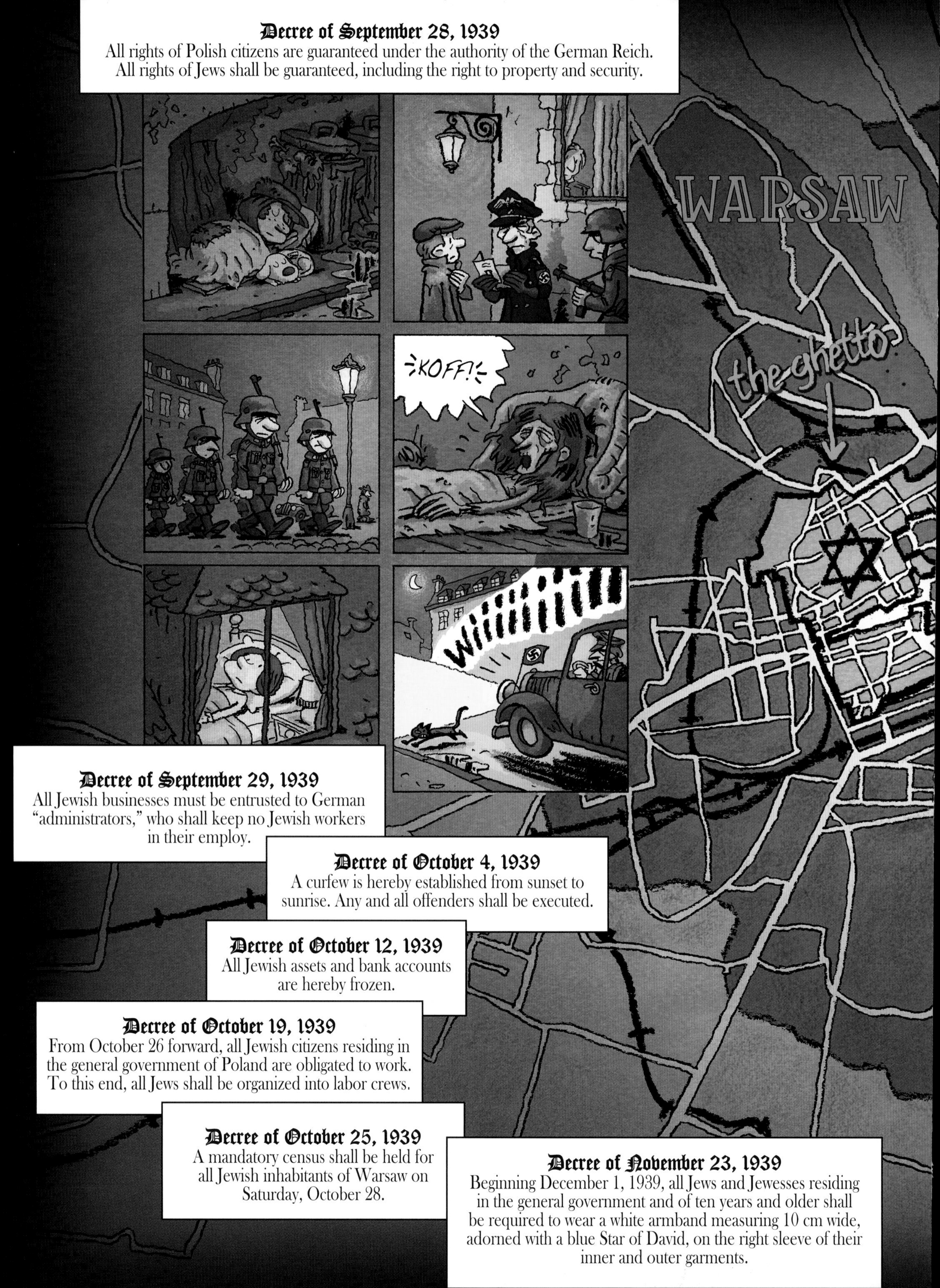
Decree of September 28, 1939
All rights of Polish citizens are guaranteed under the authority of the German Reich.
All rights of Jews shall be guaranteed, including the right to property and security.
KOFF!
WARSAW
the ghetto
Decree of September 29, 1939
All Jewish businesses must be entrusted to German "administrators," who shall keep no Jewish workers in their employ.
Decree of October 4, 1939
A curfew is hereby established from sunset to sunrise. Any and all offenders shall be executed.
Decree of October 12, 1939
All Jewish assets and bank accounts are hereby frozen.
Decree of October 19, 1939
From October 26 forward, all Jewish citizens residing in the general government of Poland are obligated to work. To this end, all Jews shall be organized into labor crews.
Decree of October 25, 1939
A mandatory census shall be held for all Jewish inhabitants of Warsaw on Saturday, October 28.
Decree of November 23, 1939
Beginning December 1, 1939, all Jews and Jewesses residing in the general government and of ten years and older shall be required to wear a white armband measuring 10 cm wide, adorned with a blue Star of David, on the right sleeve of their inner and outer garments.

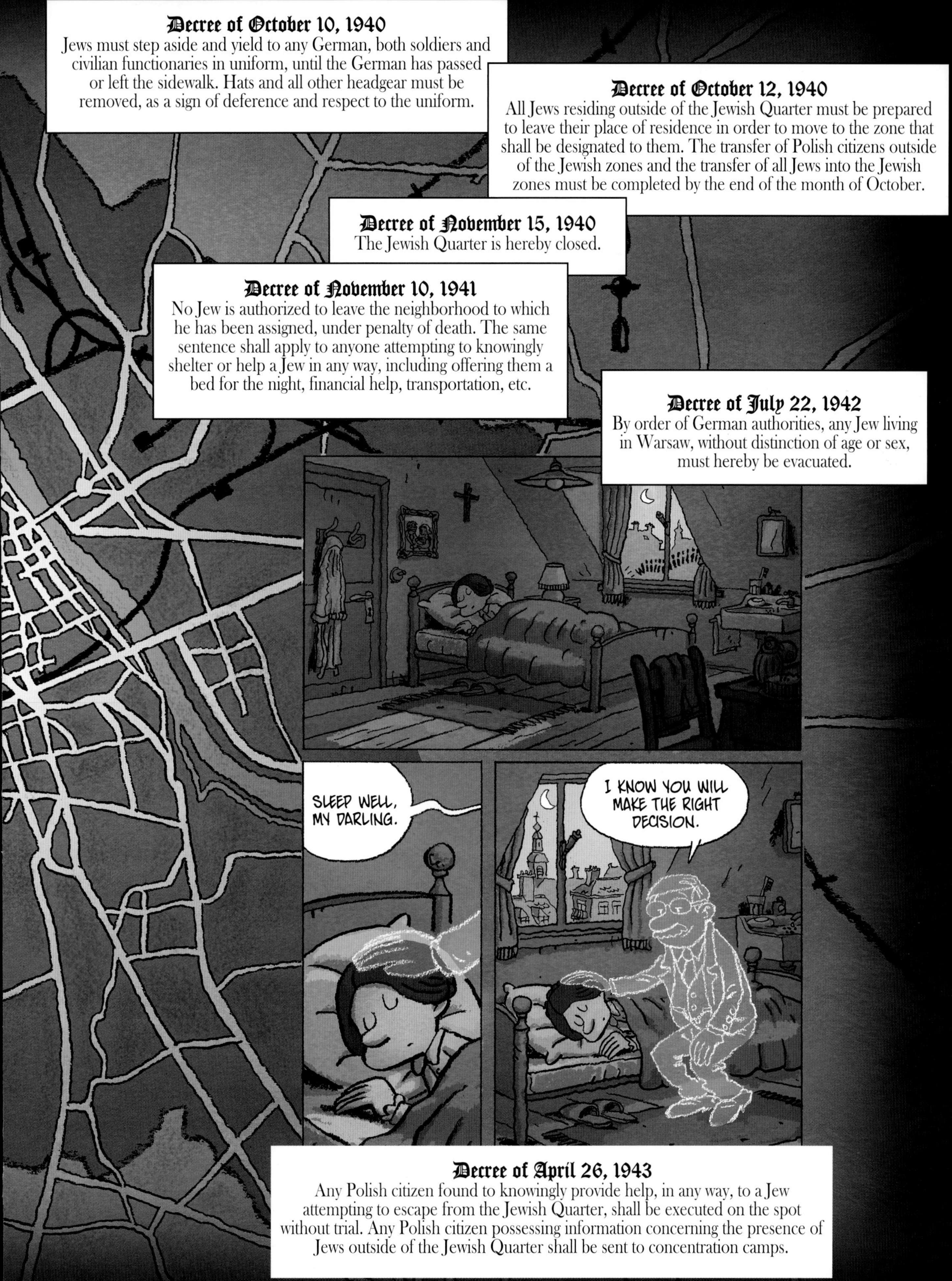
Decree of October 10, 1940
Jews must step aside and yield to any German, both soldiers and civilian functionaries in uniform, until the German has passed or left the sidewalk. Hats and all other headgear must be removed, as a sign of deference and respect to the uniform.
Decree of October 12, 1940
All Jews residing outside of the Jewish Quarter must be prepared to leave their place of residence in order to move to the zone that shall be designated to them. The transfer of Polish citizens outside of the Jewish zones and the transfer of all Jews into the Jewish zones must be completed by the end of the month of October.
Decree of November 15, 1940
The Jewish Quarter is hereby closed.
Decree of November 10, 1941
No Jew is authorized to leave the neighborhood to which he has been assigned, under penalty of death. The same sentence shall apply to anyone attempting to knowingly shelter or help a Jew in any way, including offering them a bed for the night, financial help, transportation, etc.
Decree of July 22, 1942
By order of German authorities, any Jew living in Warsaw, without distinction of age or sex, must hereby be evacuated.
SLEEP WELL, MY DARLING.
I KNOW YOU WILL MAKE THE RIGHT DECISION.
Decree of April 26, 1943
Any Polish citizen found to knowingly provide help, in any way, to a Jew attempting to escape from the Jewish Quarter, shall be executed on the spot without trial. Any Polish citizen possessing information concerning the presence of Jews outside of the Jewish Quarter shall be sent to concentration camps.

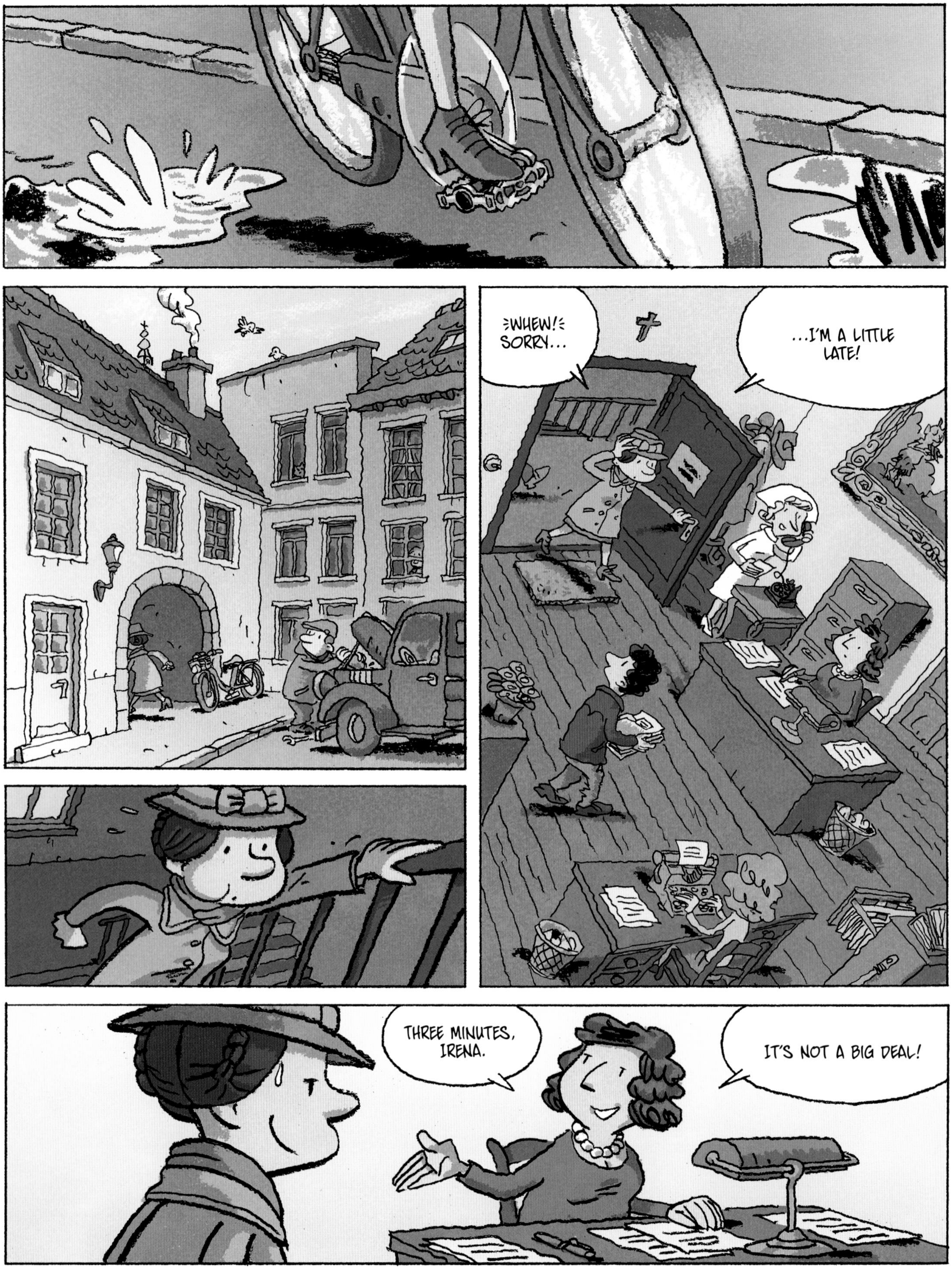
WHEW! SORRY...
...I'M A LITTLE LATE!
THREE MINUTES, IRENA.
IT'S NOT A BIG DEAL!

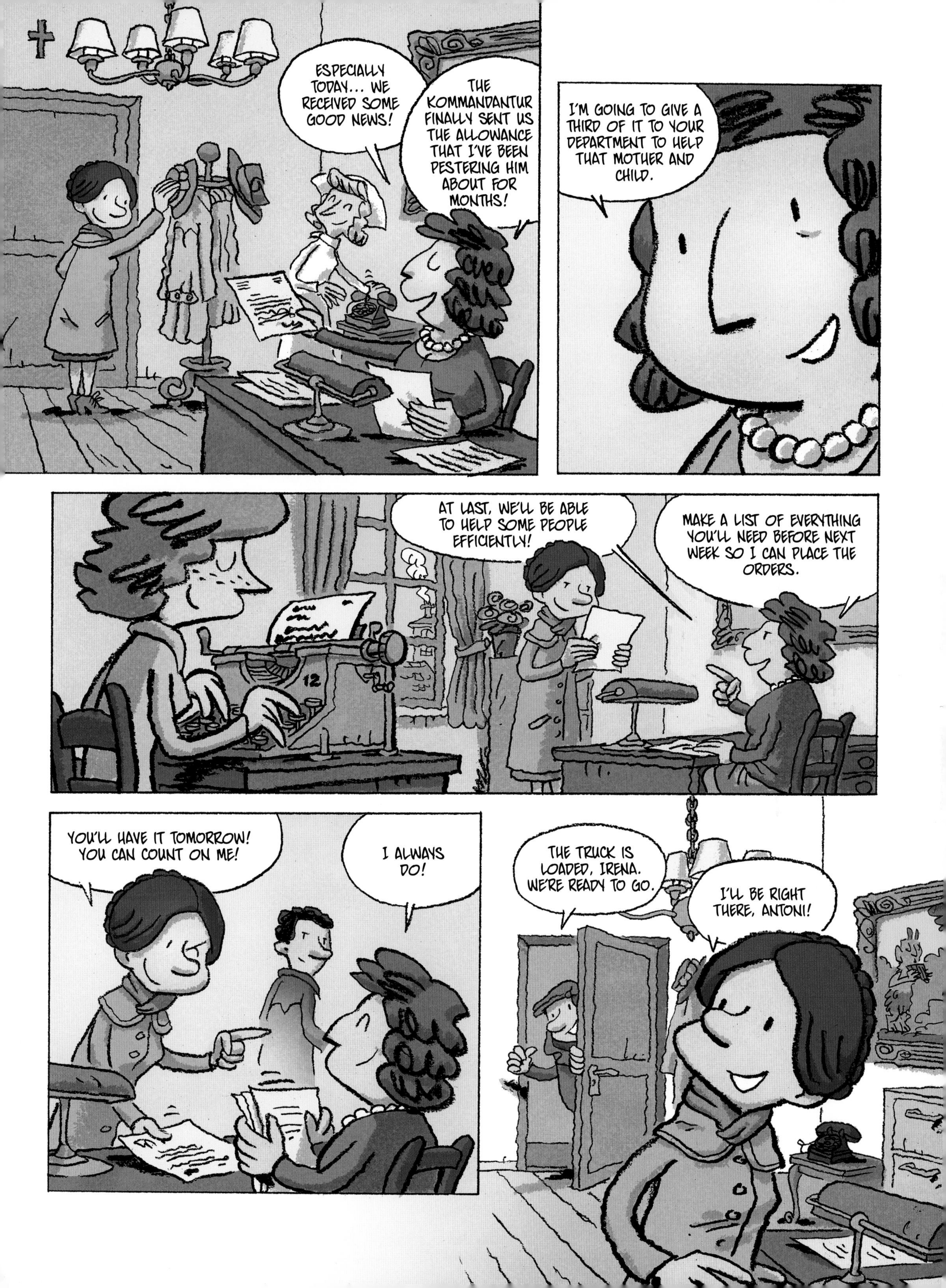
ESPECIALLY TODAY... WE RECEIVED SOME GOOD NEWS!
THE KOMMANDANTUR FINALLY SENT US THE ALLOWANCE THAT I'VE BEEN PESTERING HIM ABOUT FOR MONTHS!
I'M GOING TO GIVE A THIRD OF IT TO YOUR DEPARTMENT TO HELP THAT MOTHER AND CHILD.
AT LAST, WE'LL BE ABLE TO HELP SOME PEOPLE EFFICIENTLY!
MAKE A LIST OF EVERYTHING YOU'LL NEED BEFORE NEXT WEEK SO I CAN PLACE THE ORDERS.
YOU'LL HAVE IT TOMORROW! YOU CAN COUNT ON ME!
I ALWAYS DO!
THE TRUCK IS LOADED, IRENA. WE'RE READY TO GO.
I'LL BE RIGHT THERE, ANTONI!

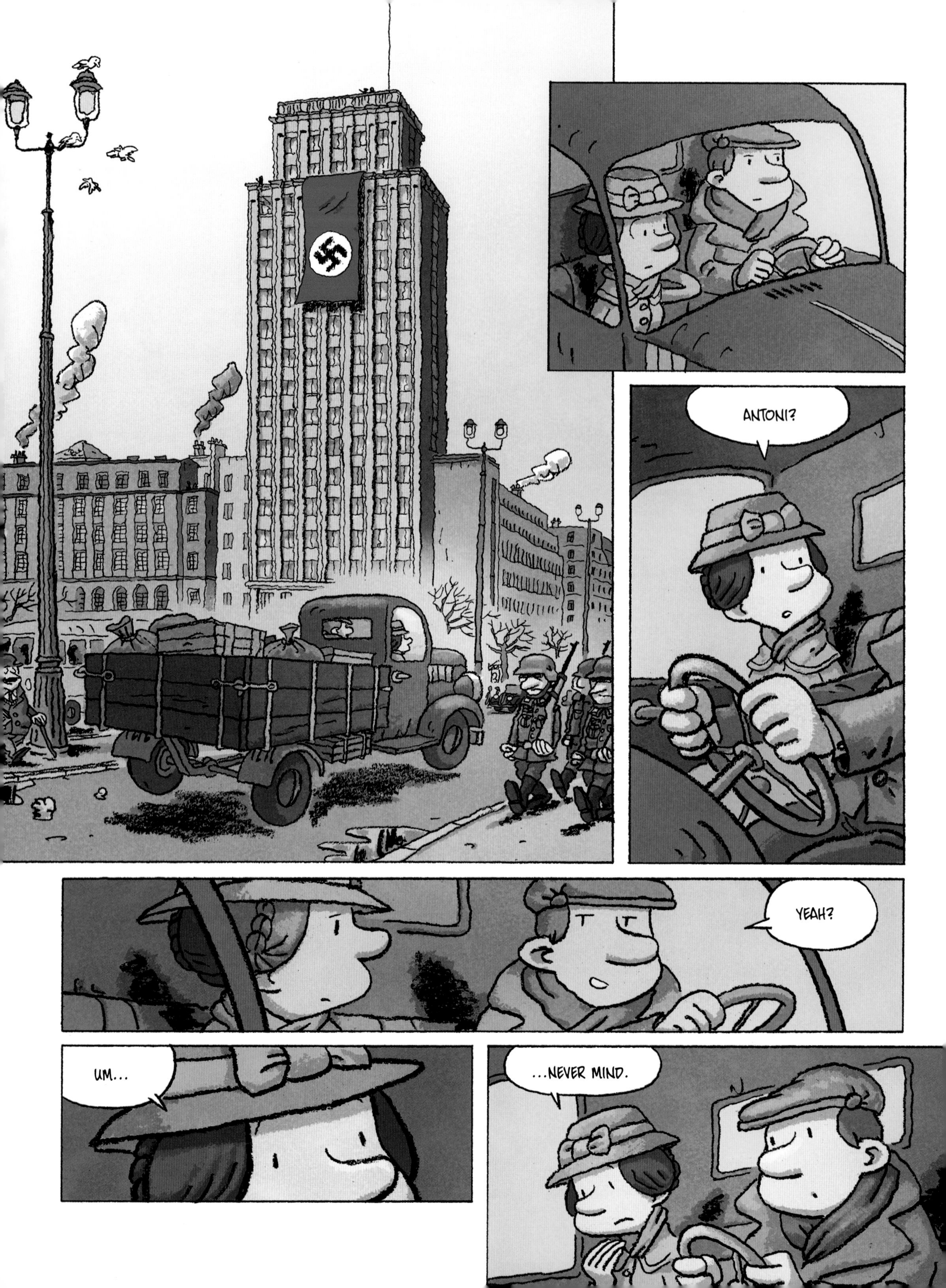
ANTONI?
YEAH?
UM...
...NEVER MIND.

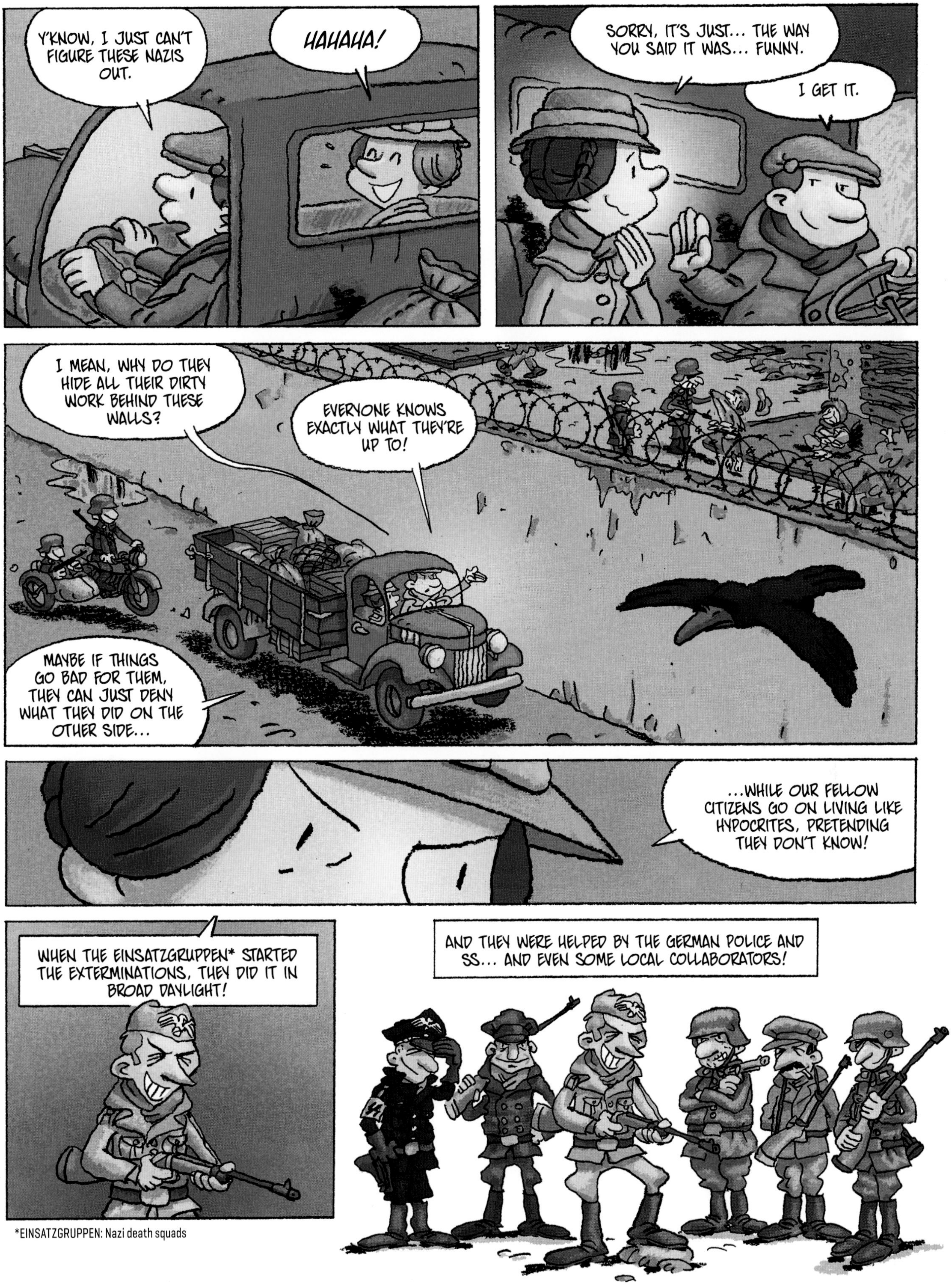
Y'KNOW, I JUST CAN'T FIGURE THESE NAZIS OUT.
HAHAHA!
SORRY, IT'S JUST... THE WAY YOU SAID IT WAS... FUNNY.
I GET IT.
I MEAN, WHY DO THEY HIDE ALL THEIR DIRTY WORK BEHIND THESE WALLS?
EVERYONE KNOWS EXACTLY WHAT THEY'RE UP TO!
MAYBE IF THINGS GO BAD FOR THEM, THEY CAN JUST DENY WHAT THEY DID ON THE OTHER SIDE...
...WHILE OUR FELLOW CITIZENS GO ON LIVING LIKE HYPOCRITES, PRETENDING THEY DON'T KNOW!
WHEN THE EINSATZGRUPPEN* STARTED THE EXTERMINATIONS, THEY DID IT IN BROAD DAYLIGHT!
AND THEY WERE HELPED BY THE GERMAN POLICE AND SS... AND EVEN SOME LOCAL COLLABORATORS!

*EINSATZGRUPPEN: Nazi death squads

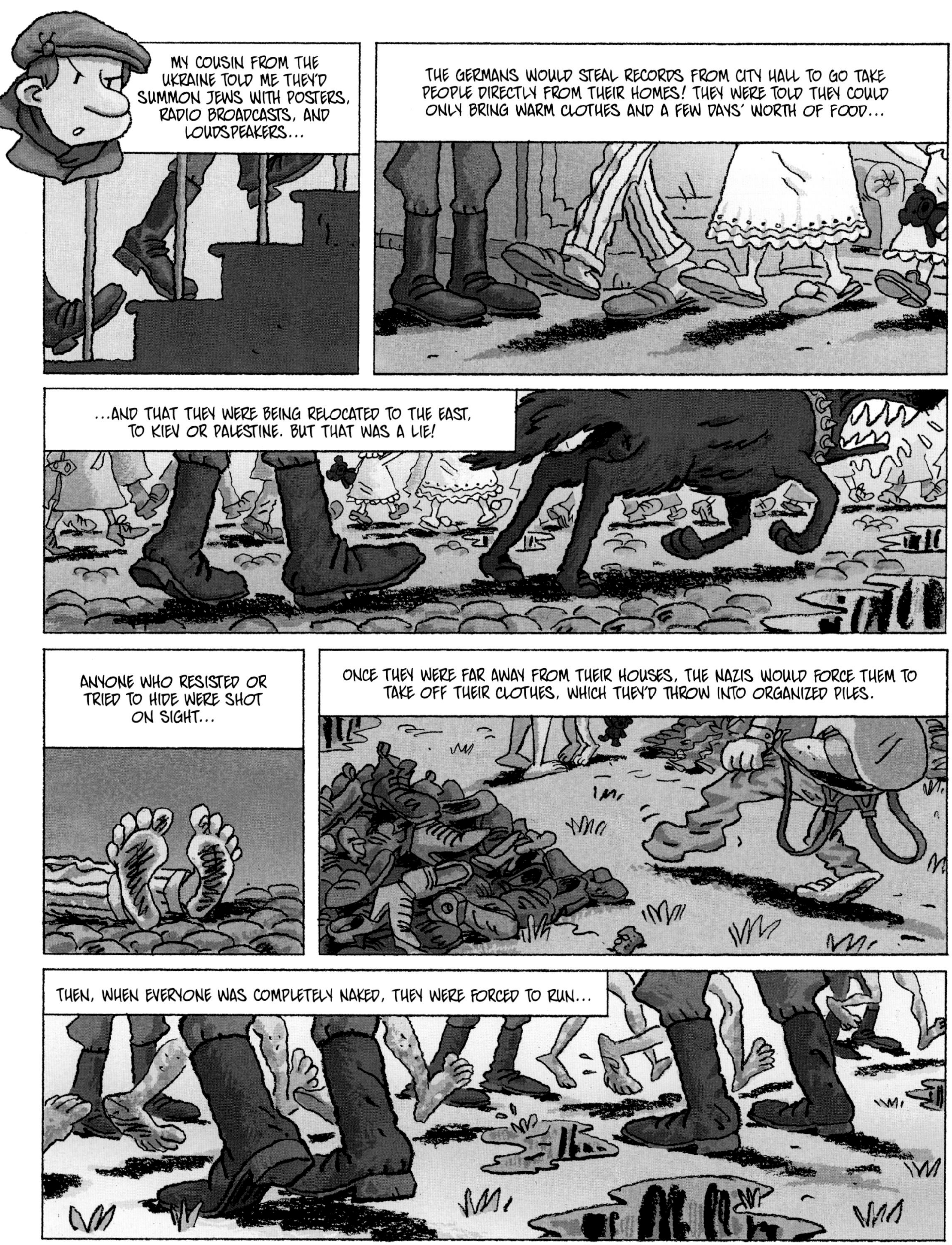
MY COUSIN FROM THE UKRAINE TOLD ME THEY'D SUMMON JEWS WITH POSTERS, RADIO BROADCASTS, AND LOUDSPEAKERS...
THE GERMANS WOULD STEAL RECORDS FROM CITY HALL TO GO TAKE PEOPLE DIRECTLY FROM THEIR HOMES! THEY WERE TOLD THEY COULD ONLY BRING WARM CLOTHES AND A FEW DAYS' WORTH OF FOOD...
...AND THAT THEY WERE BEING RELOCATED TO THE EAST, TO KIEV OR PALESTINE. BUT THAT WAS A LIE!
ANYONE WHO RESISTED OR TRIED TO HIDE WERE SHOT ON SIGHT...
ONCE THEY WERE FAR AWAY FROM THEIR HOUSES, THE NAZIS WOULD FORCE THEM TO TAKE OFF THEIR CLOTHES, WHICH THEY'D THROW INTO ORGANIZED PILES.
THEN, WHEN EVERYONE WAS COMPLETELY NAKED, THEY WERE FORCED TO RUN...

...IT WASN'T UNTIL THE END THAT THEY DISCOVERED THE MASS GRAVES, USUALLY DUG BY PEASANTS OR LOCAL WORKERS.

MY COUSIN WAS ONE OF THOSE WORKERS. HE HAD NIGHTMARES EVERY NIGHT...

THE LAST MOMENTS OF THEIR LIVES WERE STARING DOWN AT THE BODIES ALREADY LYING IN THE GRAVES. MEN, WOMEN, AND CHILDREN, ALL PILED UP ON EACH OTHER. SOMETIMES THEY'D EVEN RECOGNIZE MEMBERS OF THEIR OWN FAMILIES...

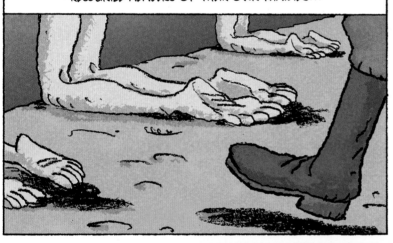

AFTER SEEING THAT, THE BULLET FIRED INTO THEIR BACKS WAS MAYBE -- JUST *MAYBE*...

BANG!

...A RELIEF.

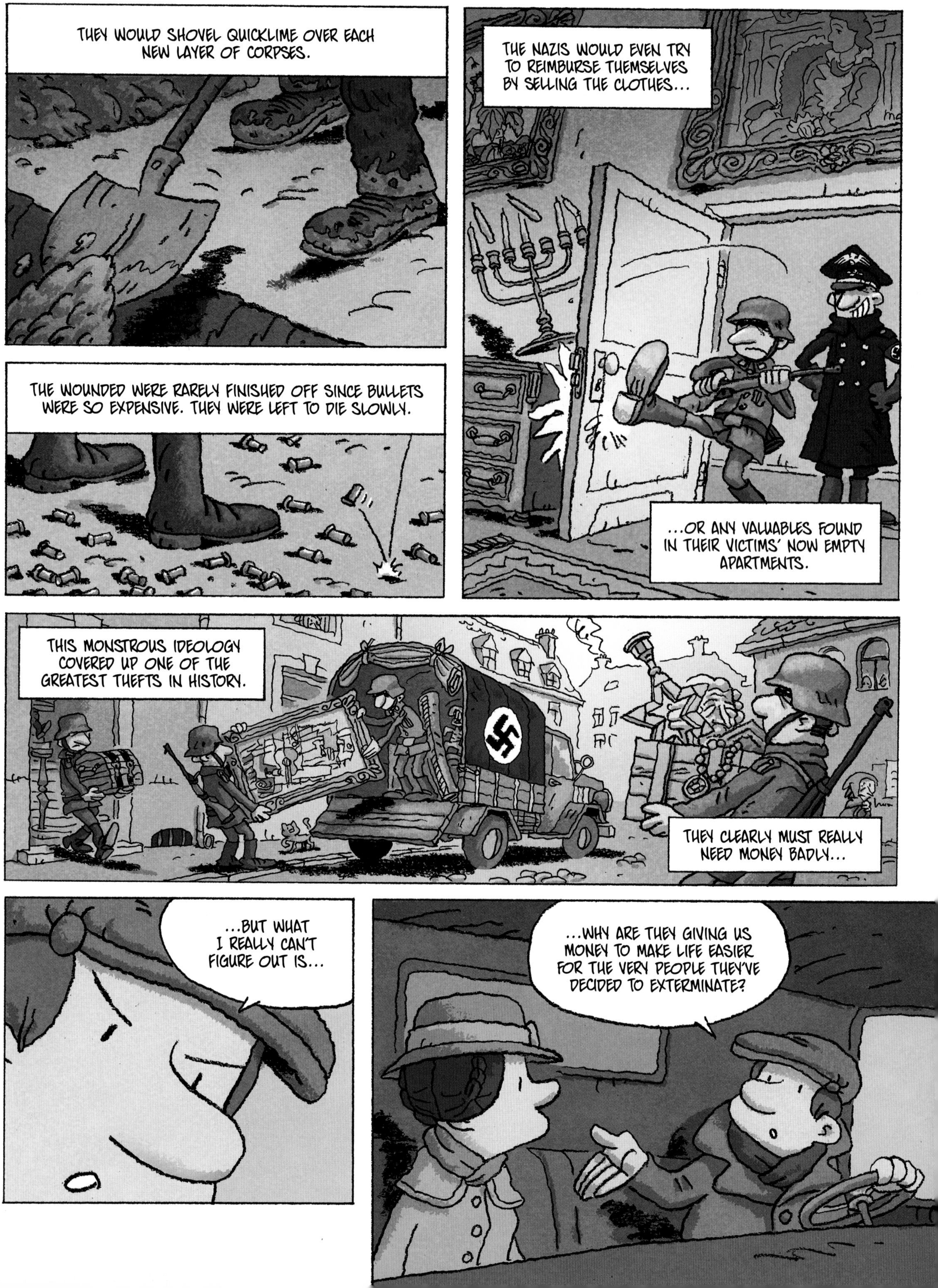
THEY WOULD SHOVEL QUICKLIME OVER EACH NEW LAYER OF CORPSES.
THE NAZIS WOULD EVEN TRY TO REIMBURSE THEMSELVES BY SELLING THE CLOTHES...
THE WOUNDED WERE RARELY FINISHED OFF SINCE BULLETS WERE SO EXPENSIVE. THEY WERE LEFT TO DIE SLOWLY.
...OR ANY VALUABLES FOUND IN THEIR VICTIMS' NOW EMPTY APARTMENTS.
THIS MONSTROUS IDEOLOGY COVERED UP ONE OF THE GREATEST THEFTS IN HISTORY.
THEY CLEARLY MUST REALLY NEED MONEY BADLY...
...BUT WHAT I REALLY CAN'T FIGURE OUT IS...
...WHY ARE THEY GIVING US MONEY TO MAKE LIFE EASIER FOR THE VERY PEOPLE THEY'VE DECIDED TO EXTERMINATE?

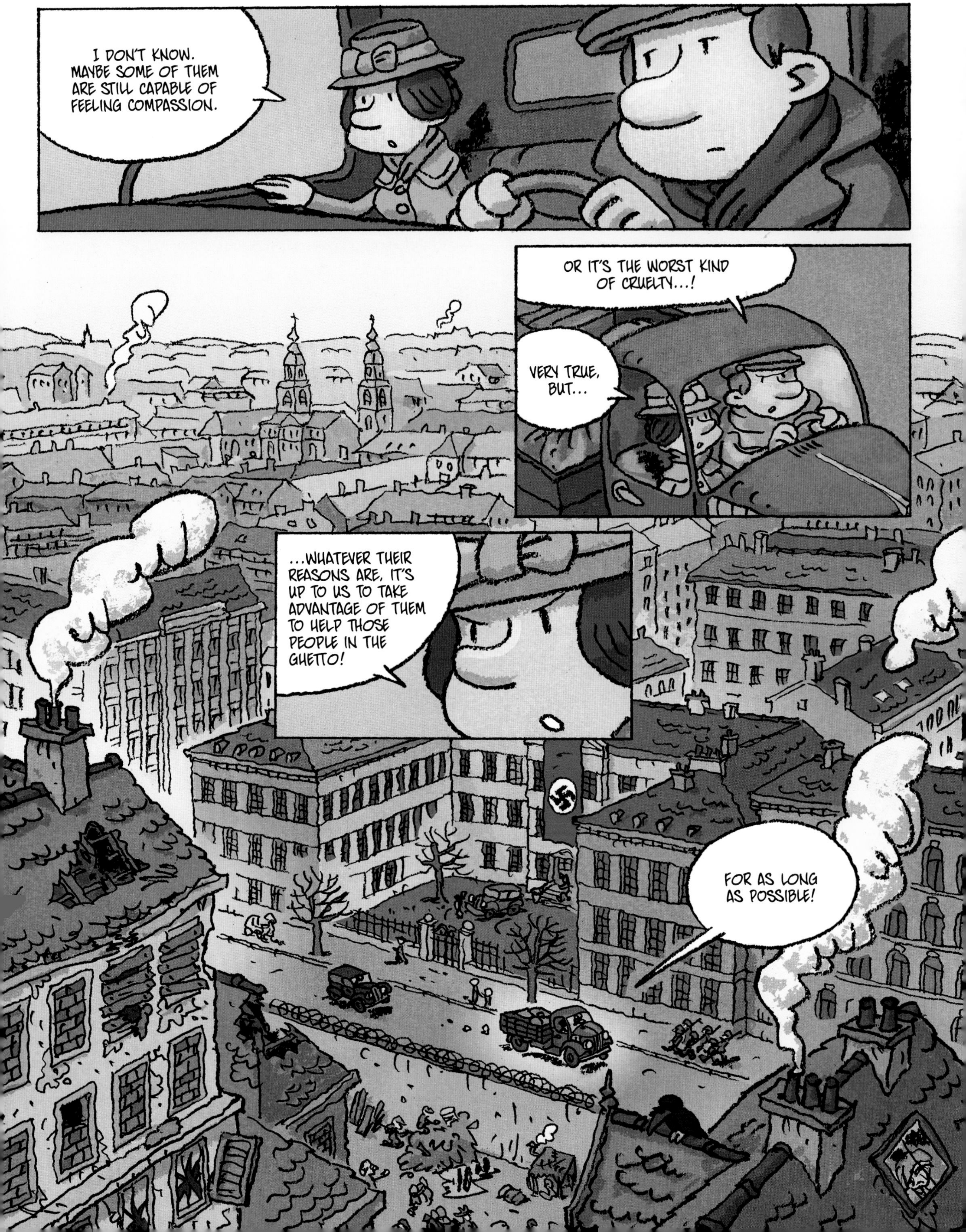
I DON'T KNOW. MAYBE SOME OF THEM ARE STILL CAPABLE OF FEELING COMPASSION.
OR IT'S THE WORST KIND OF CRUELTY...!
VERY TRUE, BUT...
...WHATEVER THEIR REASONS ARE, IT'S UP TO US TO TAKE ADVANTAGE OF THEM TO HELP THOSE PEOPLE IN THE GHETTO!
FOR AS LONG AS POSSIBLE!

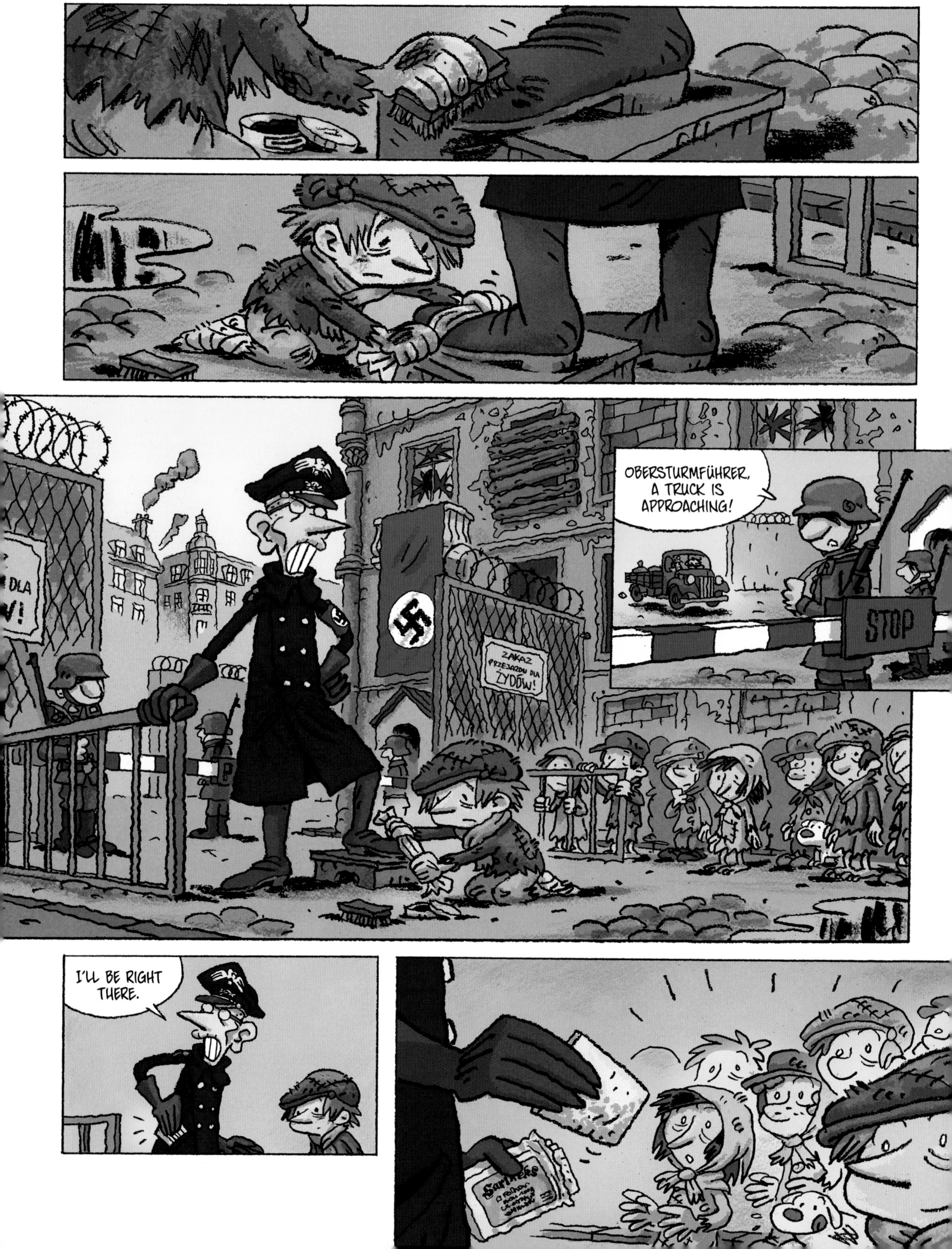
ZAKAZ
PRZEJAZDU DLA
ŻYDÓW!
OBERSTURMFÜHRER, A TRUCK IS APPROACHING!
STOP
I'LL BE RIGHT THERE.

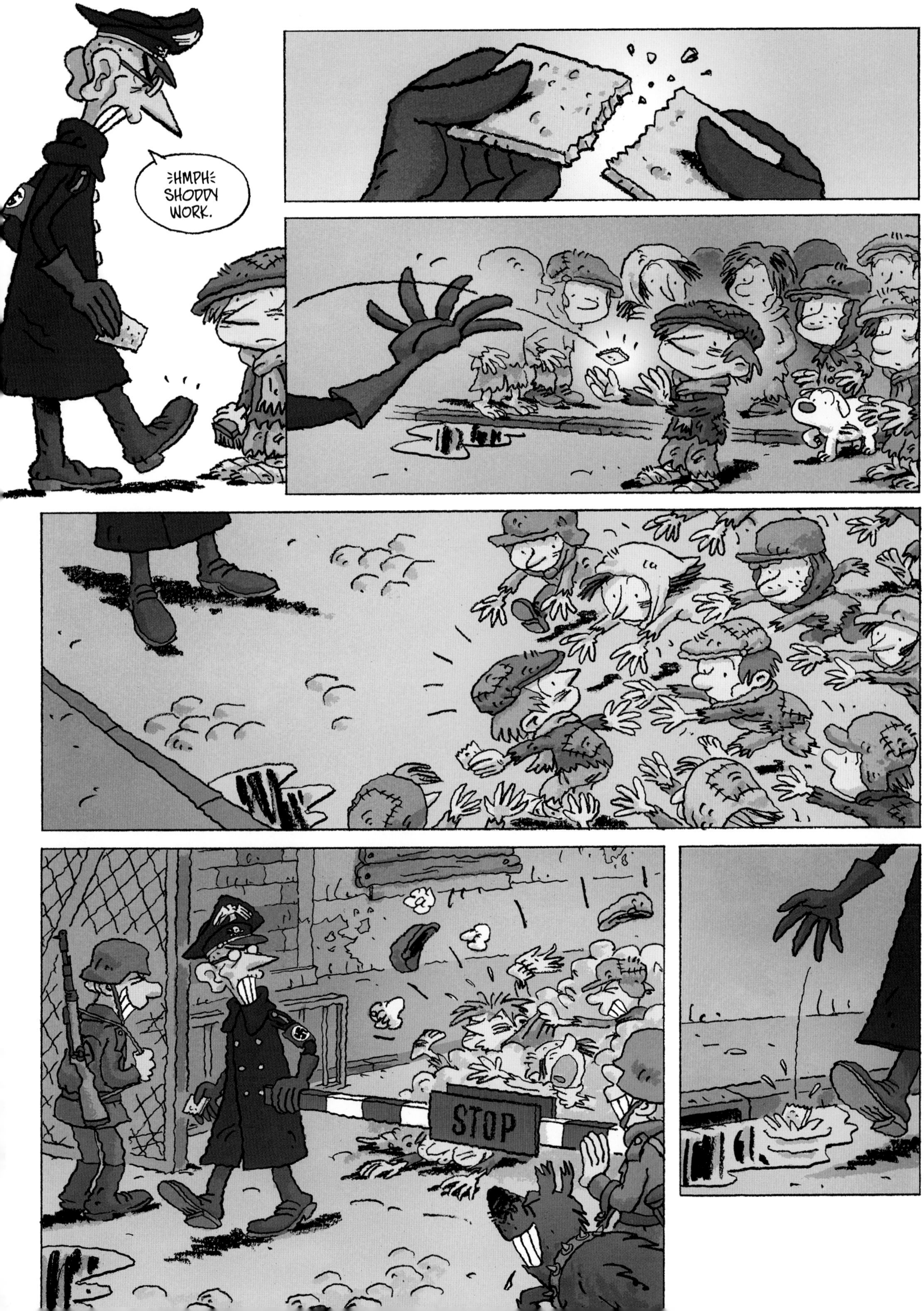
HMPH SHODDY WORK.
STOP

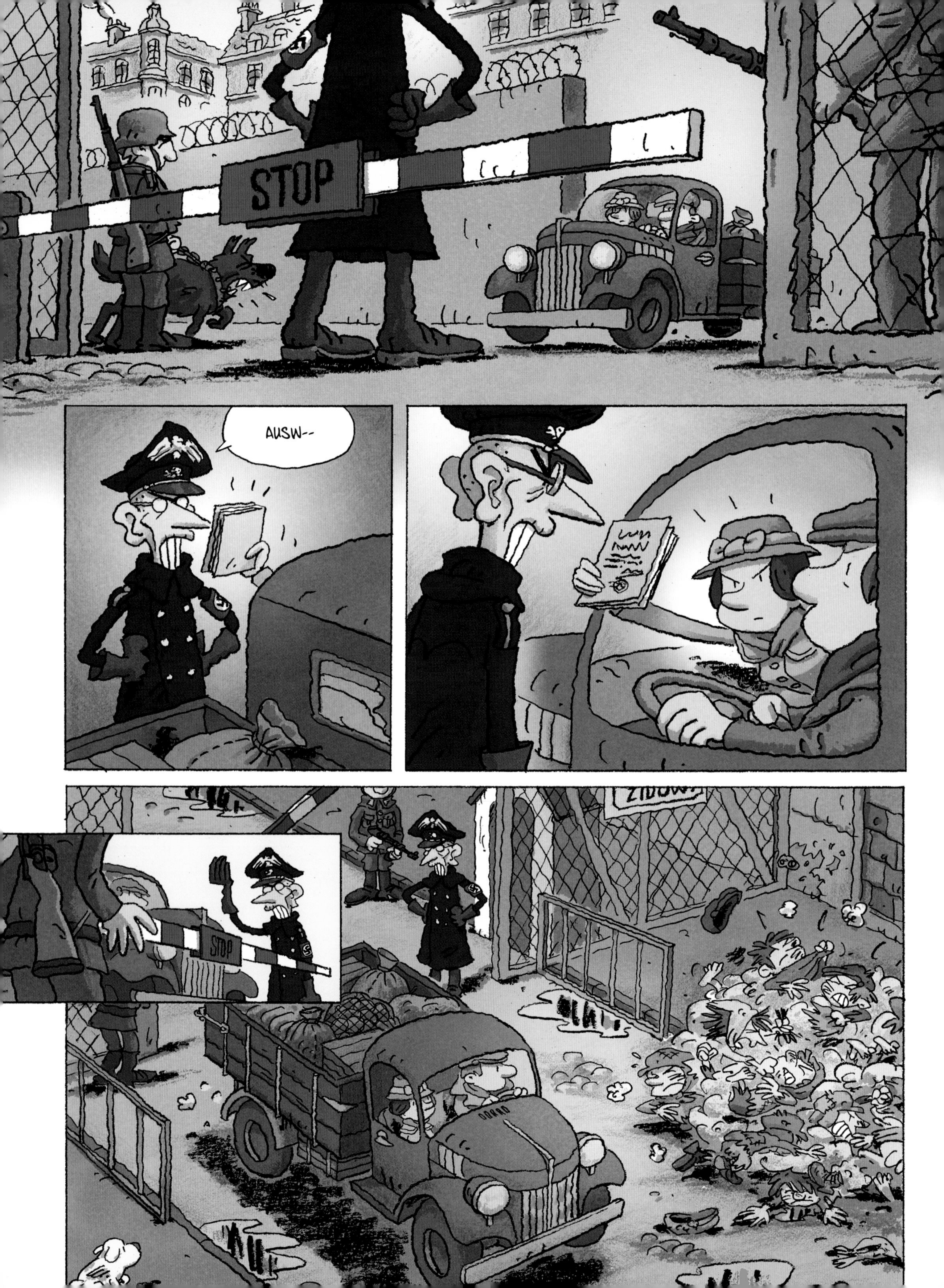
STOP
AUSW--
STOP

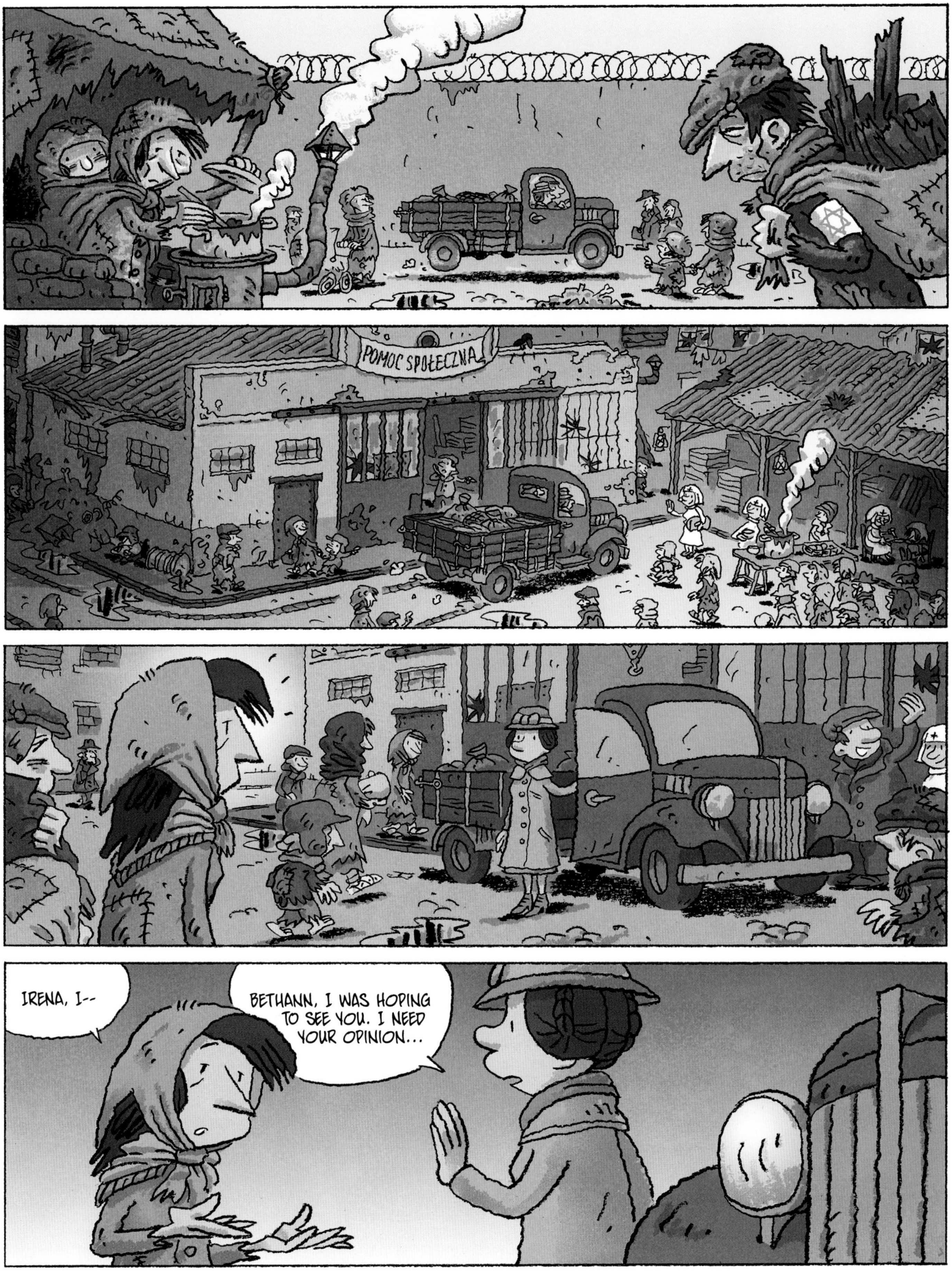

POMOC SPOŁECZNA
IRENA, I--
BETHANN, I WAS HOPING TO SEE YOU. I NEED YOUR OPINION...

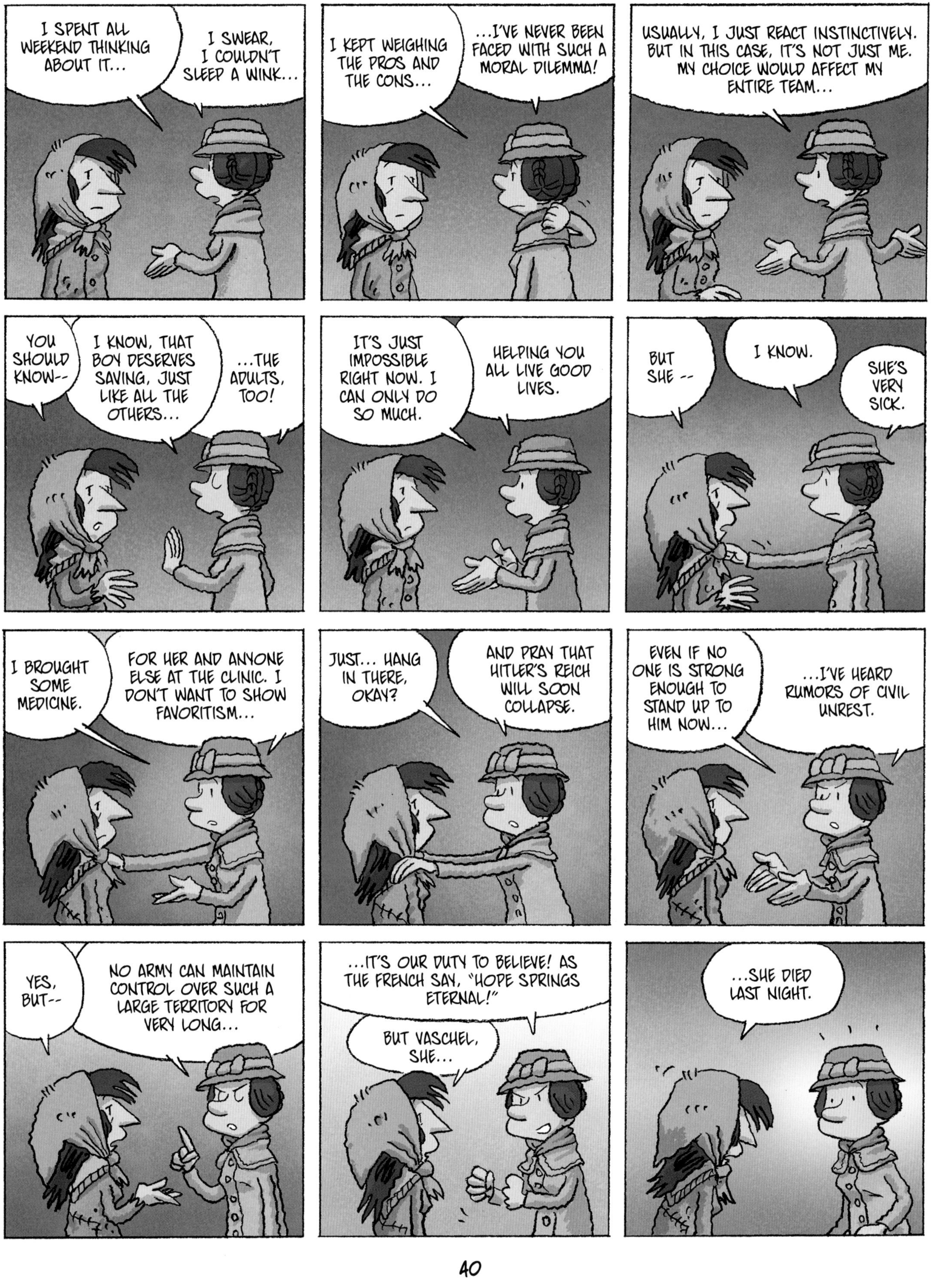
I SPENT ALL WEEKEND THINKING ABOUT IT...
I SWEAR, I COULDN'T SLEEP A WINK...
I KEPT WEIGHING THE PROS AND THE CONS...
...I'VE NEVER BEEN FACED WITH SUCH A MORAL DILEMMA!
USUALLY, I JUST REACT INSTINCTIVELY. BUT IN THIS CASE, IT'S NOT JUST ME. MY CHOICE WOULD AFFECT MY ENTIRE TEAM...
YOU SHOULD KNOW--
I KNOW, THAT BOY DESERVES SAVING, JUST LIKE ALL THE OTHERS...
...THE ADULTS, TOO!
IT'S JUST IMPOSSIBLE RIGHT NOW. I CAN ONLY DO SO MUCH.
HELPING YOU ALL LIVE GOOD LIVES.
BUT SHE --
I KNOW.
SHE'S VERY SICK.
I BROUGHT SOME MEDICINE.
FOR HER AND ANYONE ELSE AT THE CLINIC. I DON'T WANT TO SHOW FAVORITISM...
JUST... HANG IN THERE, OKAY?
AND PRAY THAT HITLER'S REICH WILL SOON COLLAPSE.
EVEN IF NO ONE IS STRONG ENOUGH TO STAND UP TO HIM NOW...
...I'VE HEARD RUMORS OF CIVIL UNREST.
YES, BUT--
NO ARMY CAN MAINTAIN CONTROL OVER SUCH A LARGE TERRITORY FOR VERY LONG...
...IT'S OUR DUTY TO BELIEVE! AS THE FRENCH SAY, "HOPE SPRINGS ETERNAL!"
BUT VASCHEL, SHE...
...SHE DIED LAST NIGHT.

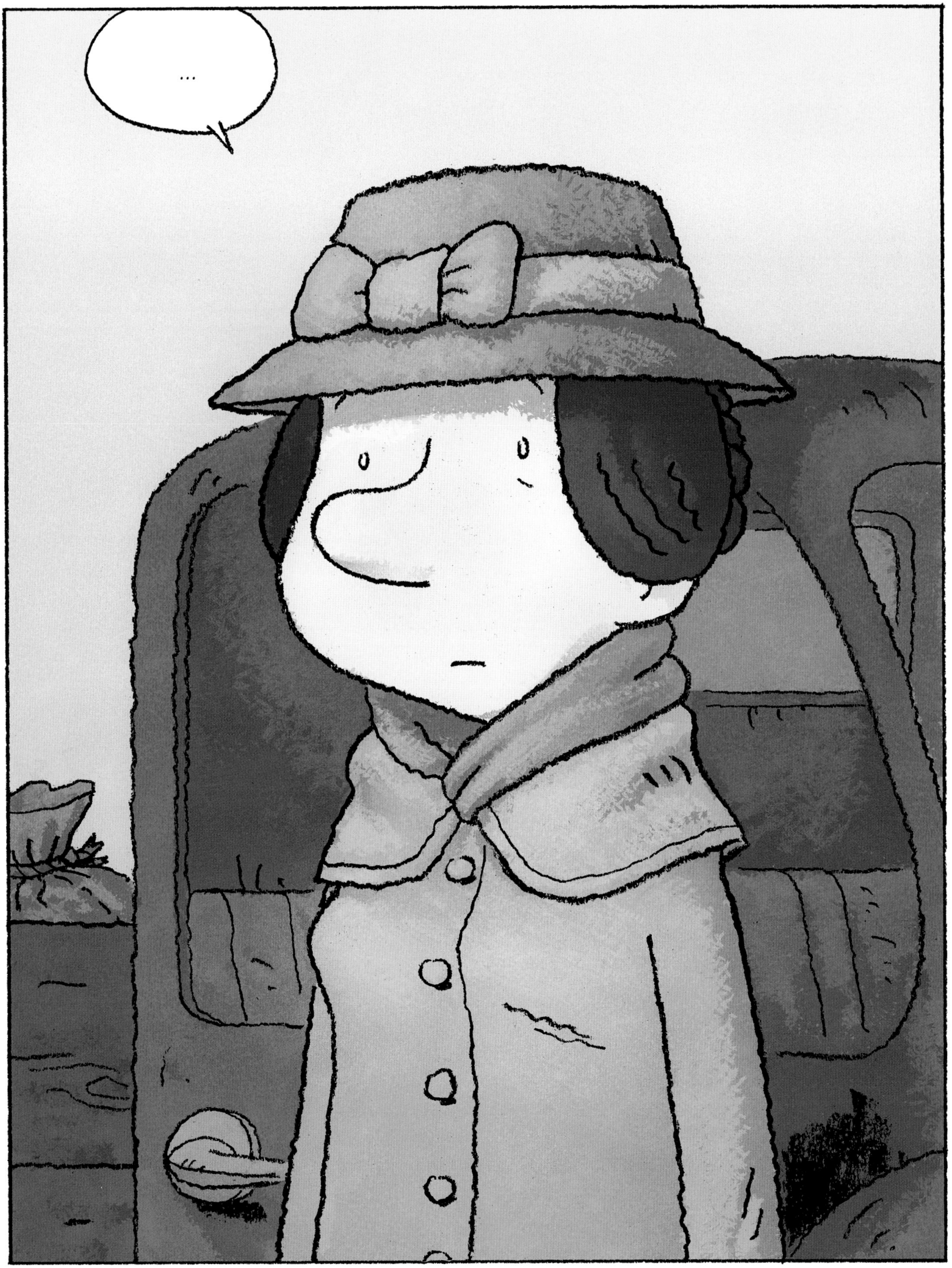
...

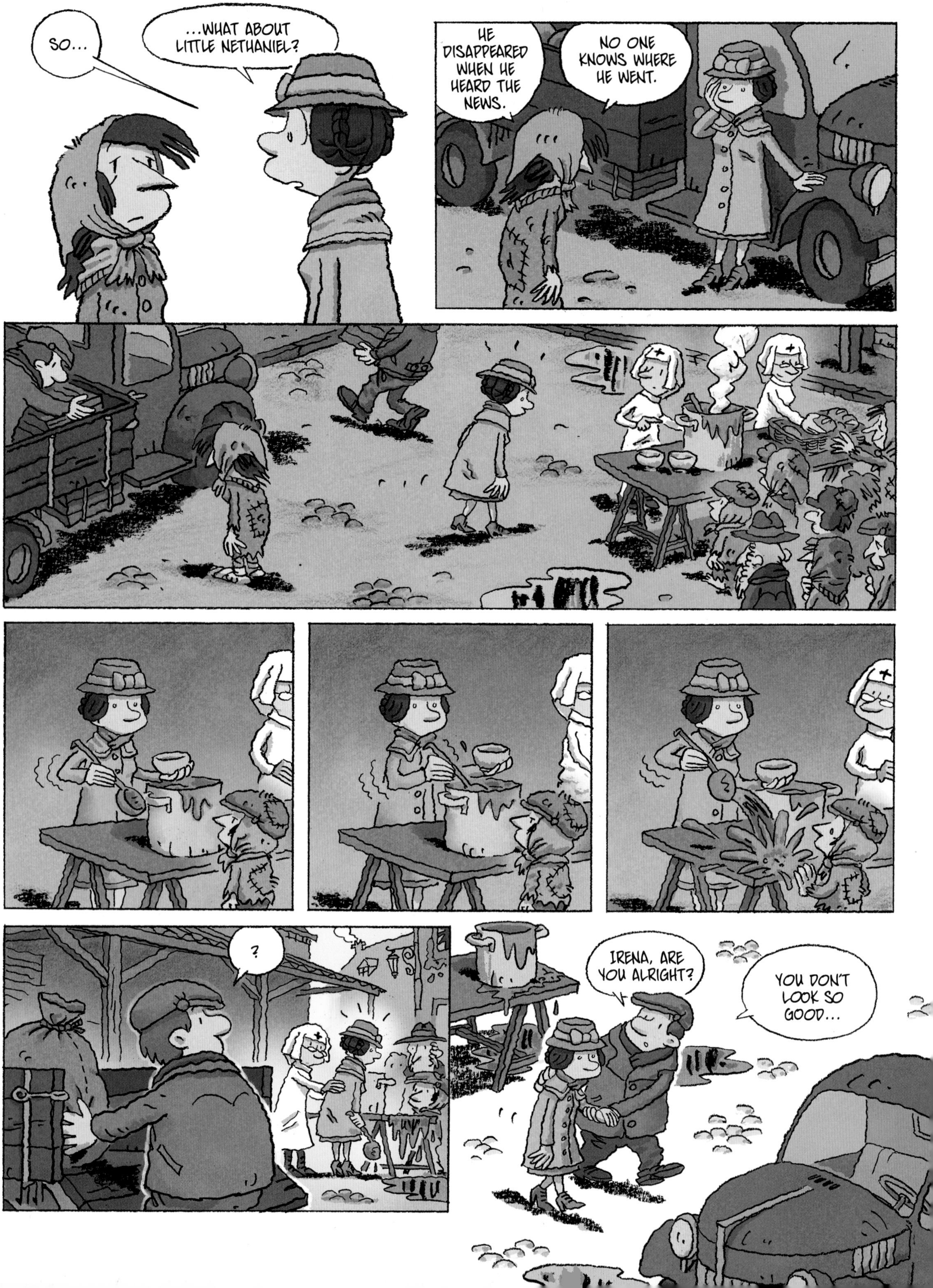
SO...
...WHAT ABOUT LITTLE NETHANIEL?
HE DISAPPEARED WHEN HE HEARD THE NEWS.
NO ONE KNOWS WHERE HE WENT.
?
IRENA, ARE YOU ALRIGHT?
YOU DON'T LOOK SO GOOD...

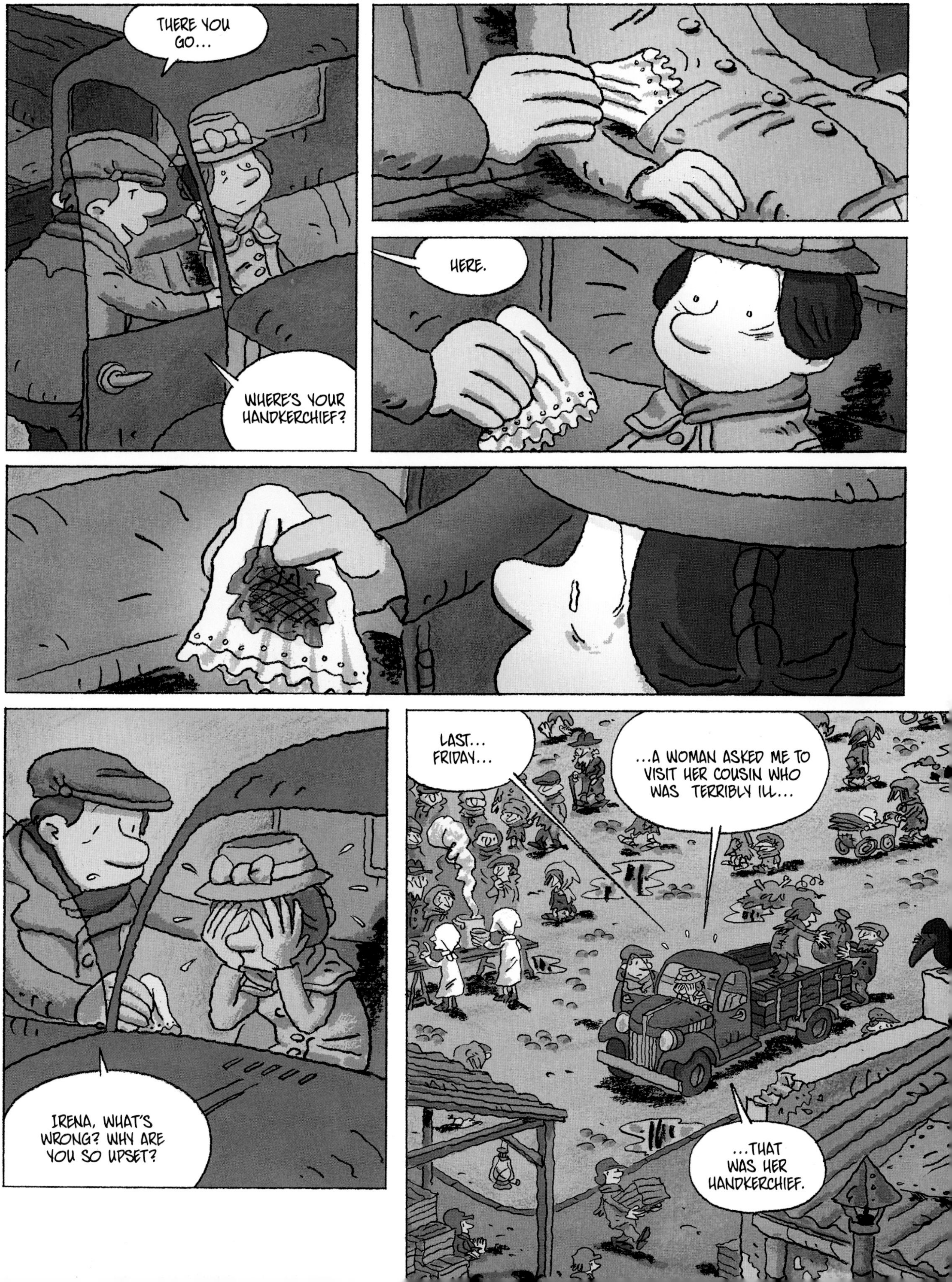
THERE YOU GO...
WHERE'S YOUR HANDKERCHIEF?
HERE.
IRENA, WHAT'S WRONG? WHY ARE YOU SO UPSET?
LAST... FRIDAY...
...A WOMAN ASKED ME TO VISIT HER COUSIN WHO WAS TERRIBLY ILL...
...THAT WAS HER HANDKERCHIEF.

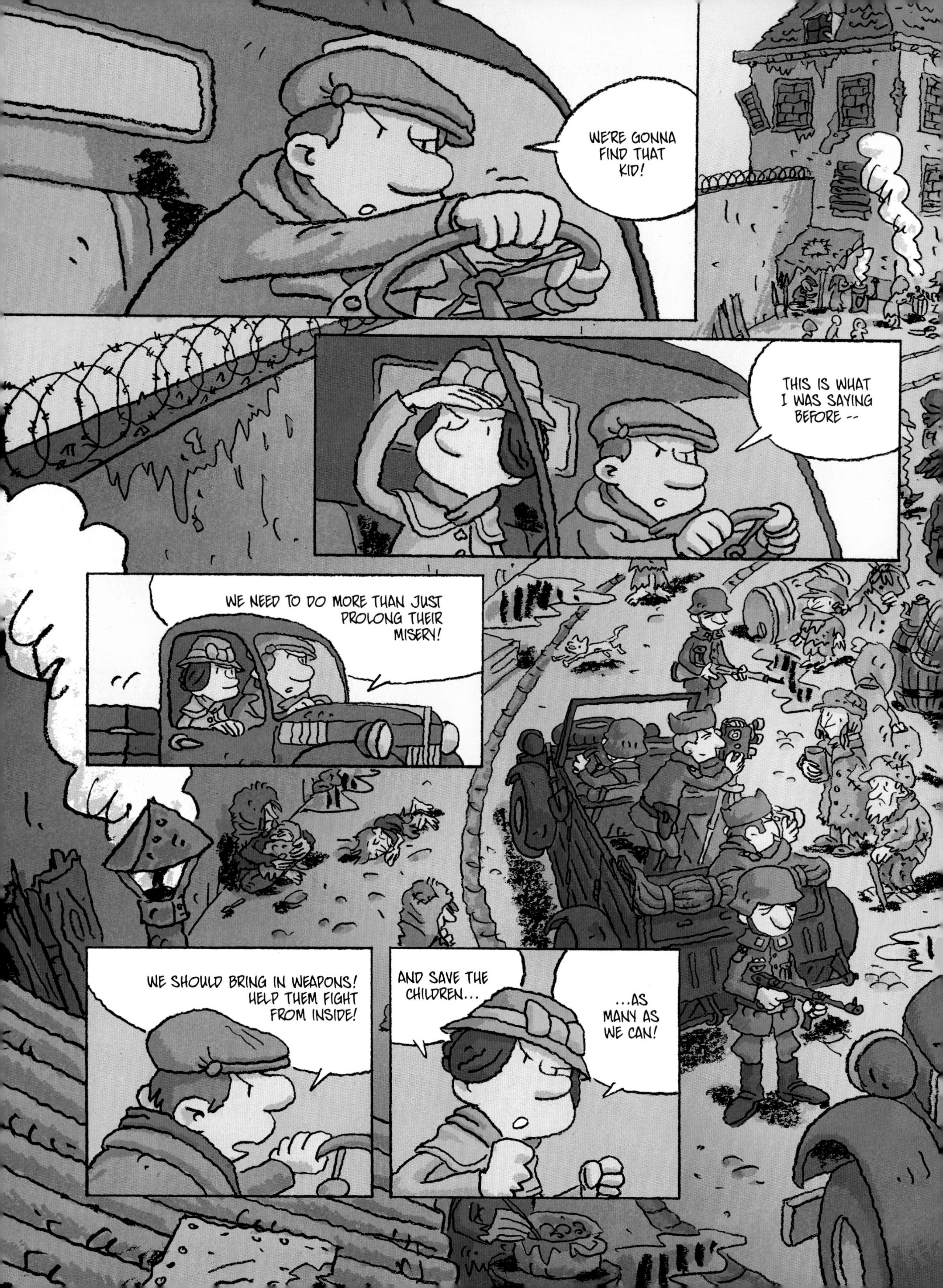
WE'RE GONNA FIND THAT KID!
THIS IS WHAT I WAS SAYING BEFORE --
WE NEED TO DO MORE THAN JUST PROLONG THEIR MISERY!
WE SHOULD BRING IN WEAPONS! HELP THEM FIGHT FROM INSIDE!
AND SAVE THE CHILDREN...
...AS MANY AS WE CAN!

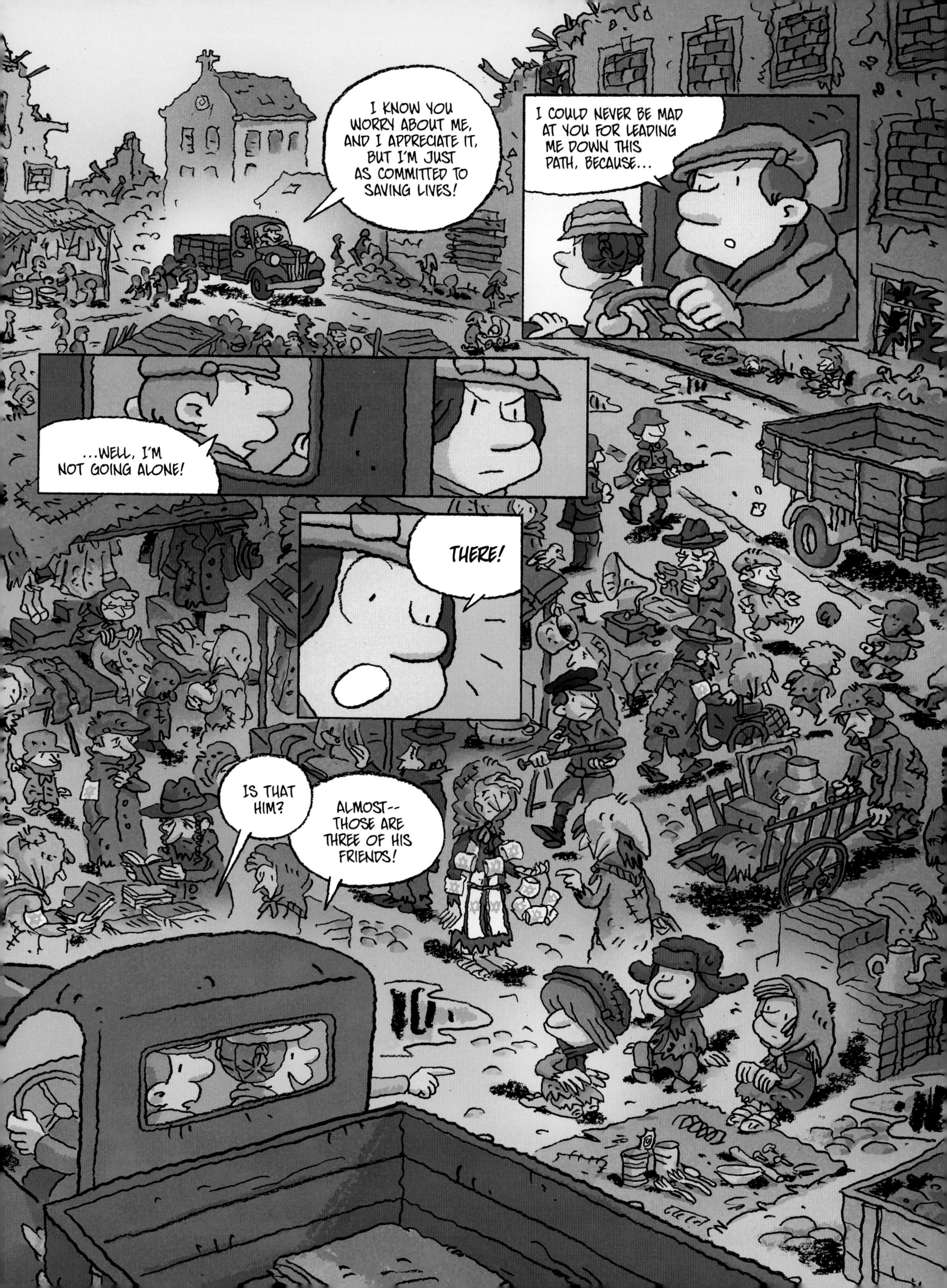
I KNOW YOU WORRY ABOUT ME, AND I APPRECIATE IT, BUT I'M JUST AS COMMITTED TO SAVING LIVES!
I COULD NEVER BE MAD AT YOU FOR LEADING ME DOWN THIS PATH, BECAUSE...
...WELL, I'M NOT GOING ALONE!
THERE!
IS THAT HIM?
ALMOST-- THOSE ARE THREE OF HIS FRIENDS!

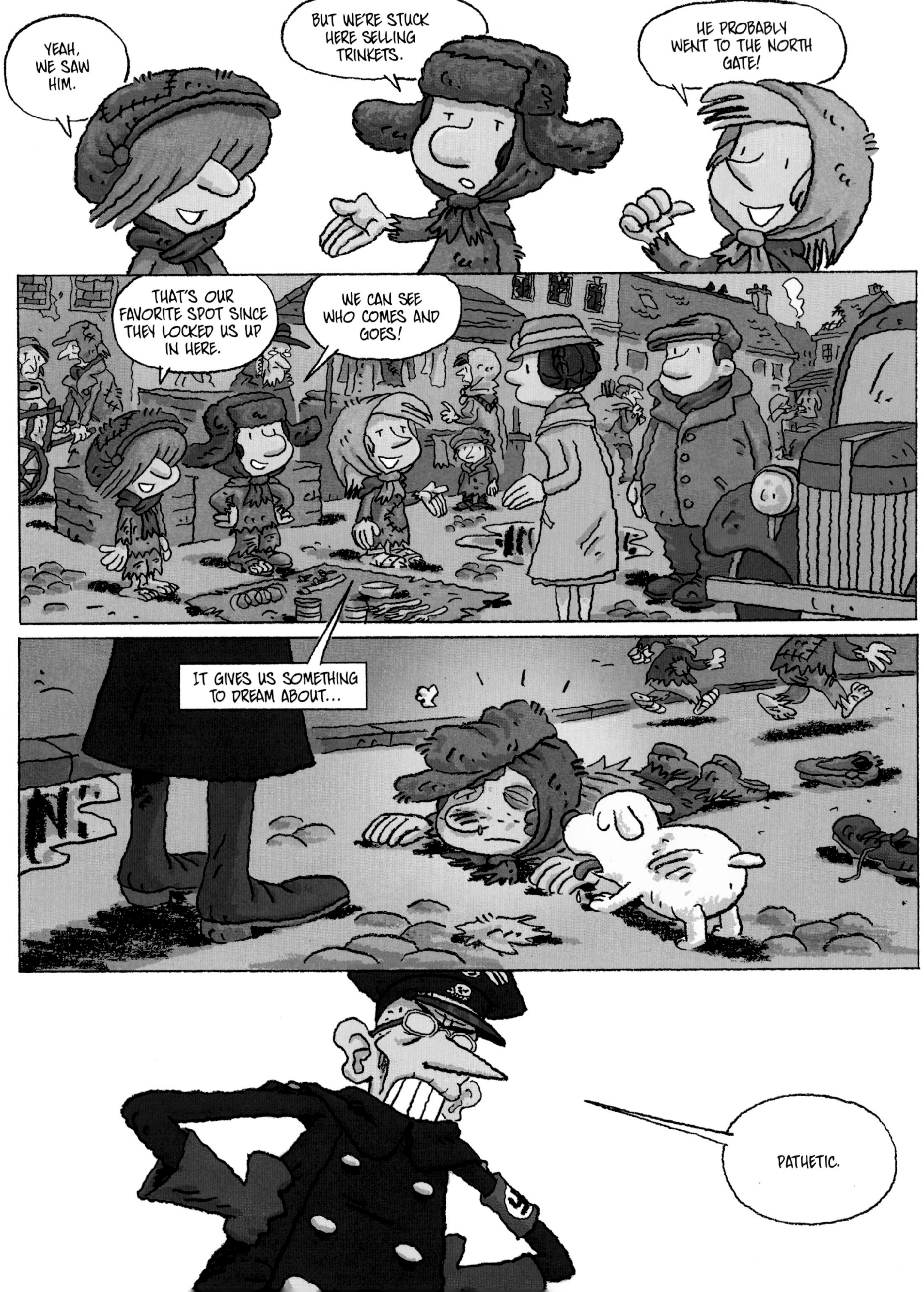
YEAH, WE SAW HIM.
BUT WE'RE STUCK HERE SELLING TRINKETS.
HE PROBABLY WENT TO THE NORTH GATE!
THAT'S OUR FAVORITE SPOT SINCE THEY LOCKED US UP IN HERE.
WE CAN SEE WHO COMES AND GOES!
IT GIVES US SOMETHING TO DREAM ABOUT...
PATHETIC.

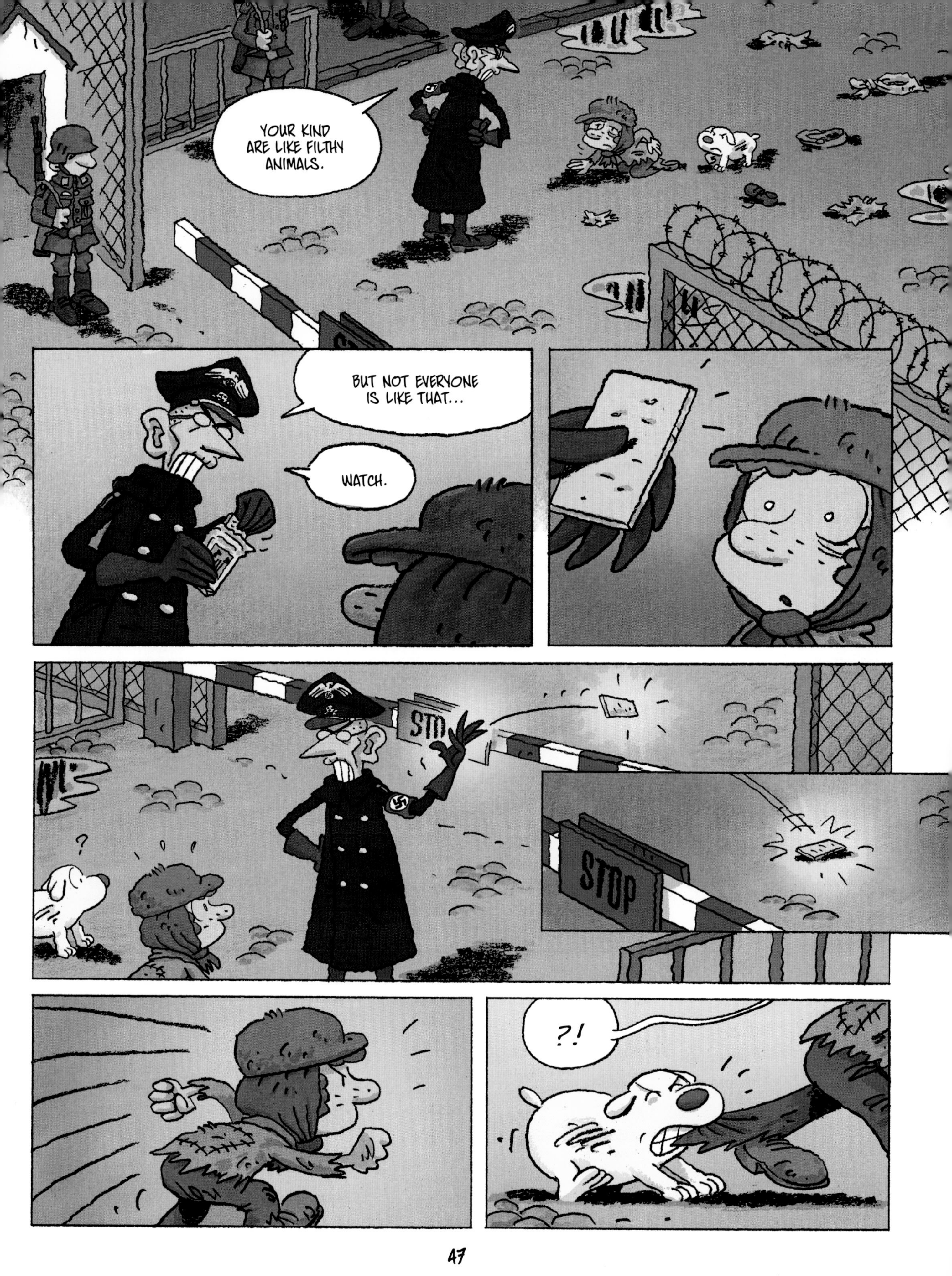
YOUR KIND ARE LIKE FILTHY ANIMALS.
BUT NOT EVERYONE IS LIKE THAT...
WATCH.
STOP
?!

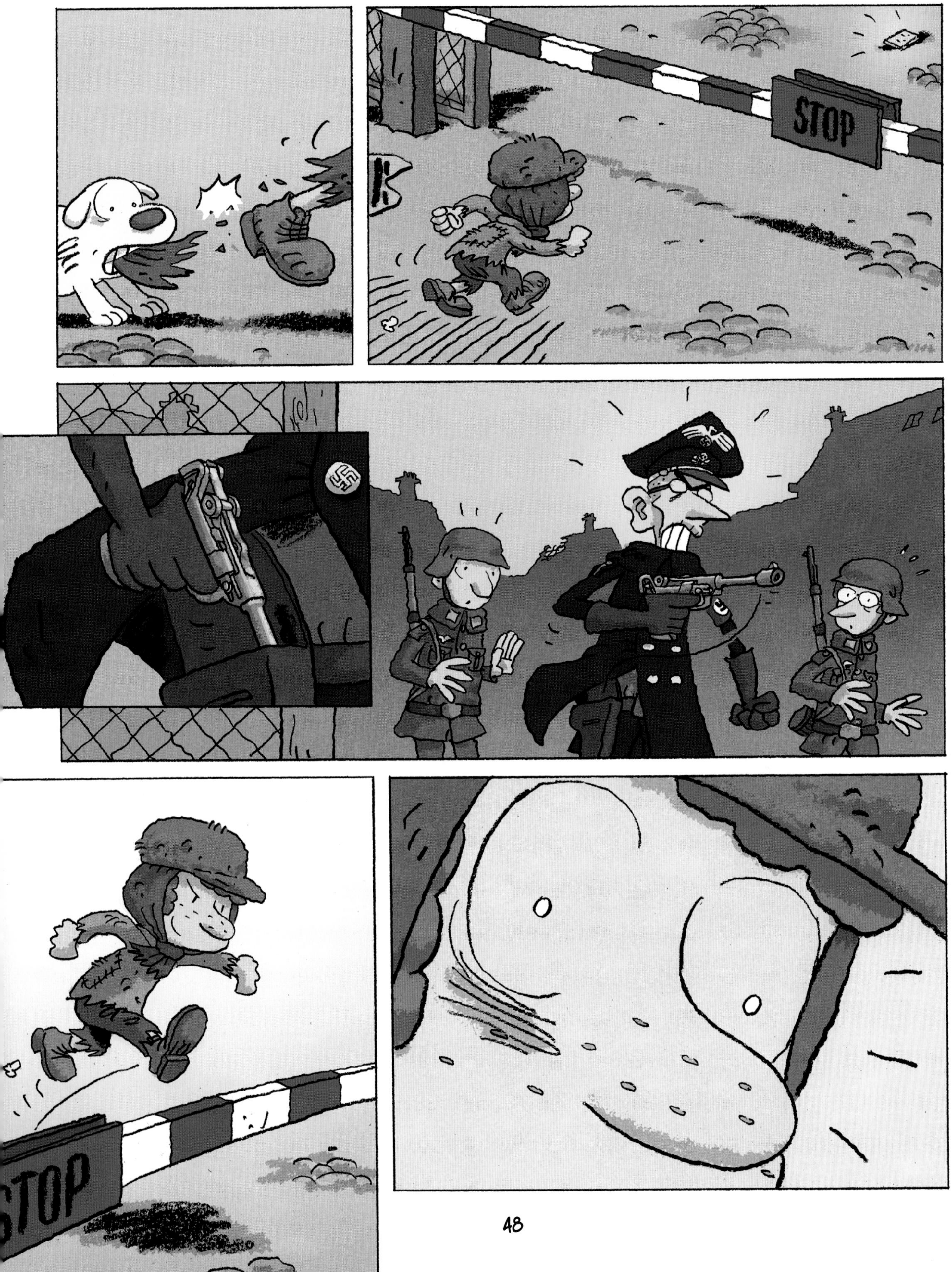
STOP
STOP

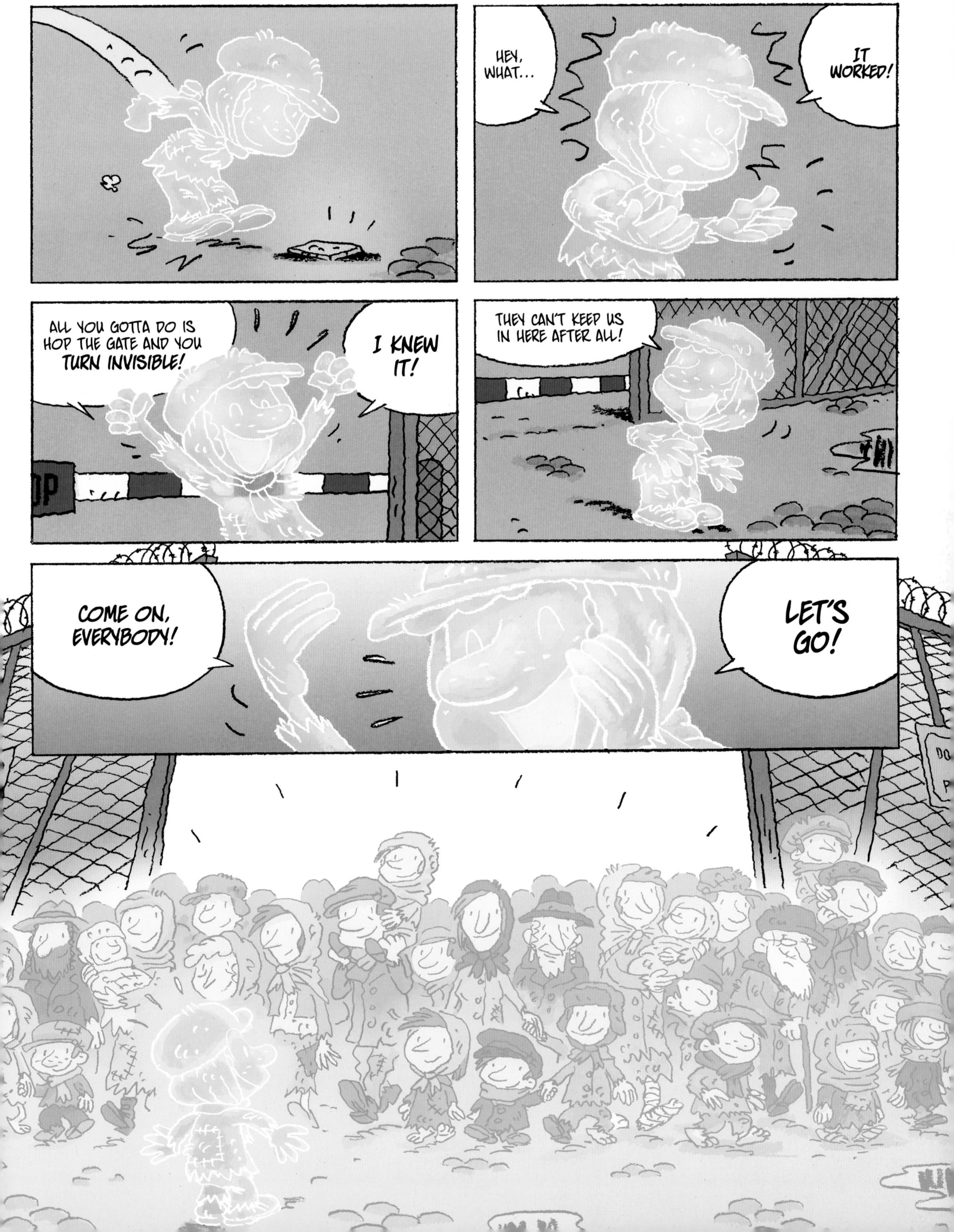
HEY, WHAT...
IT WORKED!
ALL YOU GOTTA DO IS HOP THE GATE AND YOU TURN INVISIBLE!
I KNEW IT!
THEY CAN'T KEEP US IN HERE AFTER ALL!
COME ON, EVERYBODY!
LET'S GO!

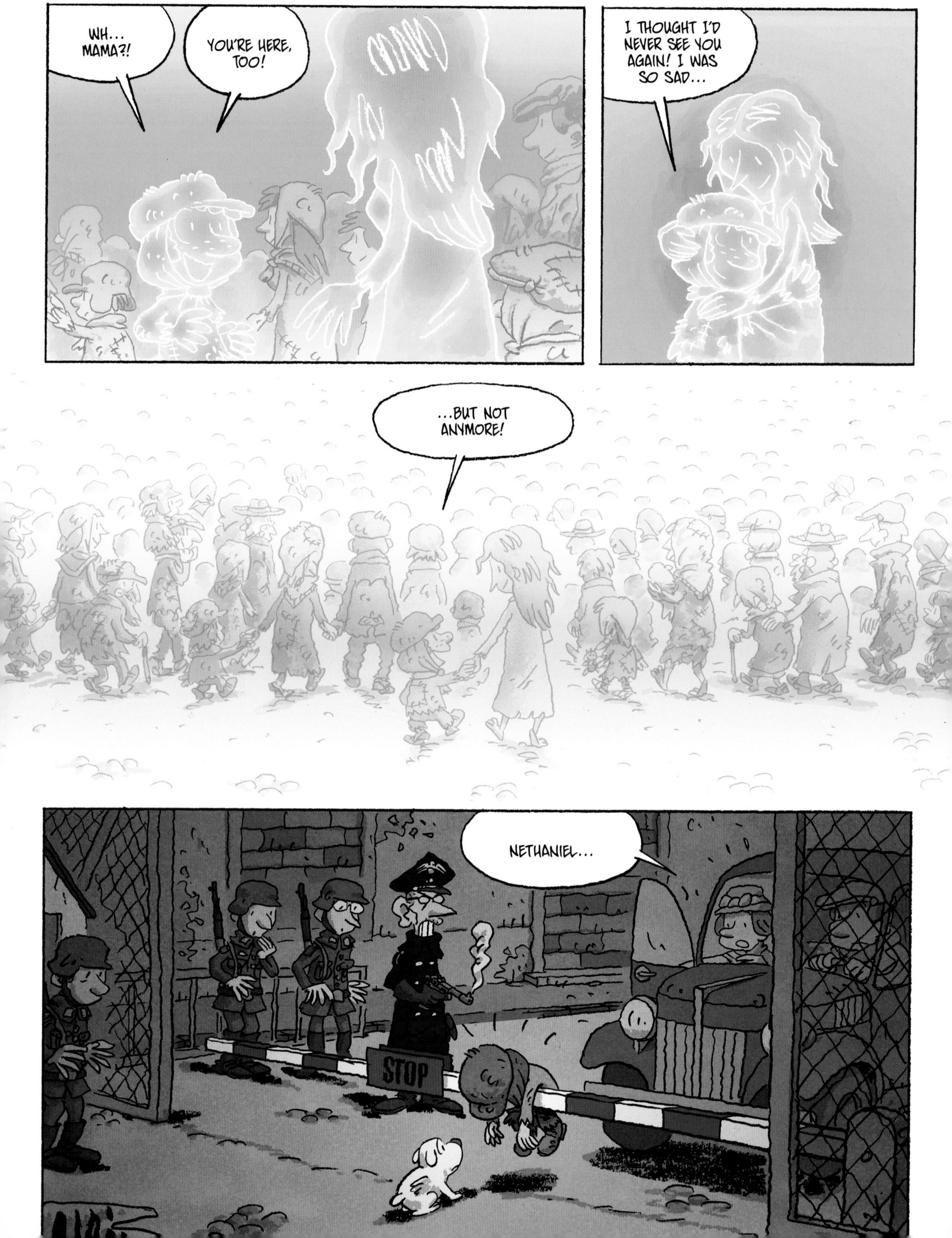
WH... MAMA?!
YOU'RE HERE, TOO!
I THOUGHT I'D NEVER SEE YOU AGAIN! I WAS SO SAD...
...BUT NOT ANYMORE!
NETHANIEL...
STOP

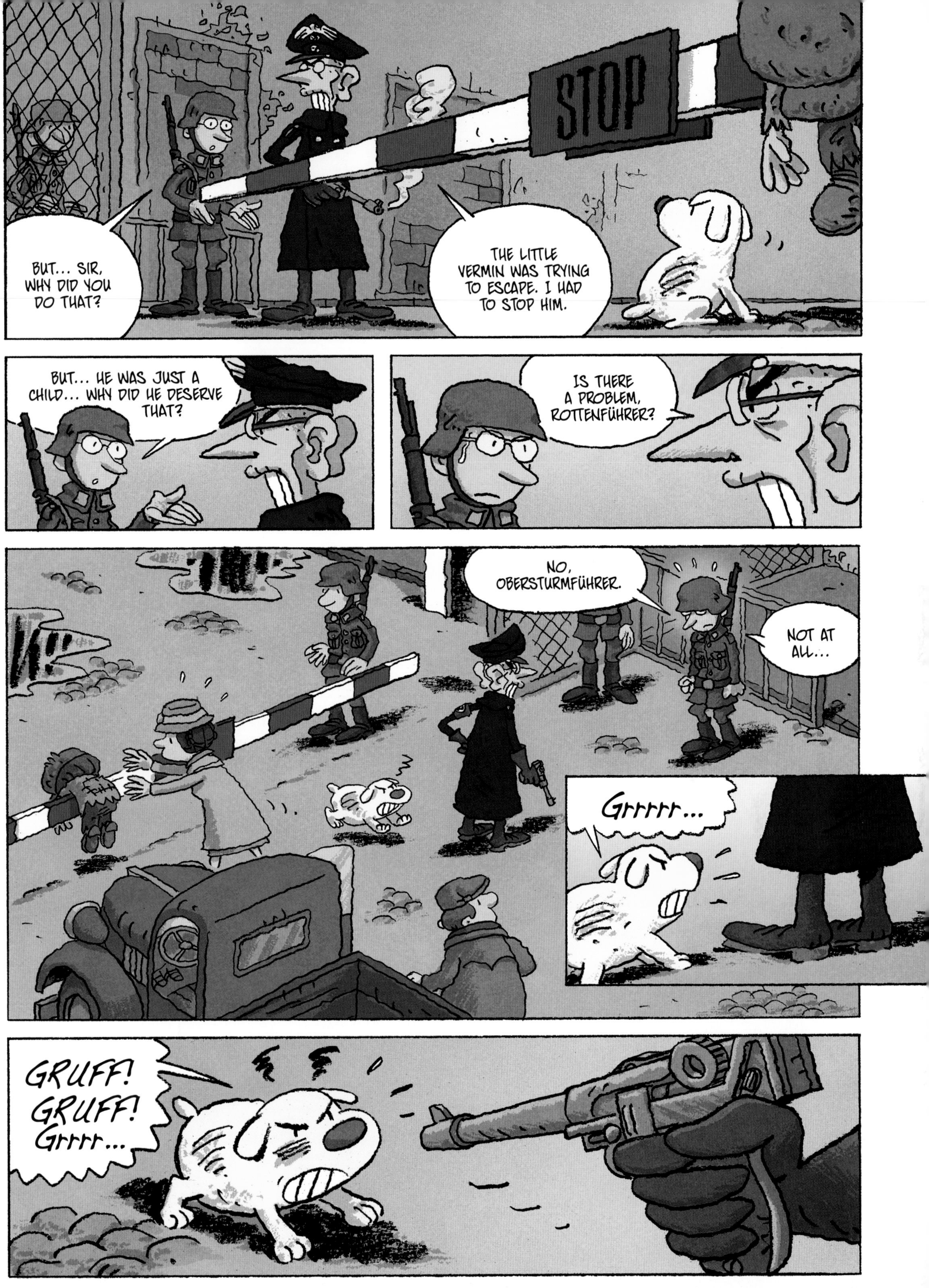
BUT... SIR, WHY DID YOU DO THAT?
THE LITTLE VERMIN WAS TRYING TO ESCAPE. I HAD TO STOP HIM.
STOP
BUT... HE WAS JUST A CHILD... WHY DID HE DESERVE THAT?
IS THERE A PROBLEM, ROTTENFÜHRER?
NO, OBERSTURMFÜHRER.
NOT AT ALL...
Grrrrr...
GRUFF! GRUFF! Grrrr...

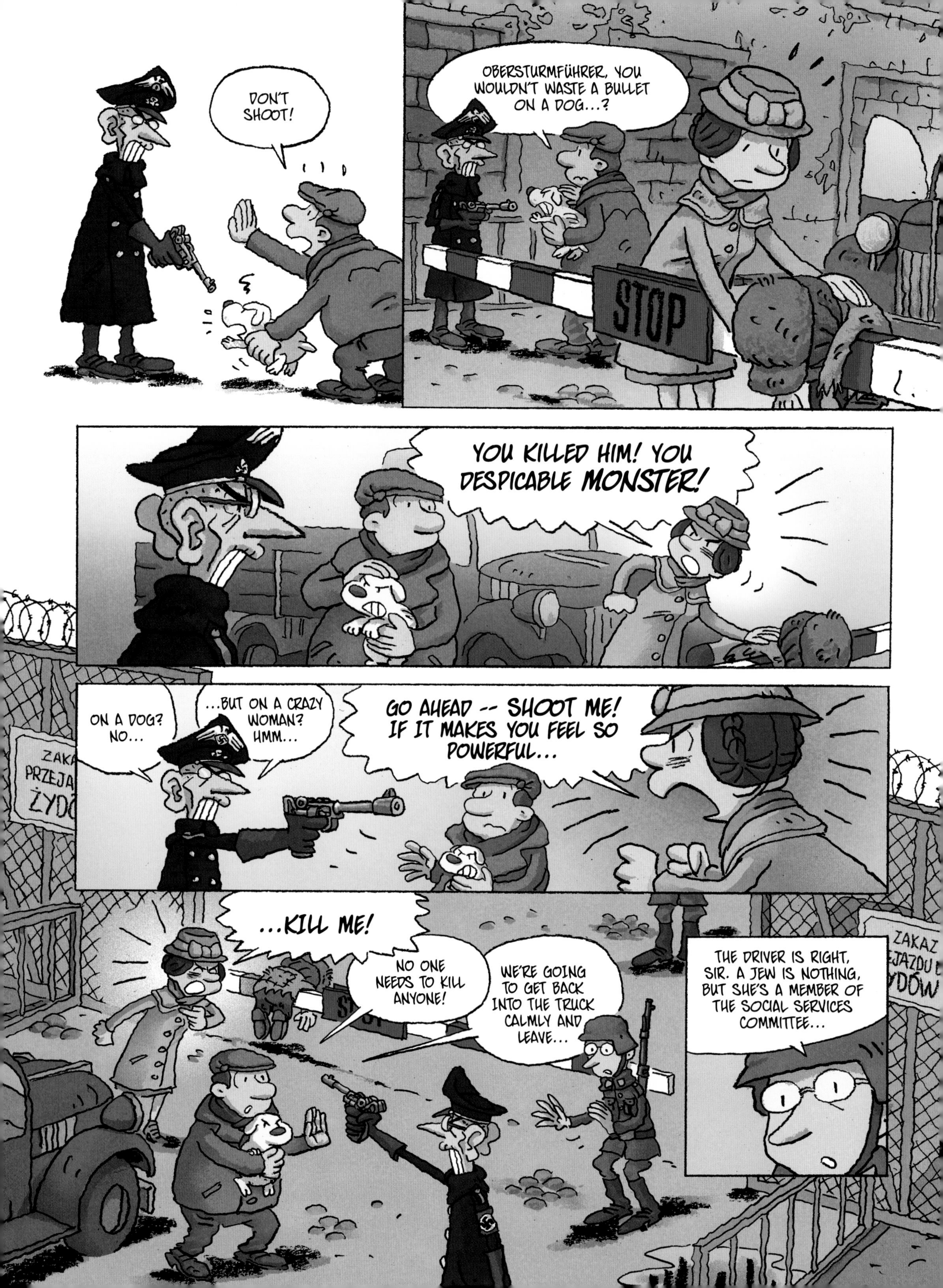
DON'T SHOOT!
OBERSTURMFÜHRER, YOU WOULDN'T WASTE A BULLET ON A DOG...?
STOP
YOU KILLED HIM! YOU DESPICABLE MONSTER!
ON A DOG? NO...
...BUT ON A CRAZY WOMAN? HMM...
GO AHEAD -- SHOOT ME! IF IT MAKES YOU FEEL SO POWERFUL...
...KILL ME!
NO ONE NEEDS TO KILL ANYONE!
WE'RE GOING TO GET BACK INTO THE TRUCK CALMLY AND LEAVE...
THE DRIVER IS RIGHT, SIR. A JEW IS NOTHING, BUT SHE'S A MEMBER OF THE SOCIAL SERVICES COMMITTEE...

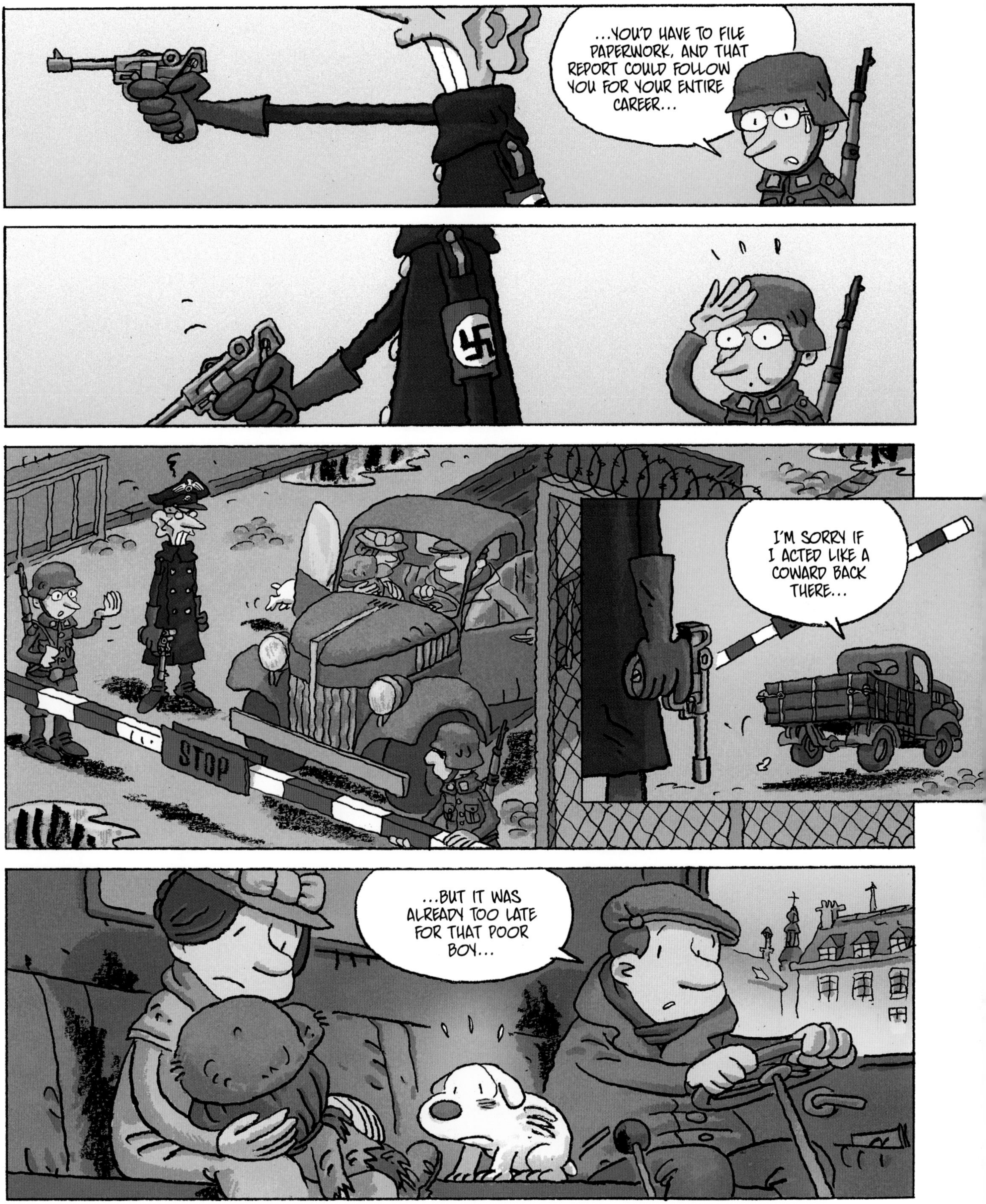

...YOU'D HAVE TO FILE PAPERWORK, AND THAT REPORT COULD FOLLOW YOU FOR YOUR ENTIRE CAREER...
STOP
I'M SORRY IF I ACTED LIKE A COWARD BACK THERE...
...BUT IT WAS ALREADY TOO LATE FOR THAT POOR BOY...

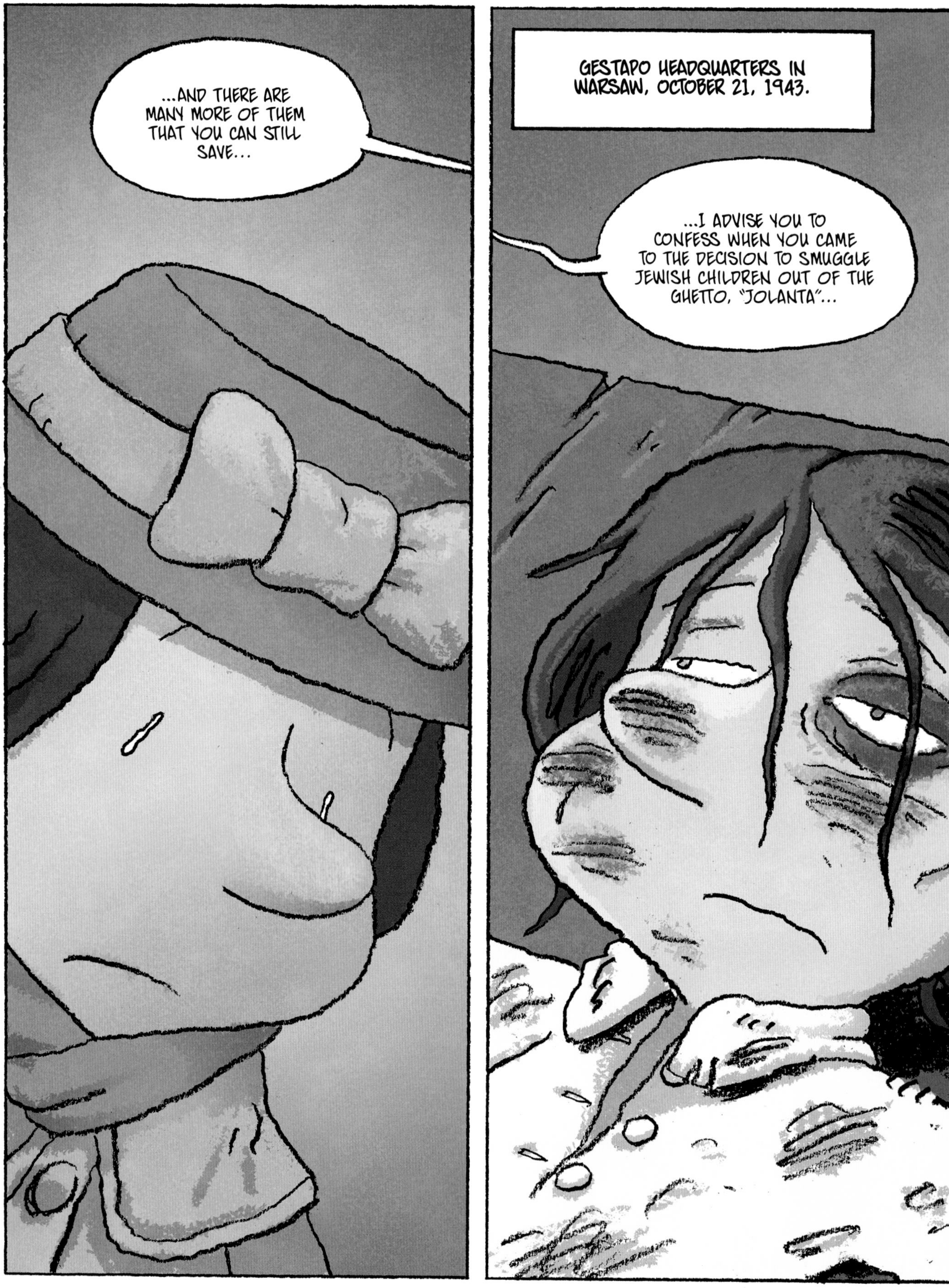
...AND THERE ARE MANY MORE OF THEM THAT YOU CAN STILL SAVE...
GESTAPO HEADQUARTERS IN WARSAW, OCTOBER 21, 1943.
...I ADVISE YOU TO CONFESS WHEN YOU CAME TO THE DECISION TO SMUGGLE JEWISH CHILDREN OUT OF THE GHETTO, "JOLANTA"...

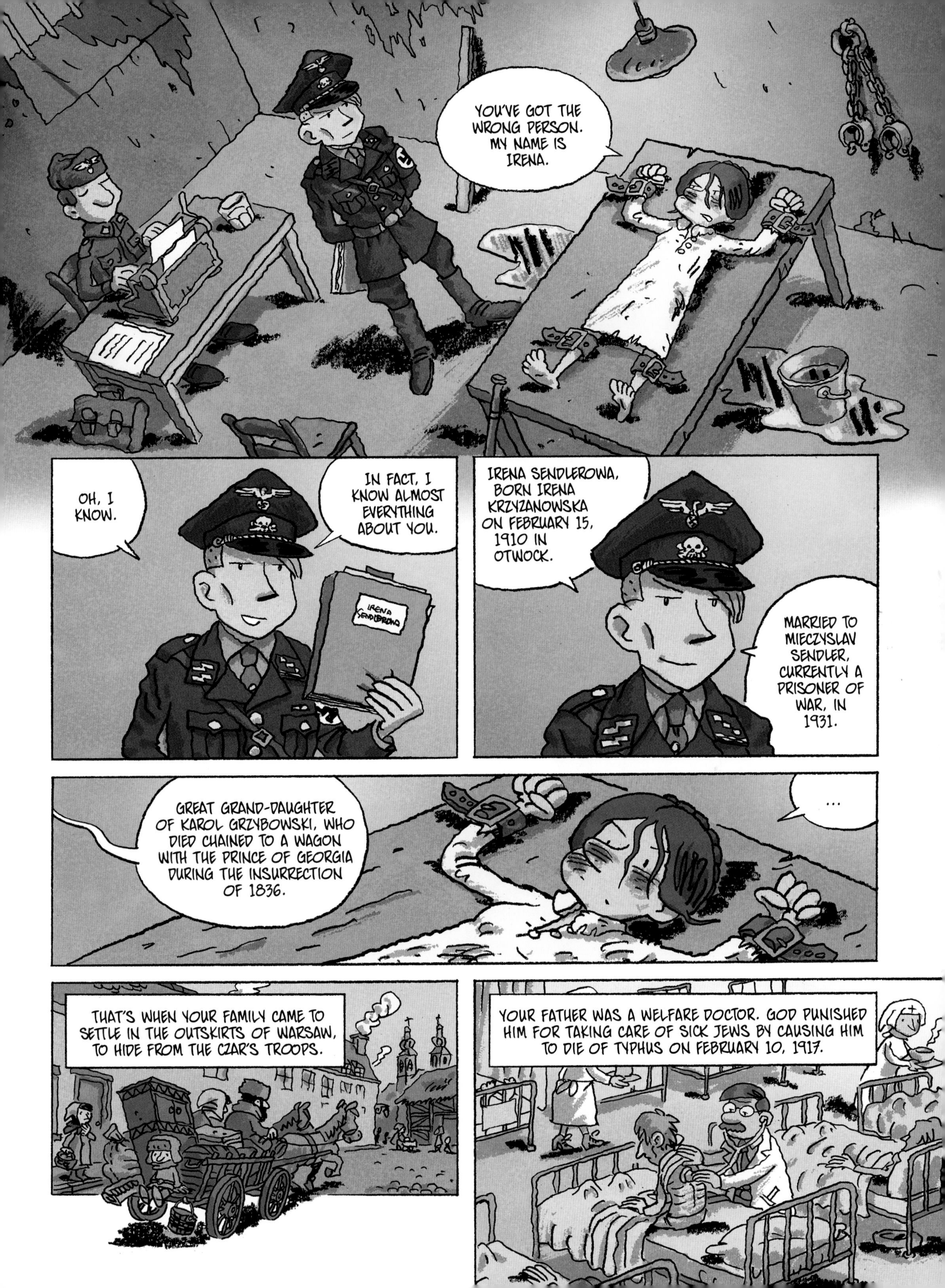
YOU'VE GOT THE WRONG PERSON. MY NAME IS IRENA.
OH, I KNOW.
IN FACT, I KNOW ALMOST EVERYTHING ABOUT YOU.
IRENA SENDLEROWA
IRENA SENDLEROWA, BORN IRENA KRZYZANOWSKA ON FEBRUARY 15, 1910 IN OTWOCK.
MARRIED TO MIECZYSLAV SENDLER, CURRENTLY A PRISONER OF WAR, IN 1931.
GREAT GRAND-DAUGHTER OF KAROL GRZYBOWSKI, WHO DIED CHAINED TO A WAGON WITH THE PRINCE OF GEORGIA DURING THE INSURRECTION OF 1836.
...
THAT'S WHEN YOUR FAMILY CAME TO SETTLE IN THE OUTSKIRTS OF WARSAW, TO HIDE FROM THE CZAR'S TROOPS.
YOUR FATHER WAS A WELFARE DOCTOR. GOD PUNISHED HIM FOR TAKING CARE OF SICK JEWS BY CAUSING HIM TO DIE OF TYPHUS ON FEBRUARY 10, 1917.

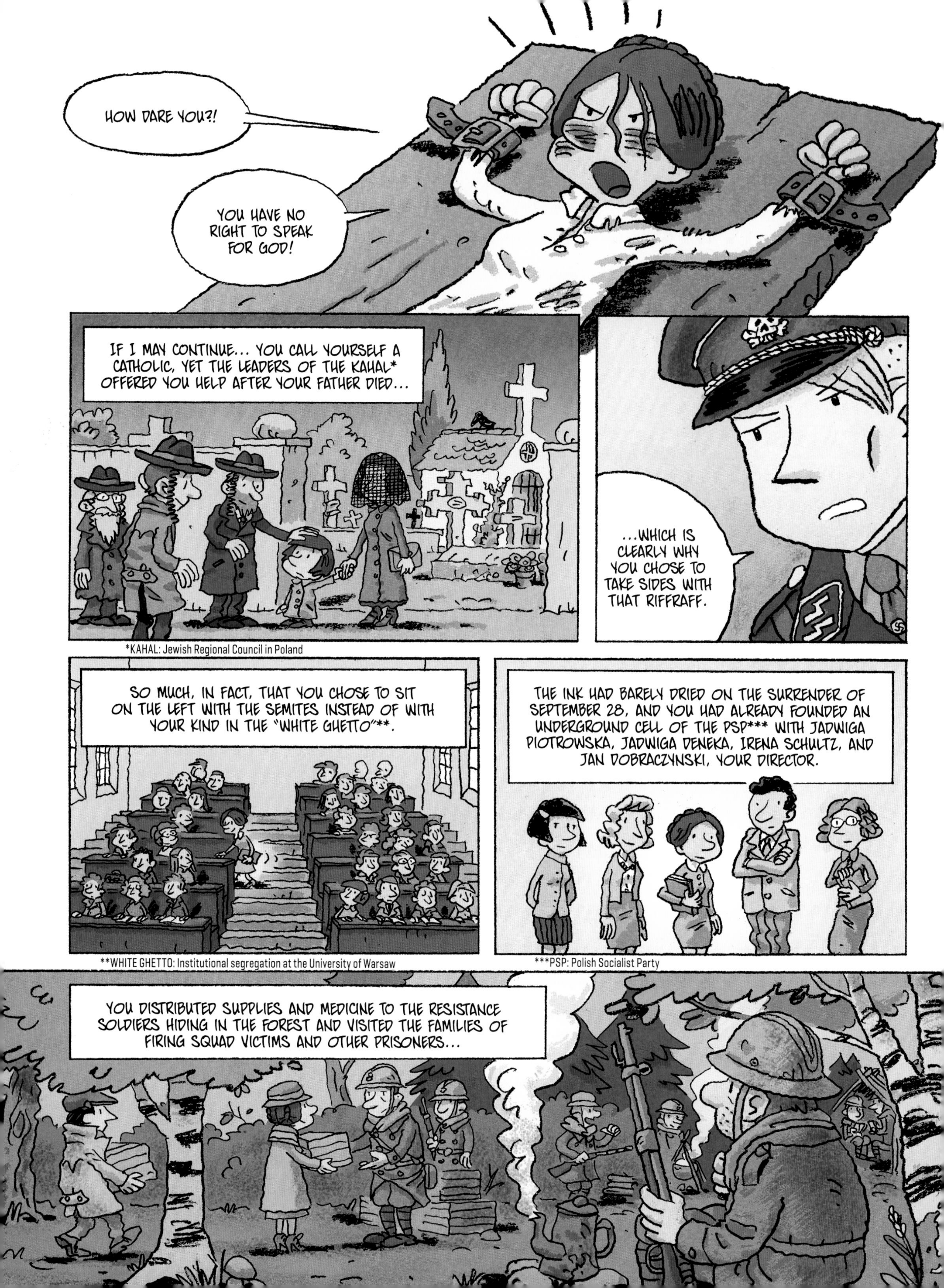
HOW DARE YOU?!
YOU HAVE NO RIGHT TO SPEAK FOR GOD!
IF I MAY CONTINUE... YOU CALL YOURSELF A CATHOLIC, YET THE LEADERS OF THE KAHAL* OFFERED YOU HELP AFTER YOUR FATHER DIED...
...WHICH IS CLEARLY WHY YOU CHOSE TO TAKE SIDES WITH THAT RIFFRAFF.
*KAHAL: Jewish Regional Council in Poland
SO MUCH, IN FACT, THAT YOU CHOSE TO SIT ON THE LEFT WITH THE SEMITES INSTEAD OF WITH YOUR KIND IN THE "WHITE GHETTO"**.
THE INK HAD BARELY DRIED ON THE SURRENDER OF SEPTEMBER 28, AND YOU HAD ALREADY FOUNDED AN UNDERGROUND CELL OF THE PSP*** WITH JADWIGA PIOTROWSKA, JADWIGA DENEKA, IRENA SCHULTZ, AND JAN DOBRACZYNSKI, YOUR DIRECTOR.
**WHITE GHETTO: Institutional segregation at the University of Warsaw
***PSP: Polish Socialist Party
YOU DISTRIBUTED SUPPLIES AND MEDICINE TO THE RESISTANCE SOLDIERS HIDING IN THE FOREST AND VISITED THE FAMILIES OF FIRING SQUAD VICTIMS AND OTHER PRISONERS...

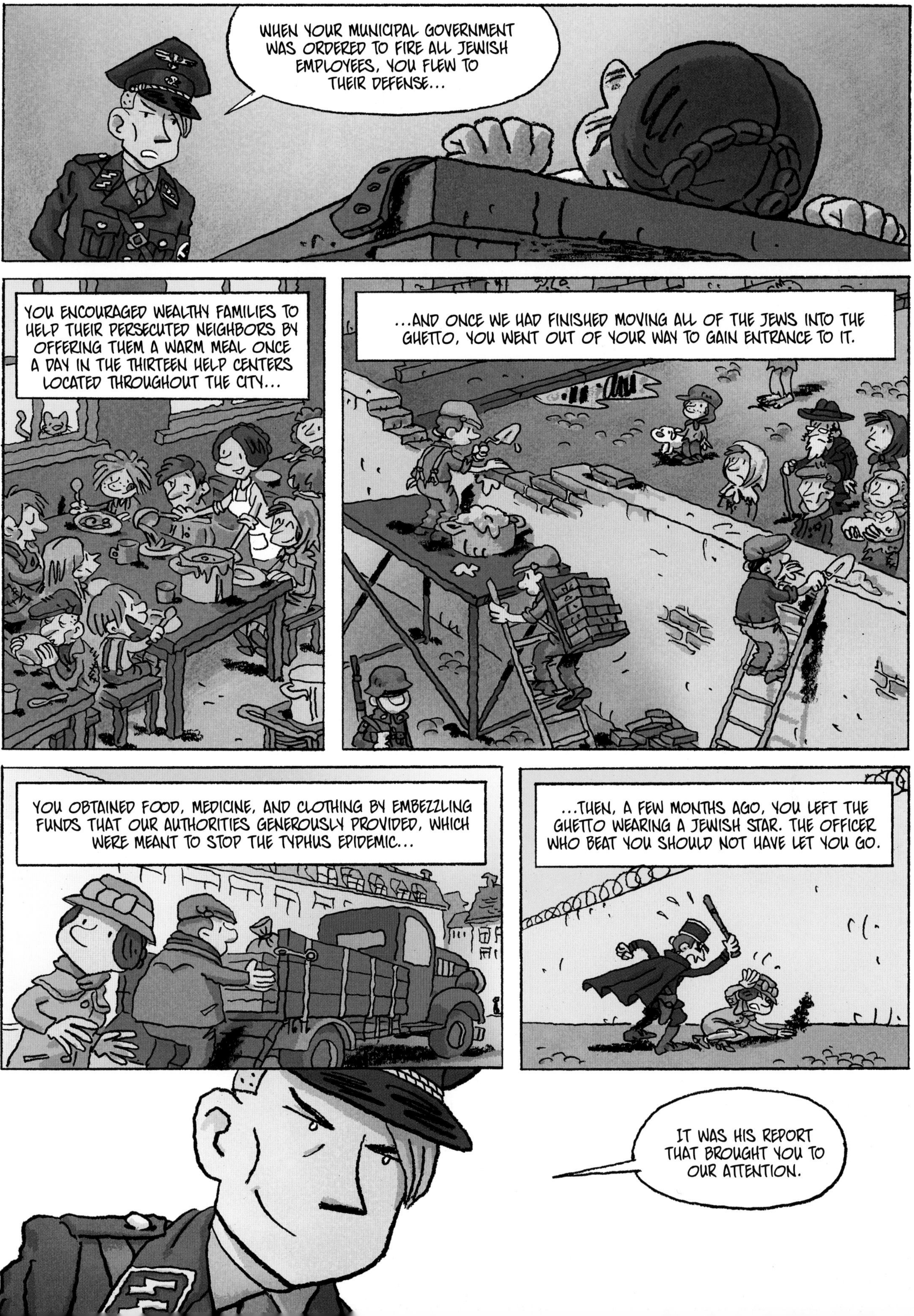
WHEN YOUR MUNICIPAL GOVERNMENT WAS ORDERED TO FIRE ALL JEWISH EMPLOYEES, YOU FLEW TO THEIR DEFENSE...
YOU ENCOURAGED WEALTHY FAMILIES TO HELP THEIR PERSECUTED NEIGHBORS BY OFFERING THEM A WARM MEAL ONCE A DAY IN THE THIRTEEN HELP CENTERS LOCATED THROUGHOUT THE CITY...
...AND ONCE WE HAD FINISHED MOVING ALL OF THE JEWS INTO THE GHETTO, YOU WENT OUT OF YOUR WAY TO GAIN ENTRANCE TO IT.
YOU OBTAINED FOOD, MEDICINE, AND CLOTHING BY EMBEZZLING FUNDS THAT OUR AUTHORITIES GENEROUSLY PROVIDED, WHICH WERE MEANT TO STOP THE TYPHUS EPIDEMIC...
...THEN, A FEW MONTHS AGO, YOU LEFT THE GHETTO WEARING A JEWISH STAR. THE OFFICER WHO BEAT YOU SHOULD NOT HAVE LET YOU GO.
IT WAS HIS REPORT THAT BROUGHT YOU TO OUR ATTENTION.

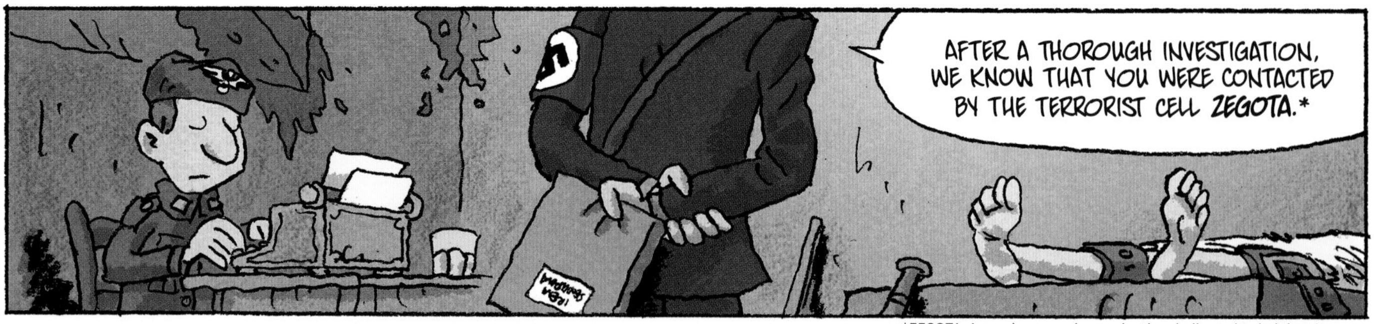
AFTER A THOROUGH INVESTIGATION, WE KNOW THAT YOU WERE CONTACTED BY THE TERRORIST CELL **ZEGOTA**.*

*ZEGOTA: An underground organization dedicated to helping Jews.

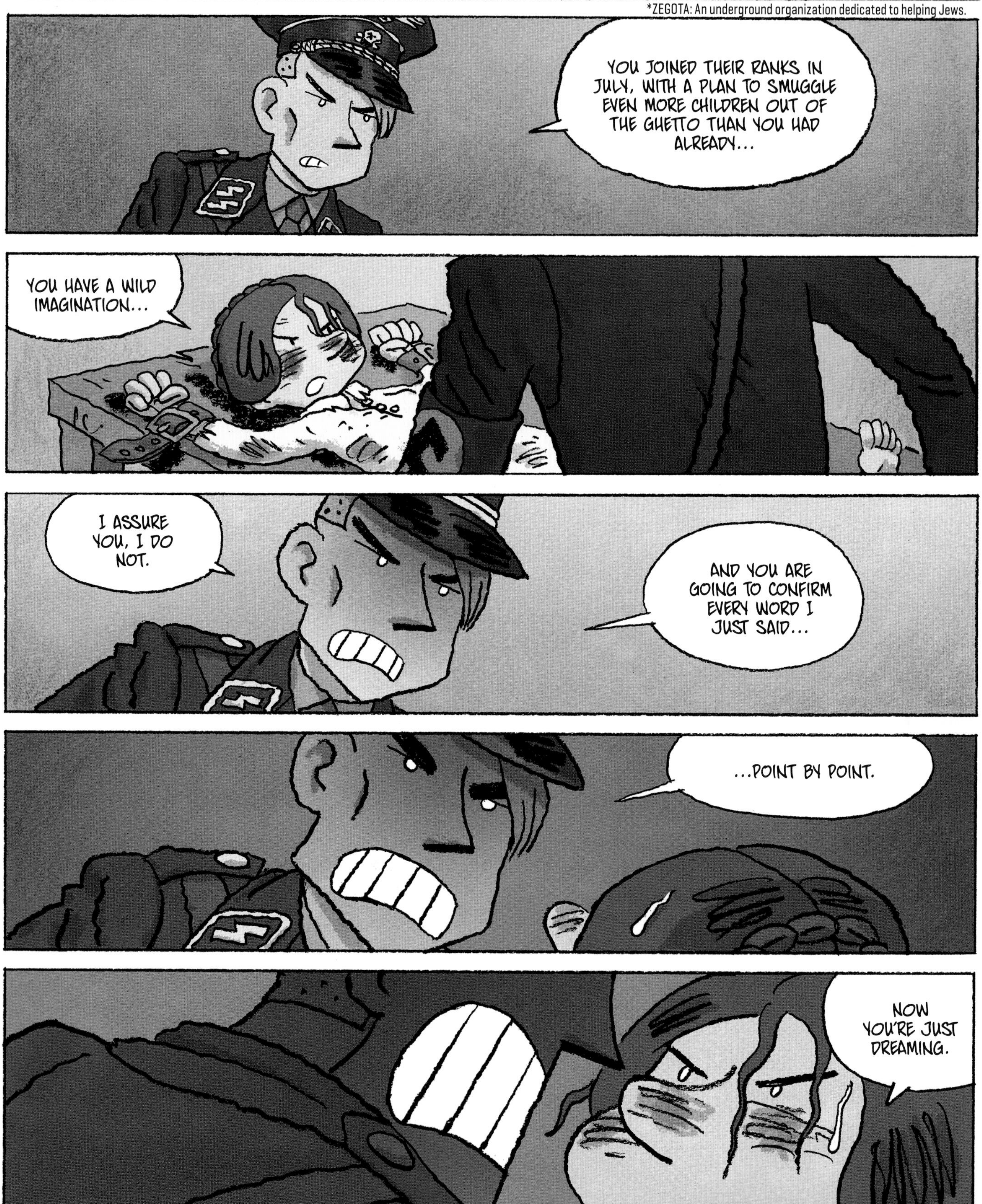
YOU JOINED THEIR RANKS IN JULY, WITH A PLAN TO SMUGGLE EVEN MORE CHILDREN OUT OF THE GHETTO THAN YOU HAD ALREADY...
YOU HAVE A WILD IMAGINATION...
I ASSURE YOU, I DO NOT.
AND YOU ARE GOING TO CONFIRM EVERY WORD I JUST SAID...
...POINT BY POINT.
NOW YOU'RE JUST DREAMING.

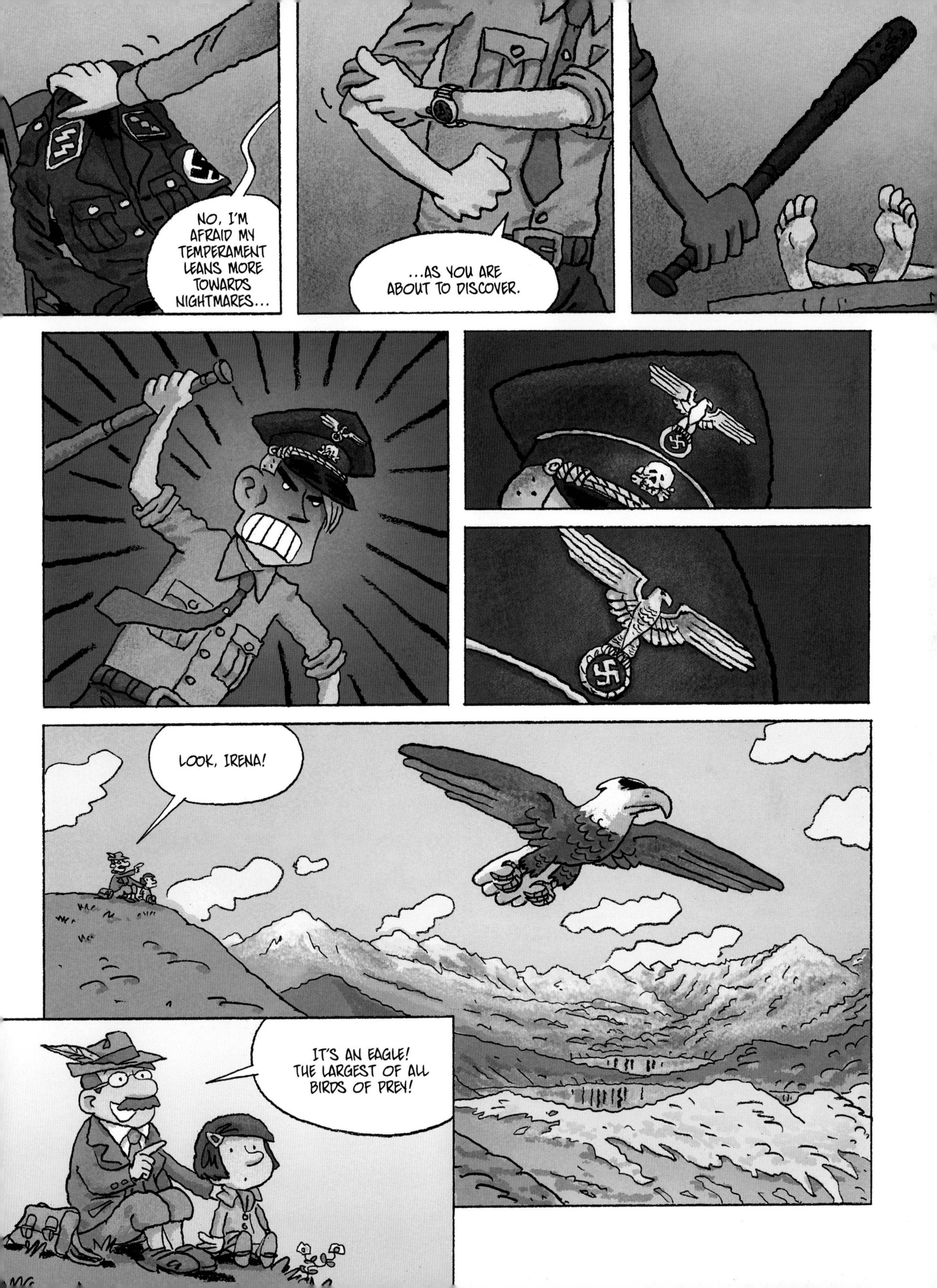
NO, I'M AFRAID MY TEMPERAMENT LEANS MORE TOWARDS NIGHTMARES...
...AS YOU ARE ABOUT TO DISCOVER.
LOOK, IRENA!
IT'S AN EAGLE! THE LARGEST OF ALL BIRDS OF PREY!

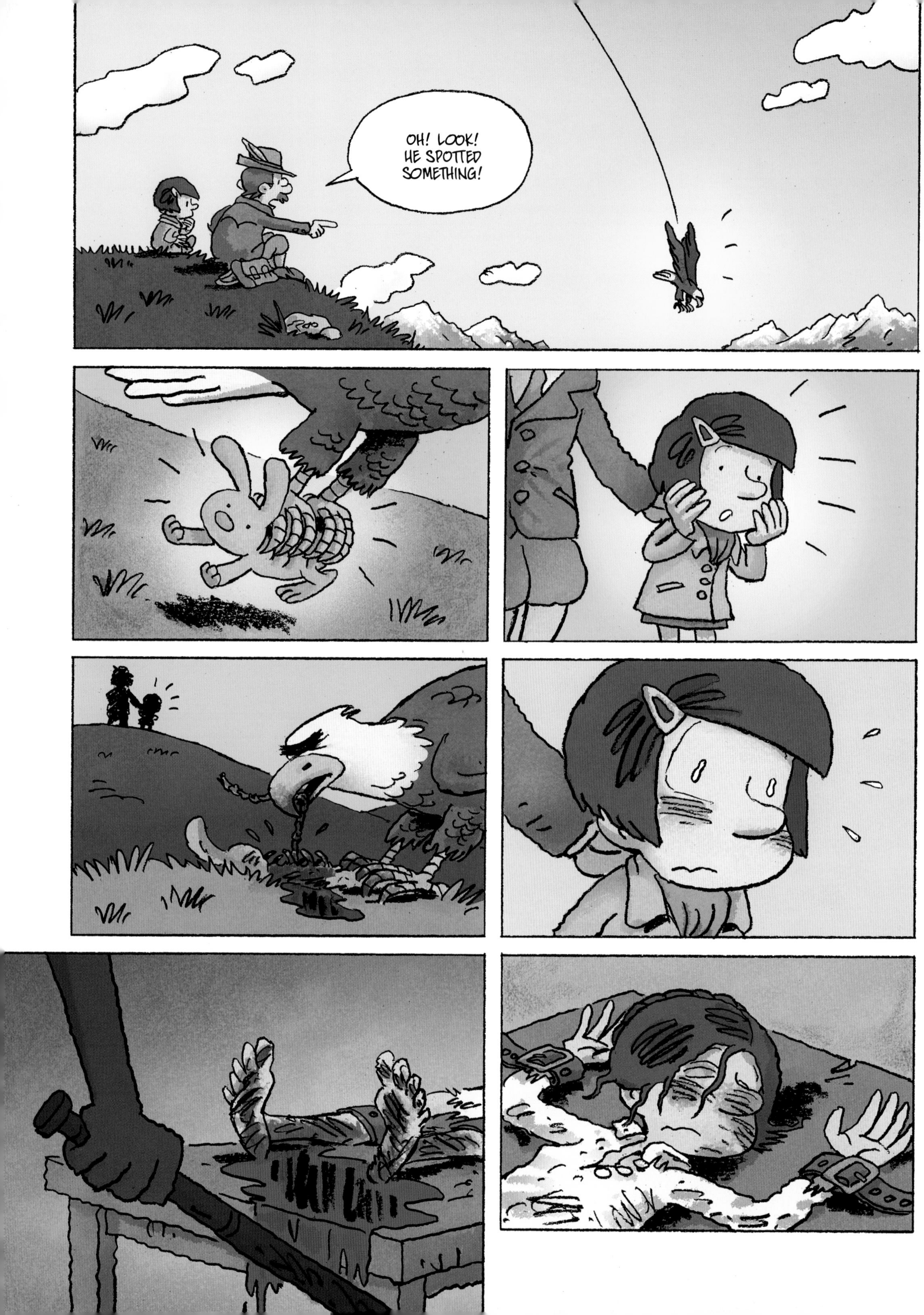
OH! LOOK!
HE SPOTTED
SOMETHING!

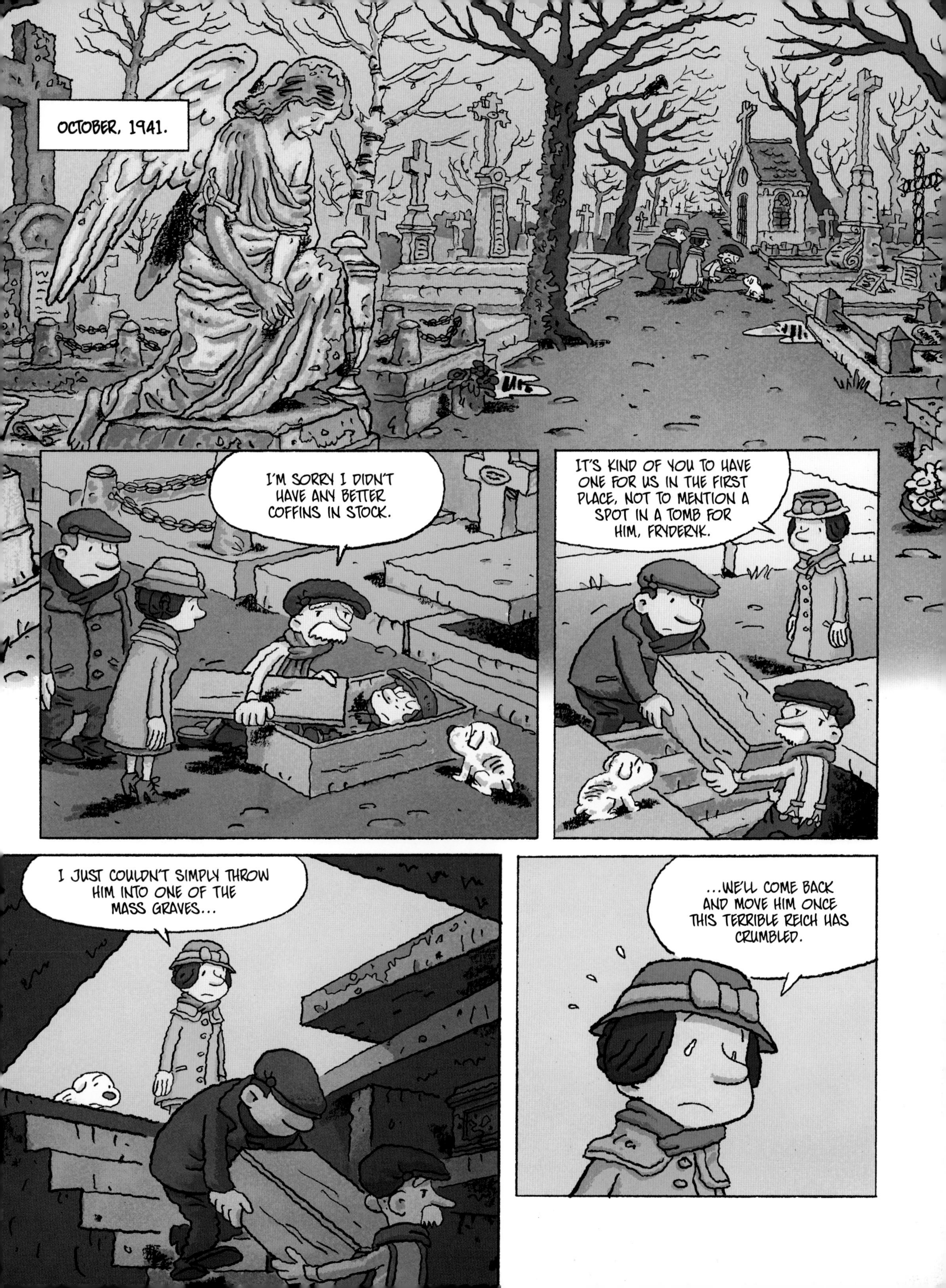
OCTOBER, 1941.
I'M SORRY I DIDN'T HAVE ANY BETTER COFFINS IN STOCK.
IT'S KIND OF YOU TO HAVE ONE FOR US IN THE FIRST PLACE, NOT TO MENTION A SPOT IN A TOMB FOR HIM, FRYDERYK.
I JUST COULDN'T SIMPLY THROW HIM INTO ONE OF THE MASS GRAVES...
...WE'LL COME BACK AND MOVE HIM ONCE THIS TERRIBLE REICH HAS CRUMBLED.

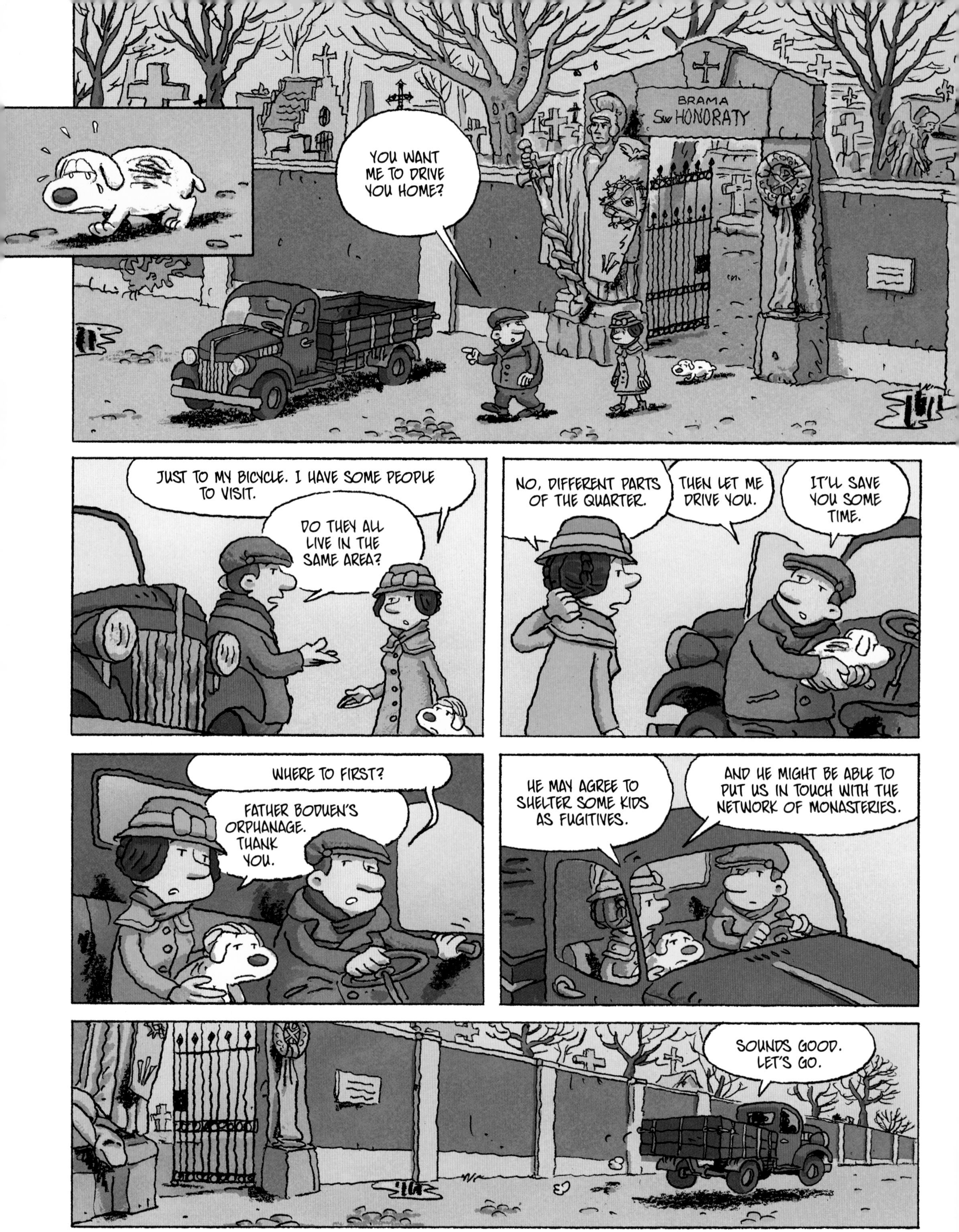
BRAMA
Św HONORATY
YOU WANT ME TO DRIVE YOU HOME?
JUST TO MY BICYCLE. I HAVE SOME PEOPLE TO VISIT.
DO THEY ALL LIVE IN THE SAME AREA?
NO, DIFFERENT PARTS OF THE QUARTER.
THEN LET ME DRIVE YOU.
IT'LL SAVE YOU SOME TIME.
WHERE TO FIRST?
FATHER BODUEN'S ORPHANAGE. THANK YOU.
HE MAY AGREE TO SHELTER SOME KIDS AS FUGITIVES.
AND HE MIGHT BE ABLE TO PUT US IN TOUCH WITH THE NETWORK OF MONASTERIES.
SOUNDS GOOD. LET'S GO.

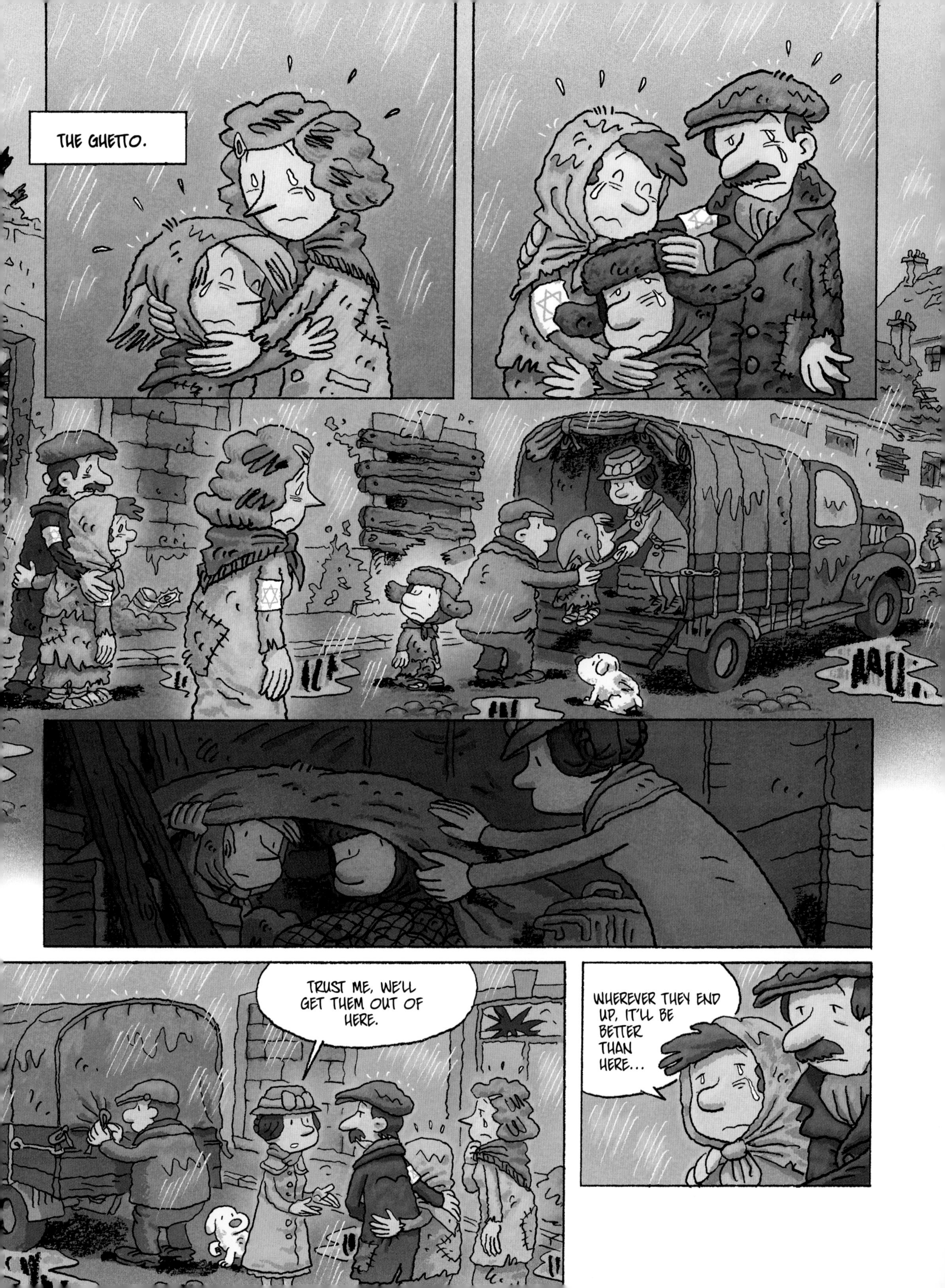
THE GHETTO.
TRUST ME, WE'LL GET THEM OUT OF HERE.
WHEREVER THEY END UP, IT'LL BE BETTER THAN HERE...

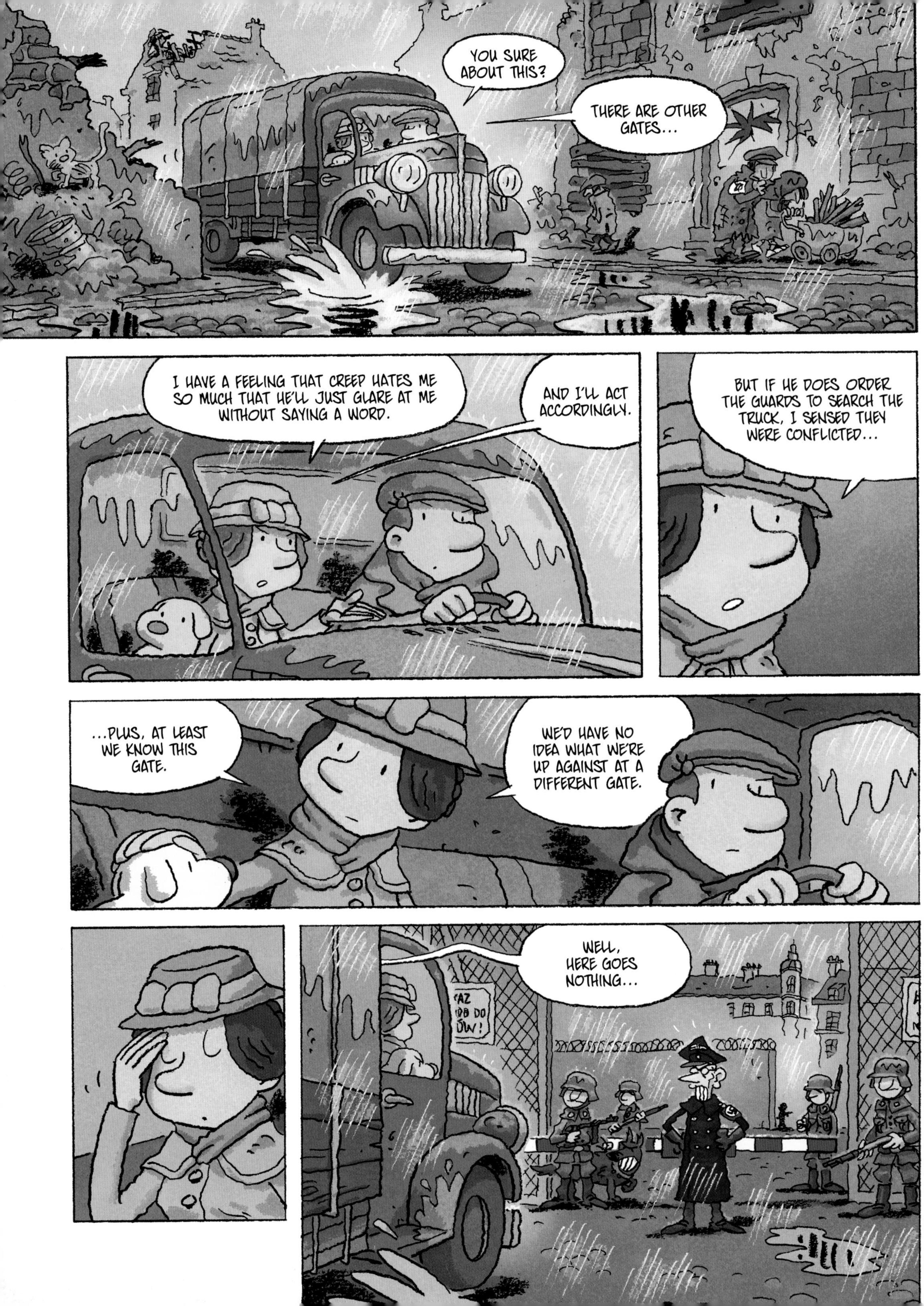
YOU SURE ABOUT THIS?
THERE ARE OTHER GATES...
I HAVE A FEELING THAT CREEP HATES ME SO MUCH THAT HE'LL JUST GLARE AT ME WITHOUT SAYING A WORD.
AND I'LL ACT ACCORDINGLY.
BUT IF HE DOES ORDER THE GUARDS TO SEARCH THE TRUCK, I SENSED THEY WERE CONFLICTED...
...PLUS, AT LEAST WE KNOW THIS GATE.
WE'D HAVE NO IDEA WHAT WE'RE UP AGAINST AT A DIFFERENT GATE.
WELL, HERE GOES NOTHING...

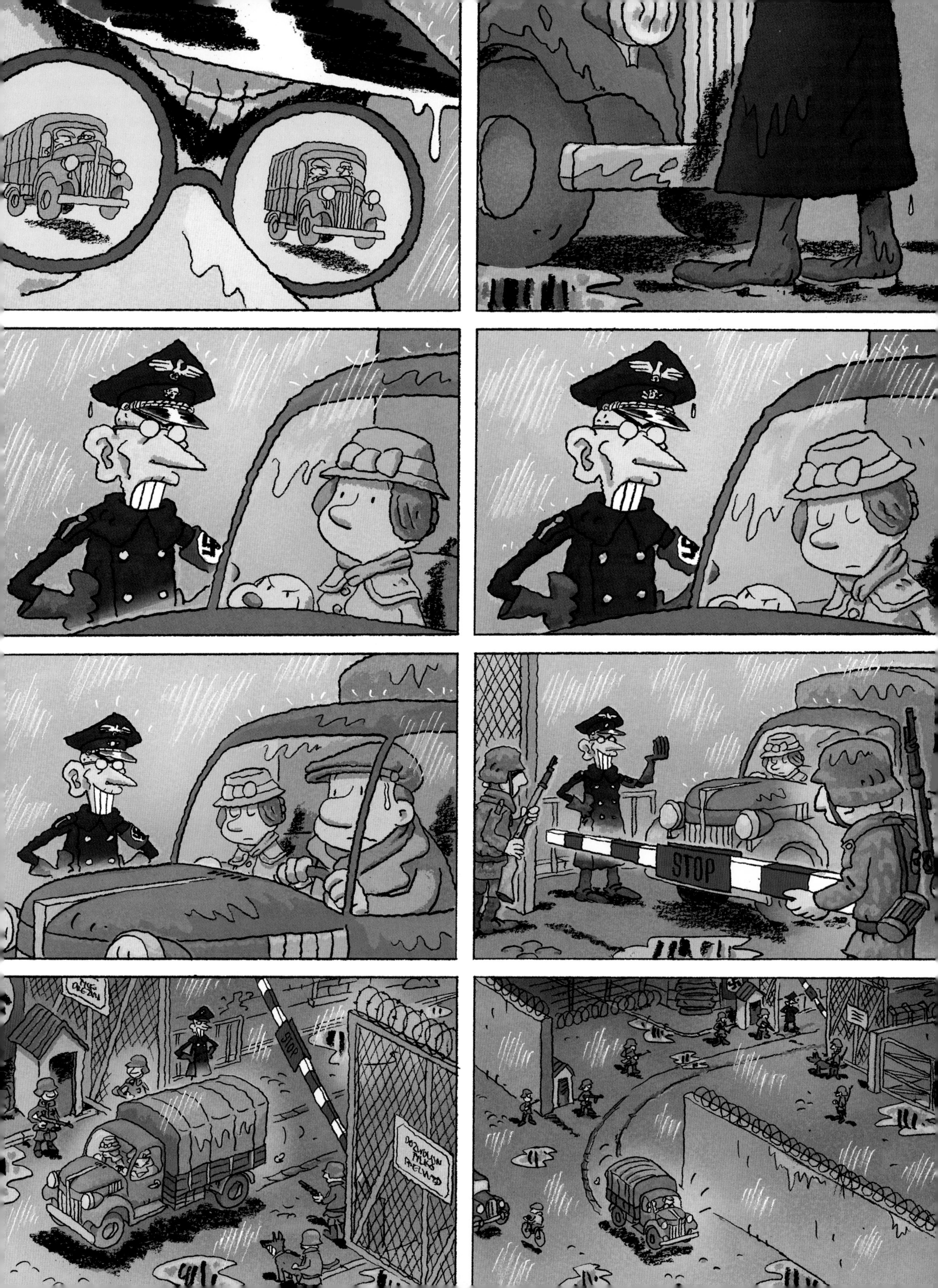
STOP
STOP

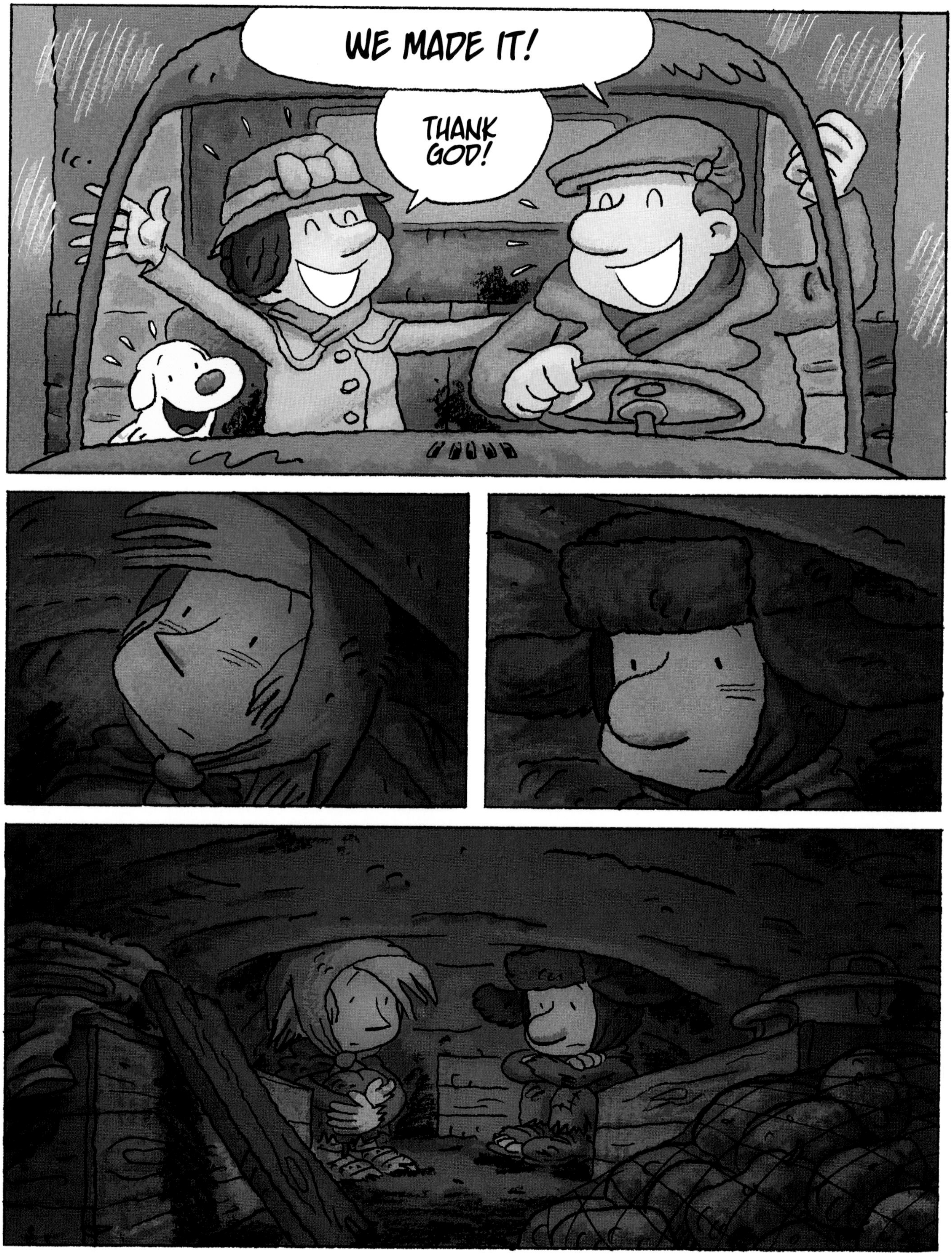
WE MADE IT!
THANK GOD!

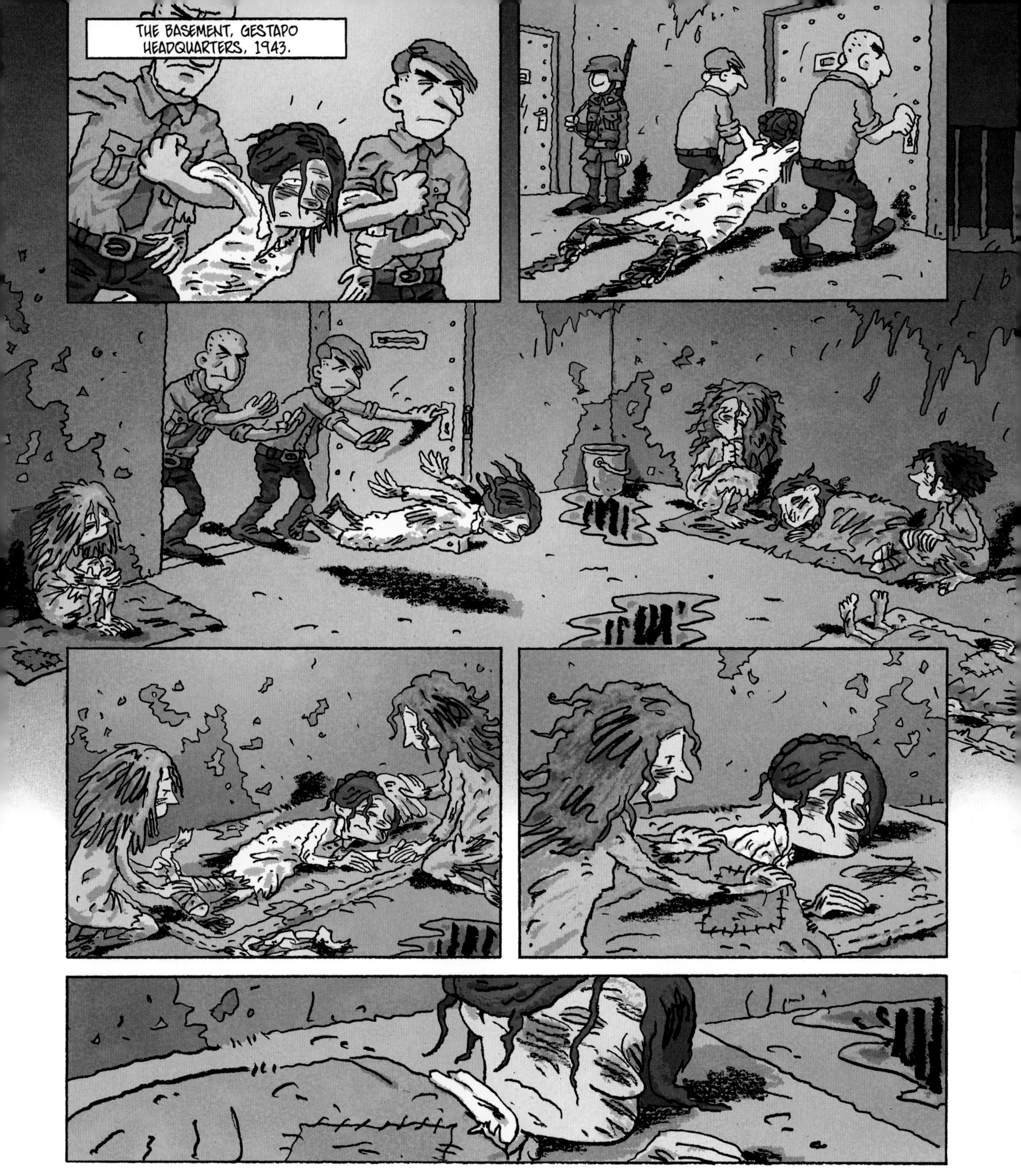
THE BASEMENT, GESTAPO HEADQUARTERS, 1943.

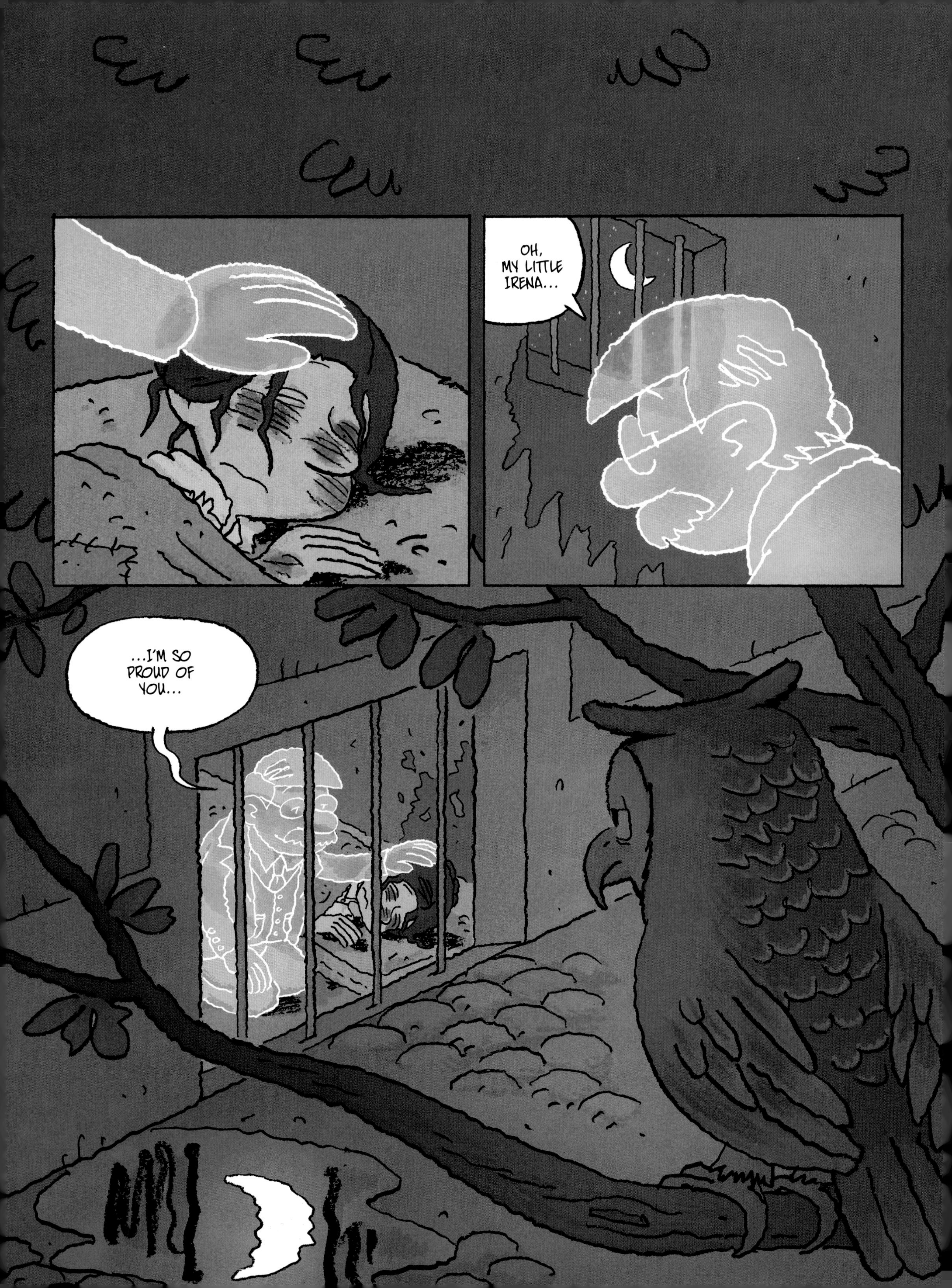
OH, MY LITTLE IRENA...
...I'M SO PROUD OF YOU...

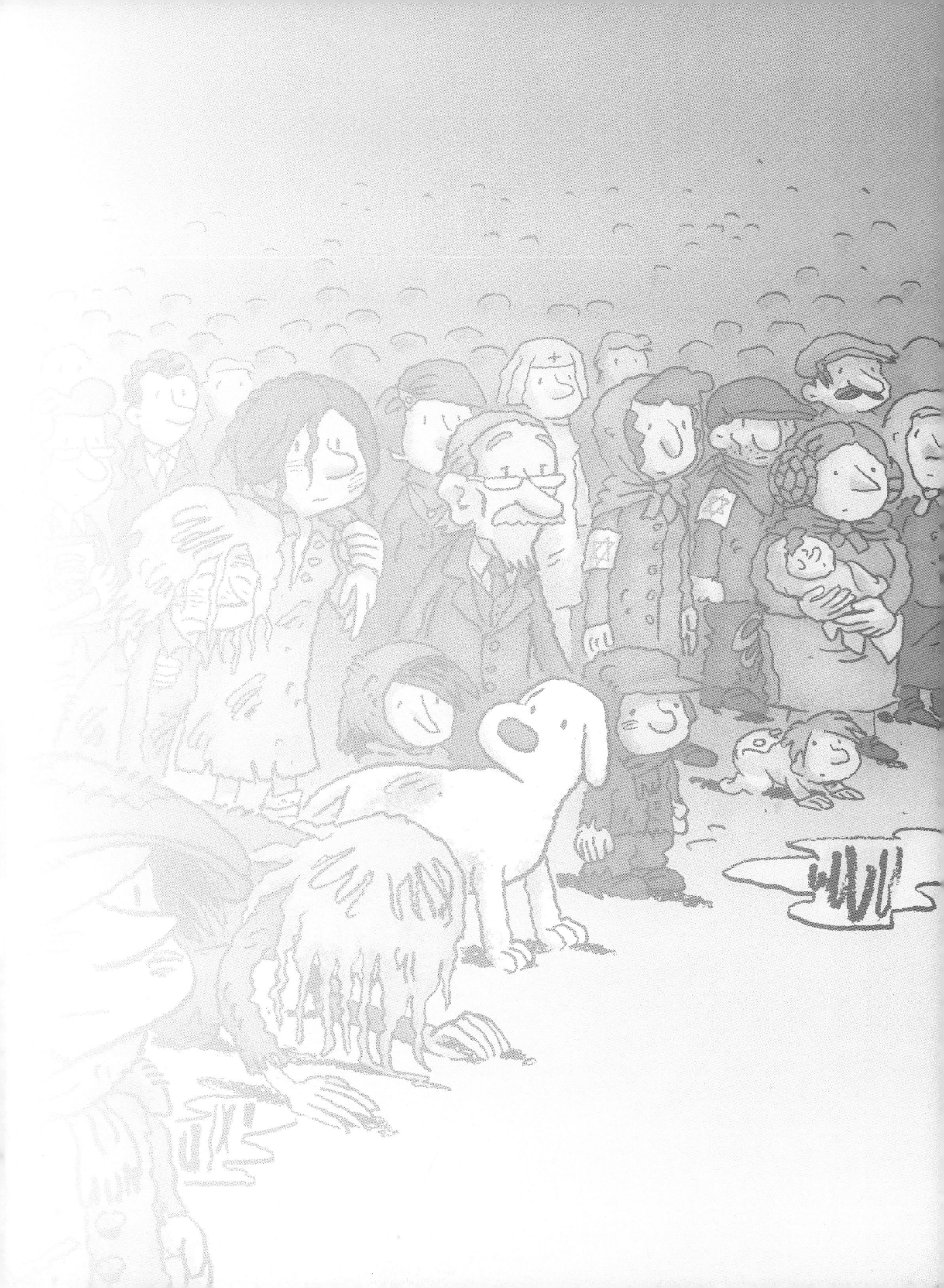

Irena

CHAPTER 2 – THE RIGHTEOUS

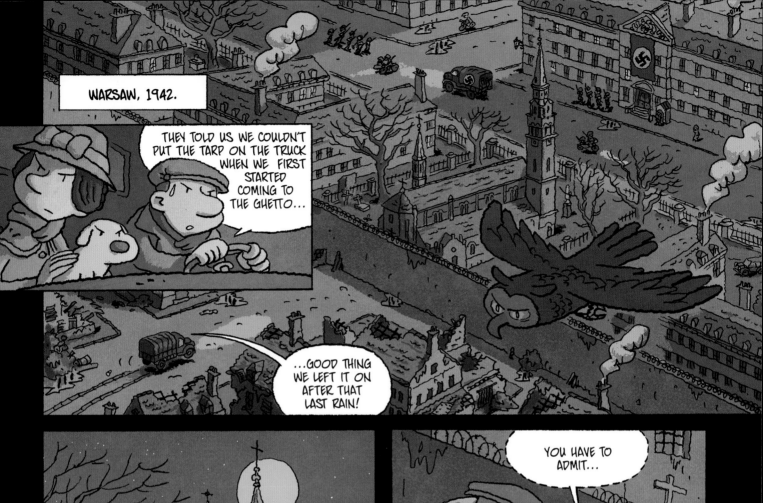

WARSAW, 1942.

THEY TOLD US WE COULDN'T PUT THE TARP ON THE TRUCK WHEN WE FIRST STARTED COMING TO THE GHETTO...

...GOOD THING WE LEFT IT ON AFTER THAT LAST RAIN!

THE NAZIS AND THE JÜDISCHER ORDNUNGSDIEST* HAVEN'T TOLD US TO REMOVE IT SINCE!

*JÜDISCHER ORDNUNGSDIEST: Jewish Ghetto Police.

YOU HAVE TO ADMIT...

...IT DOES COME IN HANDY!

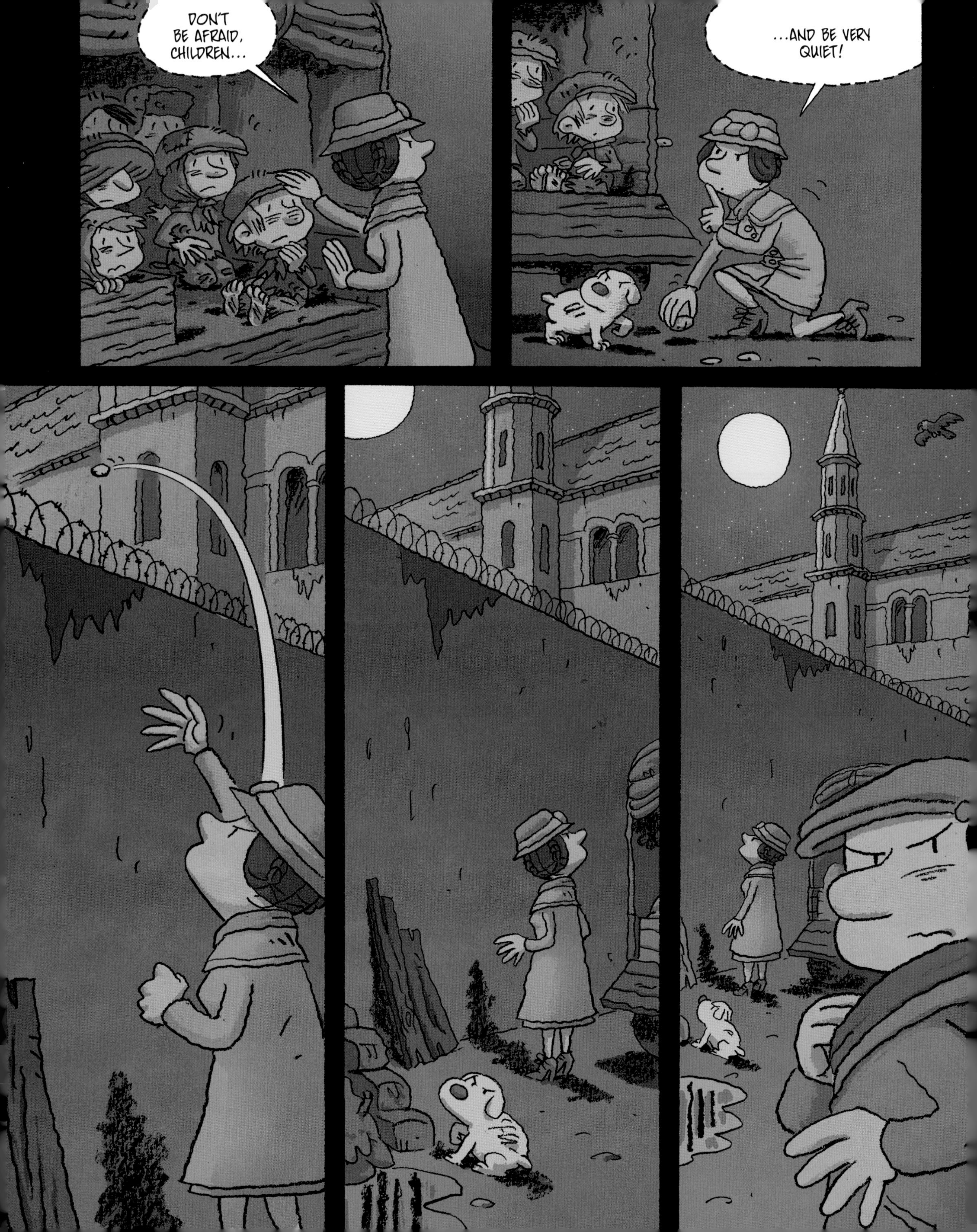
DON'T BE AFRAID, CHILDREN...
...AND BE VERY QUIET!

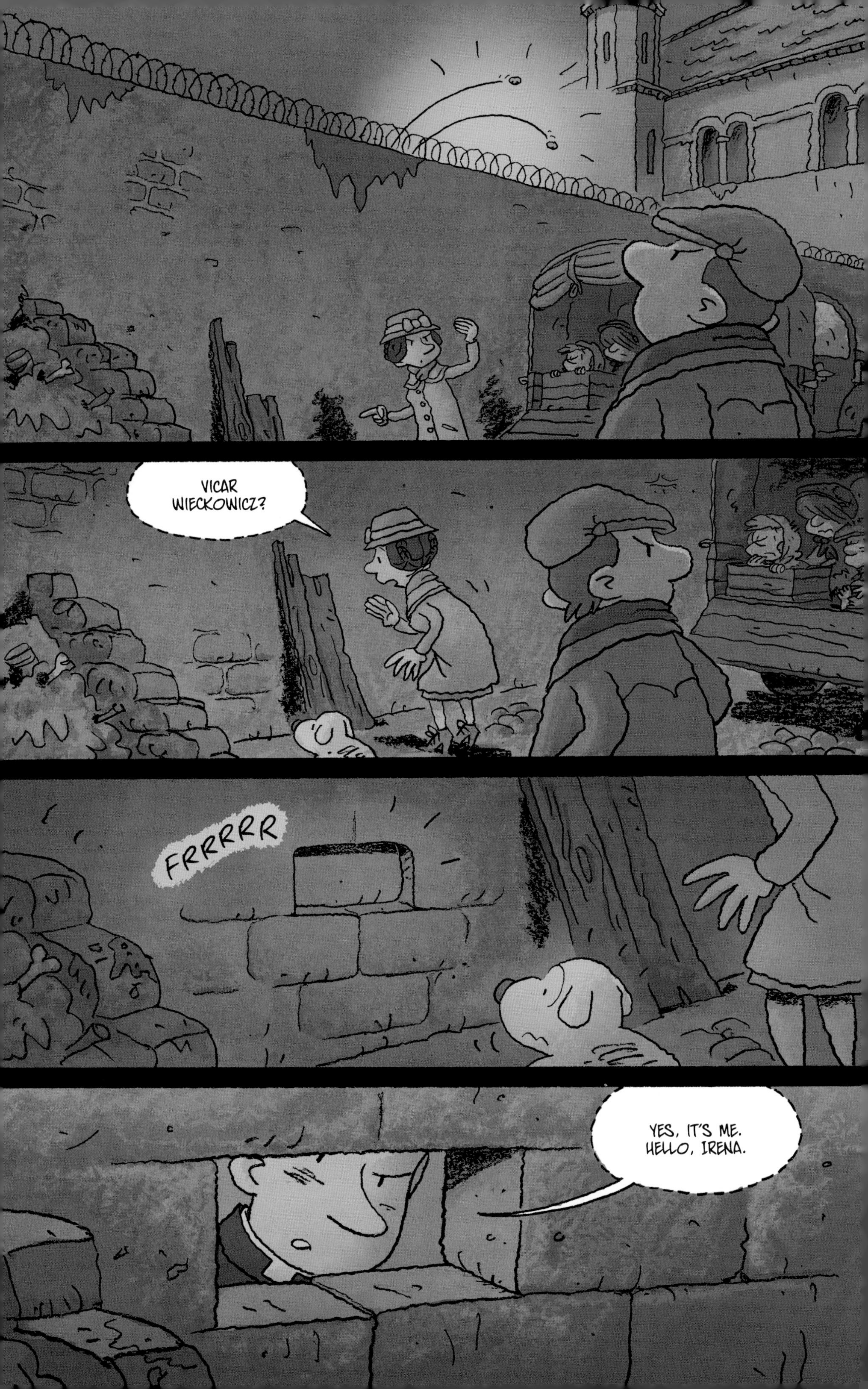
VICAR WIECKOWICZ?
FRRRRR
YES, IT'S ME. HELLO, IRENA.

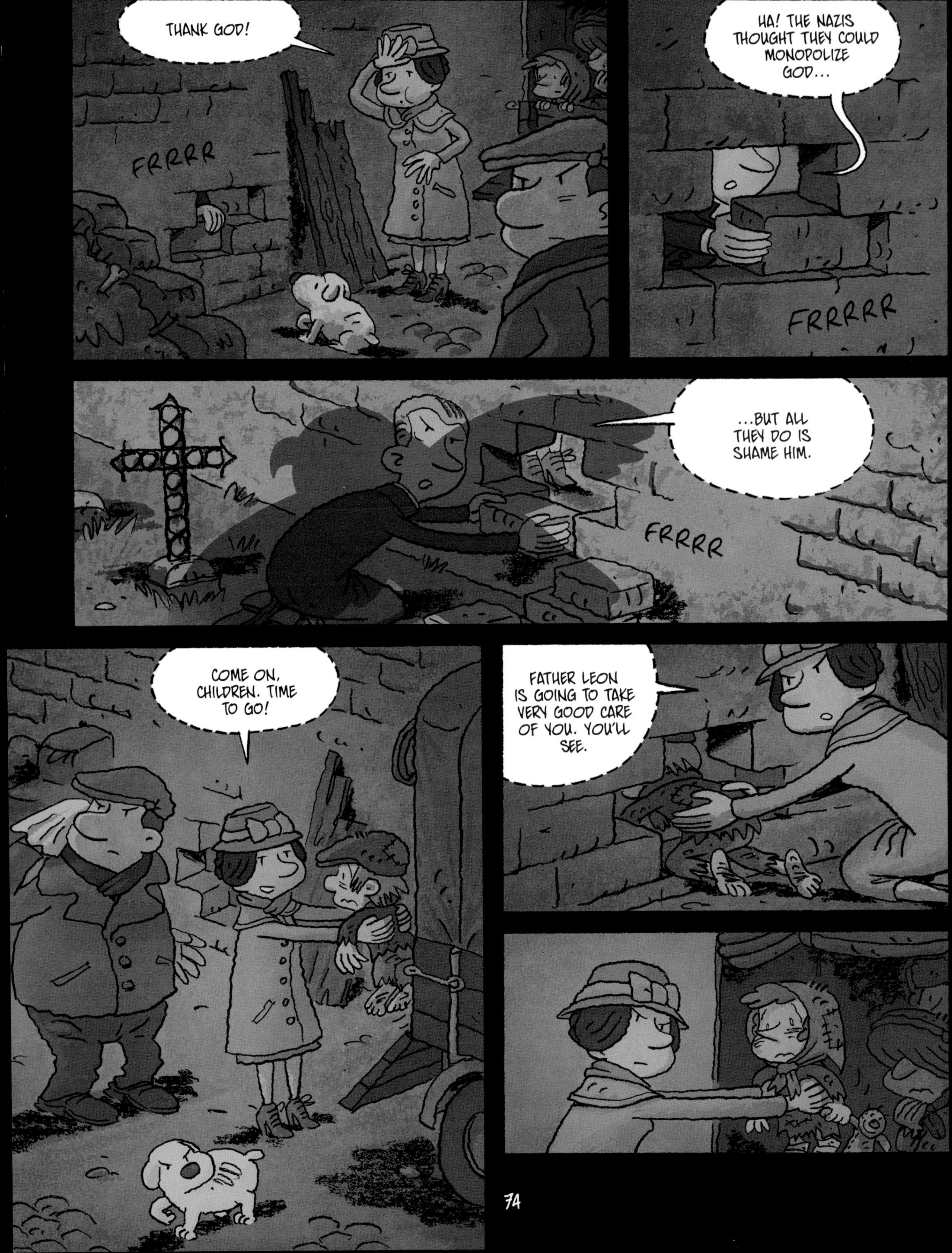
THANK GOD!
FRRRR
HA! THE NAZIS THOUGHT THEY COULD MONOPOLIZE GOD...
FRRRRR
...BUT ALL THEY DO IS SHAME HIM.
FRRRR
COME ON, CHILDREN. TIME TO GO!
FATHER LEON IS GOING TO TAKE VERY GOOD CARE OF YOU. YOU'LL SEE.

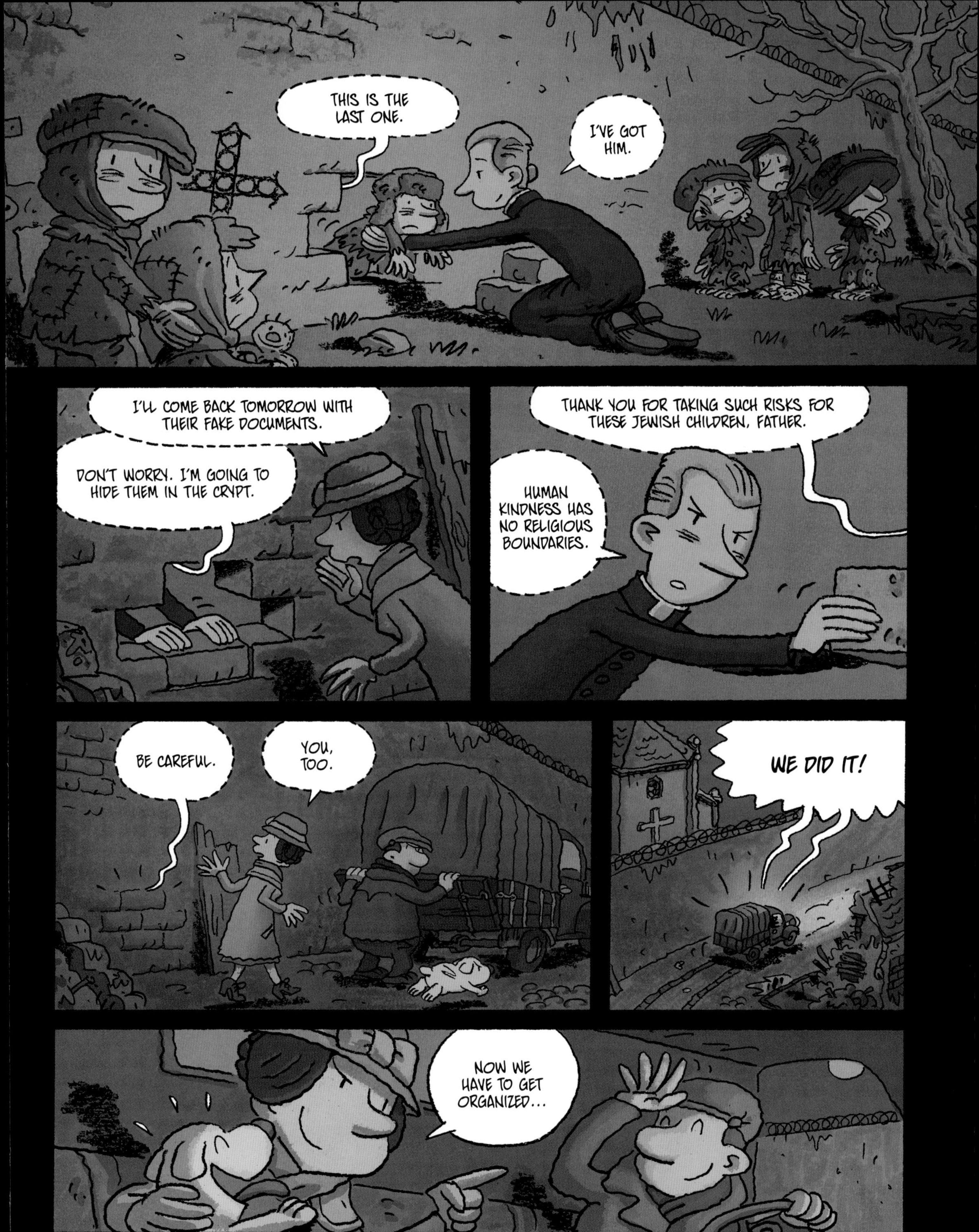
THIS IS THE LAST ONE.
I'VE GOT HIM.
I'LL COME BACK TOMORROW WITH THEIR FAKE DOCUMENTS.
DON'T WORRY. I'M GOING TO HIDE THEM IN THE CRYPT.
THANK YOU FOR TAKING SUCH RISKS FOR THESE JEWISH CHILDREN, FATHER.
HUMAN KINDNESS HAS NO RELIGIOUS BOUNDARIES.
BE CAREFUL.
YOU, TOO.
WE DID IT!
NOW WE HAVE TO GET ORGANIZED...

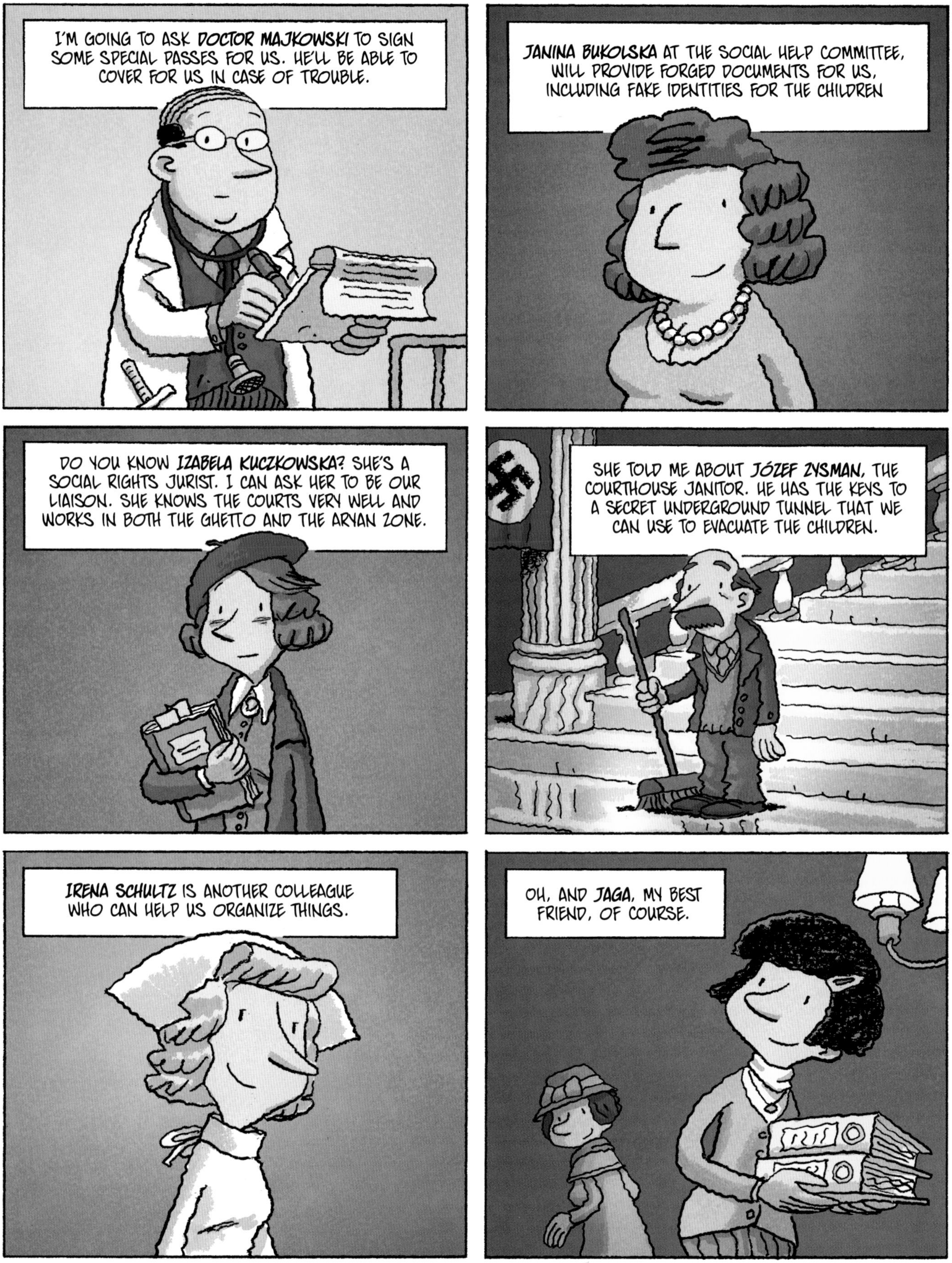
I'M GOING TO ASK DOCTOR MAJKOWSKI TO SIGN SOME SPECIAL PASSES FOR US. HE'LL BE ABLE TO COVER FOR US IN CASE OF TROUBLE.
JANINA BUKOLSKA AT THE SOCIAL HELP COMMITTEE, WILL PROVIDE FORGED DOCUMENTS FOR US, INCLUDING FAKE IDENTITIES FOR THE CHILDREN
DO YOU KNOW IZABELA KUCZKOWSKA? SHE'S A SOCIAL RIGHTS JURIST. I CAN ASK HER TO BE OUR LIAISON. SHE KNOWS THE COURTS VERY WELL AND WORKS IN BOTH THE GHETTO AND THE ARYAN ZONE.
SHE TOLD ME ABOUT JÓZEF ZYSMAN, THE COURTHOUSE JANITOR. HE HAS THE KEYS TO A SECRET UNDERGROUND TUNNEL THAT WE CAN USE TO EVACUATE THE CHILDREN.
IRENA SCHULTZ IS ANOTHER COLLEAGUE WHO CAN HELP US ORGANIZE THINGS.
OH, AND JAGA, MY BEST FRIEND, OF COURSE.

WE CAN ASK **LEON SZESZKO**, WHO DRIVES THE TROLLEY THAT RUNS THROUGH THE GHETTO, TO HELP EVACUATE THE CHILDREN,

DW.GDANSKI

I'M GOOD FRIENDS WITH HIS WIFE, **MARIA**, WHO I'M SURE WILL BE HAPPY TO COORDINATE THINGS FOR US.

I CAN ALSO TALK TO **HENRYK**, A MASON WHO TRANSPORTS TRUCKLOADS OF BRICKS... HE COULD HIDE SOME CHILDREN IN THOSE SHIPMENTS.

AND **DOBRACZYNSKI**, WHO CAN SIGN WAREHOUSE ORDERS FOR PROVISIONS! AND MAYBE EVEN HELP FINANCE OUR OPERATIONS...

WARSZAWA

INSIDE THE GHETTO, THERE'S **EWA RECHTMAN** AT THE CENTOS* YOUTH CENTER. THEY'LL BE ABLE TO HELP WITH SOME OF OUR MISSIONS. SHE COULD HIDE A FEW FUGITIVES IN HER HOME...

AND THEN THERE'S HER BROTHER, **ADAM**, A MEMBER OF THE OJC.** HE KNOWS THE SEWERS AND TUNNELS UNDER THE CITY LIKE THE BACK OF HIS HAND.

*CENTOS: A National organization created to help orphans.

**OJC: A Jewish resistance group founded in the Ghetto in 1942

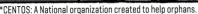

77

AND **SCHUMUEL**, EWA'S FIANCÉ, WHO SAYS HE ONLY WANTS TO MARRY HER TO KEEP HER SAFE. HE INFILTRATED THE JEWISH POLICE AND STANDS GUARD NEAR THE GATE TO TWARDA. HE HELPS BRING FOOD INTO THE GHETTO WITH BRIBES.

HE WORKS WITH A BUNCH OF SMUGGLERS, INCLUDING **HIRSCH**, WHO I HAVEN'T MET YET.

WE'LL ALSO NEED TO CREATE A NETWORK OF PLACES TO HIDE THE CHILDREN, LIKE **MOTHER MATYLDA GETTER**, WHO I'M SURE WILL BE GLAD TO TAKE THEM INTO HER CONVENT...

...OR **JANUSZ KORCZAK**, THE PEDIATRICIAN WHO OWNS THE SIENNA STREET ORPHANAGE. BOTH OF THEM WILL KNOW HOW TO LOOK AFTER THE KIDS...

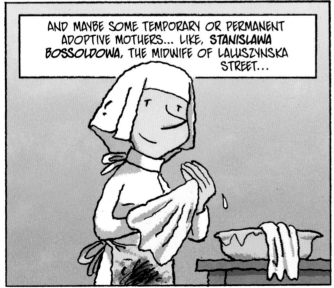

AND MAYBE SOME TEMPORARY OR PERMANENT ADOPTIVE MOTHERS... LIKE, **STANISLAWA BOSSOLDOWA**, THE MIDWIFE OF LALUSZYNSKA STREET...

...OR **JANINA**, THE NANNY, IN MICHALIN...

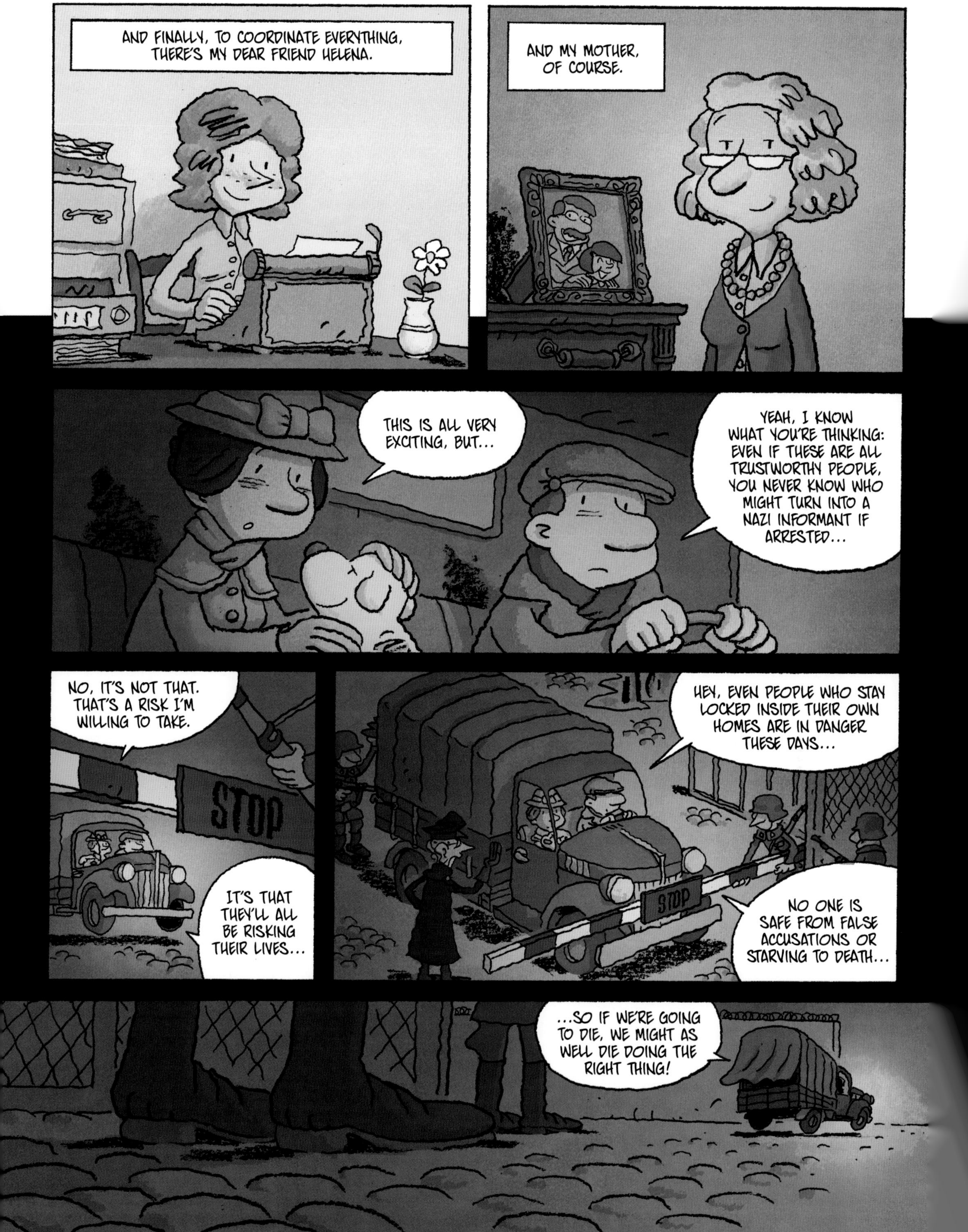
AND FINALLY, TO COORDINATE EVERYTHING, THERE'S MY DEAR FRIEND HELENA.
AND MY MOTHER, OF COURSE.
THIS IS ALL VERY EXCITING, BUT...
YEAH, I KNOW WHAT YOU'RE THINKING: EVEN IF THESE ARE ALL TRUSTWORTHY PEOPLE, YOU NEVER KNOW WHO MIGHT TURN INTO A NAZI INFORMANT IF ARRESTED...
NO, IT'S NOT THAT. THAT'S A RISK I'M WILLING TO TAKE.
STOP
IT'S THAT THEY'LL ALL BE RISKING THEIR LIVES...
HEY, EVEN PEOPLE WHO STAY LOCKED INSIDE THEIR OWN HOMES ARE IN DANGER THESE DAYS...
STOP
NO ONE IS SAFE FROM FALSE ACCUSATIONS OR STARVING TO DEATH...
...SO IF WE'RE GOING TO DIE, WE MIGHT AS WELL DIE DOING THE RIGHT THING!

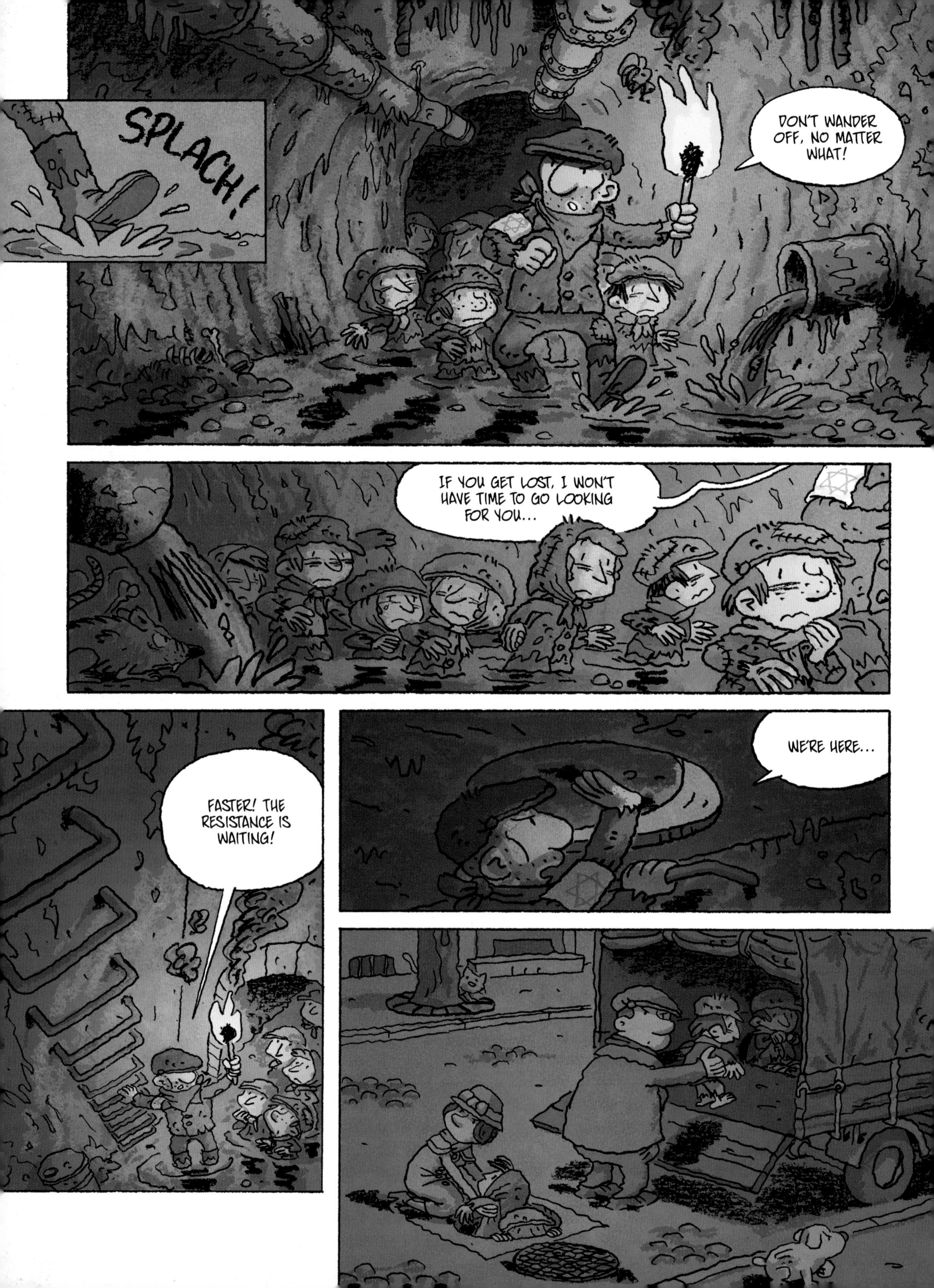
SPLACH!
DON'T WANDER OFF, NO MATTER WHAT!
IF YOU GET LOST, I WON'T HAVE TIME TO GO LOOKING FOR YOU...
FASTER! THE RESISTANCE IS WAITING!
WE'RE HERE...

DONG DONG...

ON THE TENTH CHIME...

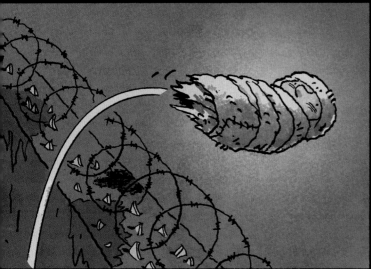

POF!

WE HAVE HIM, MA'AM! SAFE AND SOUND!

TH-THANK YOU...

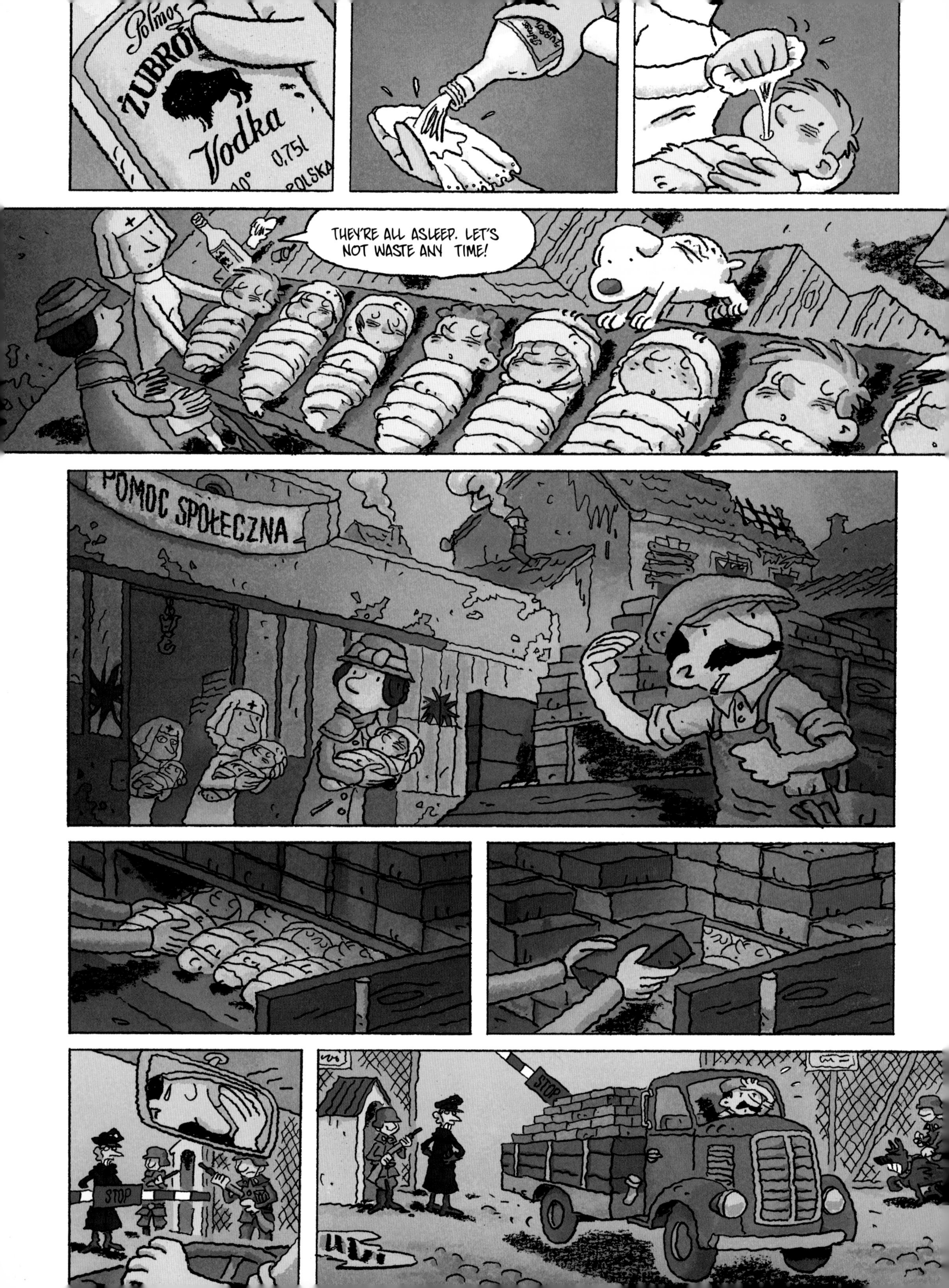
Polmos
ŻUBRÓ
Vodka
0,75l
POLSKA
THEY'RE ALL ASLEEP. LET'S NOT WASTE ANY TIME!
POMOC SPOŁECZNA
STOP
STOP

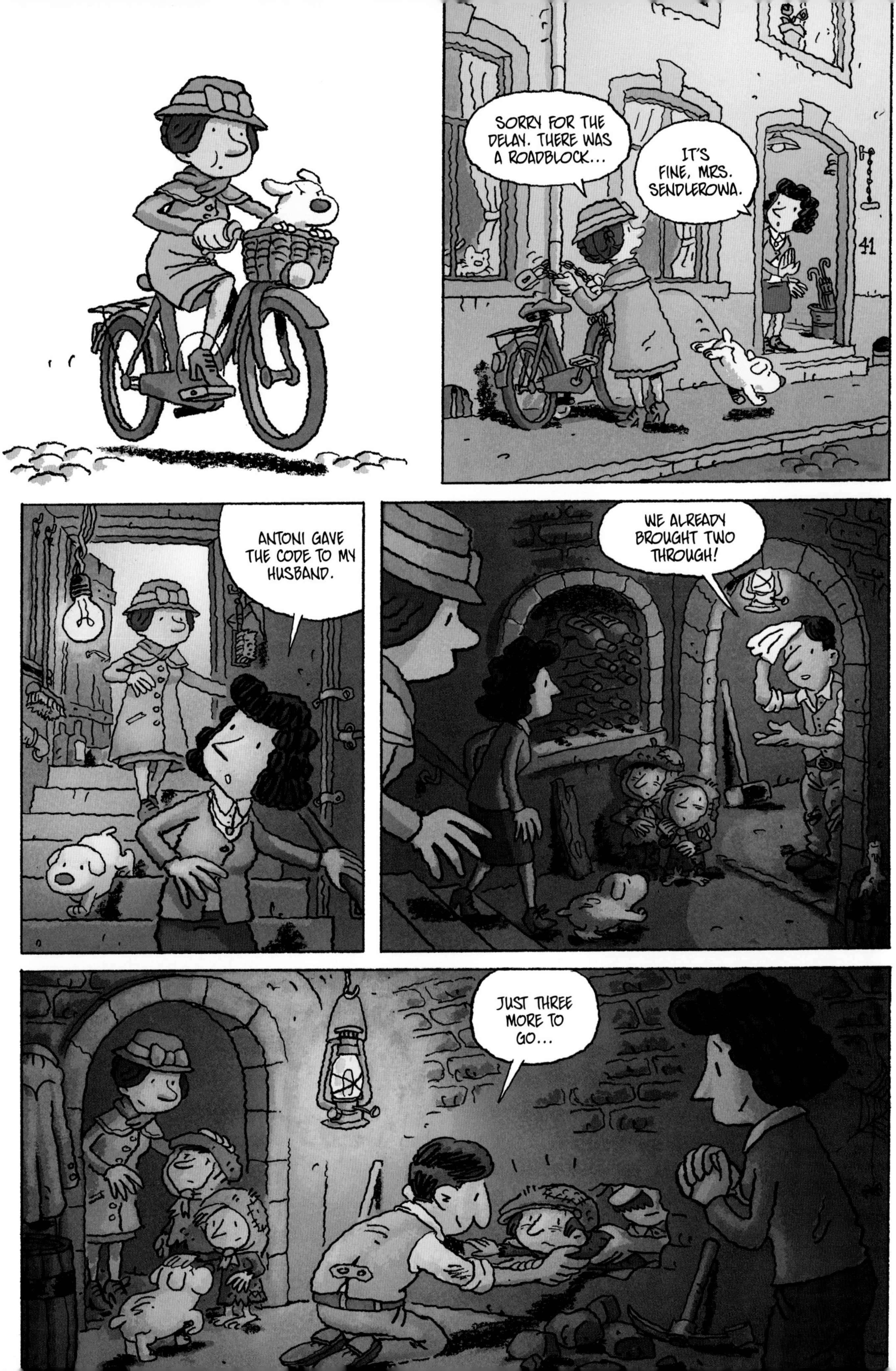
SORRY FOR THE DELAY. THERE WAS A ROADBLOCK...
IT'S FINE, MRS. SENDLEROWA.
41
ANTONI GAVE THE CODE TO MY HUSBAND.
WE ALREADY BROUGHT TWO THROUGH!
JUST THREE MORE TO GO...

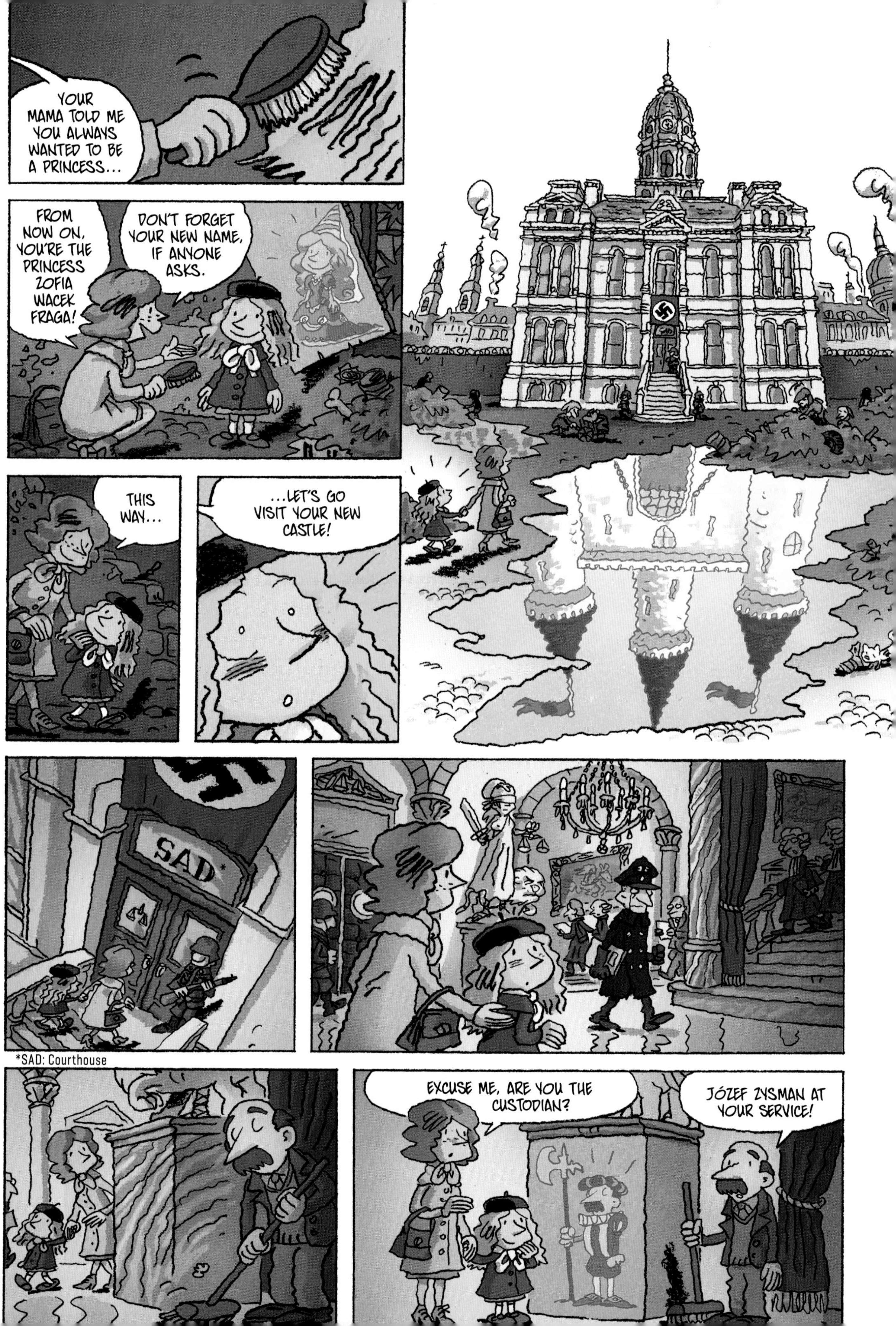
YOUR MAMA TOLD ME YOU ALWAYS WANTED TO BE A PRINCESS...
FROM NOW ON, YOU'RE THE PRINCESS ZOFIA WACEK FRAGA!
DON'T FORGET YOUR NEW NAME, IF ANYONE ASKS.
THIS WAY...
...LET'S GO VISIT YOUR NEW CASTLE!
SAD*
EXCUSE ME, ARE YOU THE CUSTODIAN?
JÓZEF ZYSMAN AT YOUR SERVICE!

*SAD: Courthouse

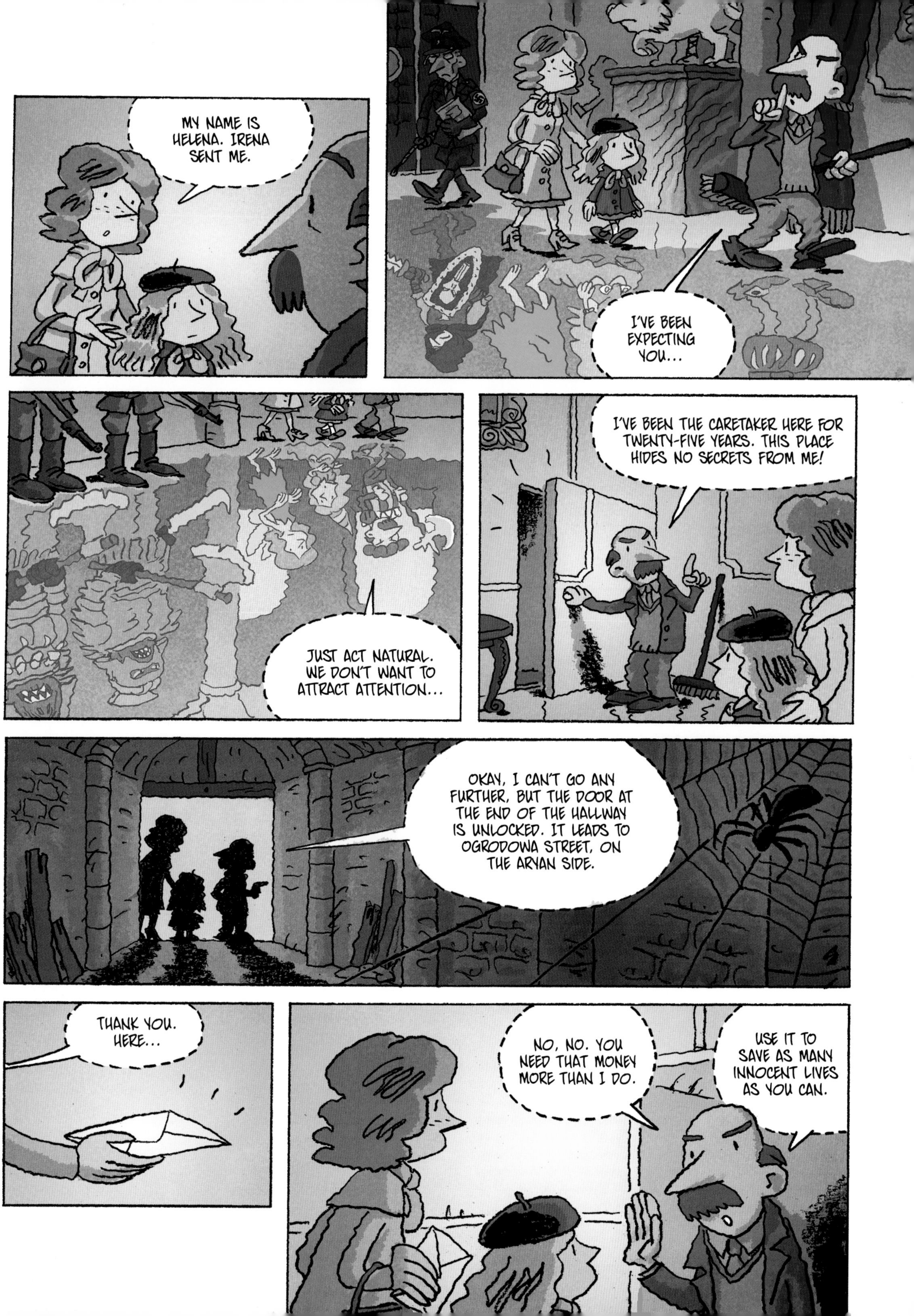
MY NAME IS HELENA. IRENA SENT ME.
I'VE BEEN EXPECTING YOU...
JUST ACT NATURAL. WE DON'T WANT TO ATTRACT ATTENTION...
I'VE BEEN THE CARETAKER HERE FOR TWENTY-FIVE YEARS. THIS PLACE HIDES NO SECRETS FROM ME!
OKAY, I CAN'T GO ANY FURTHER, BUT THE DOOR AT THE END OF THE HALLWAY IS UNLOCKED. IT LEADS TO OGRODOWA STREET, ON THE ARYAN SIDE.
THANK YOU. HERE...
NO, NO. YOU NEED THAT MONEY MORE THAN I DO.
USE IT TO SAVE AS MANY INNOCENT LIVES AS YOU CAN.

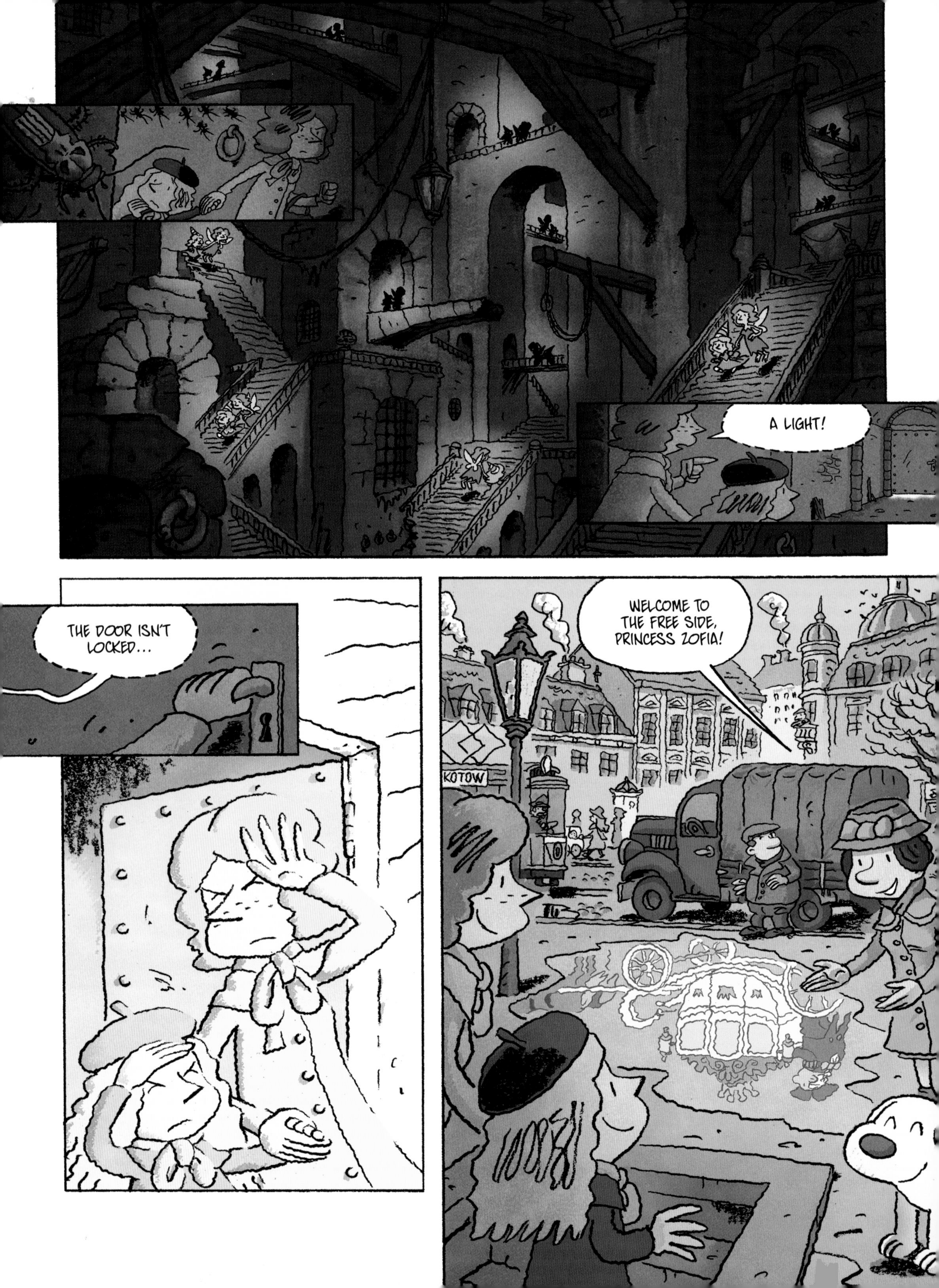
A LIGHT!
THE DOOR ISN'T LOCKED...
WELCOME TO THE FREE SIDE, PRINCESS ZOFIA!
KOTOW

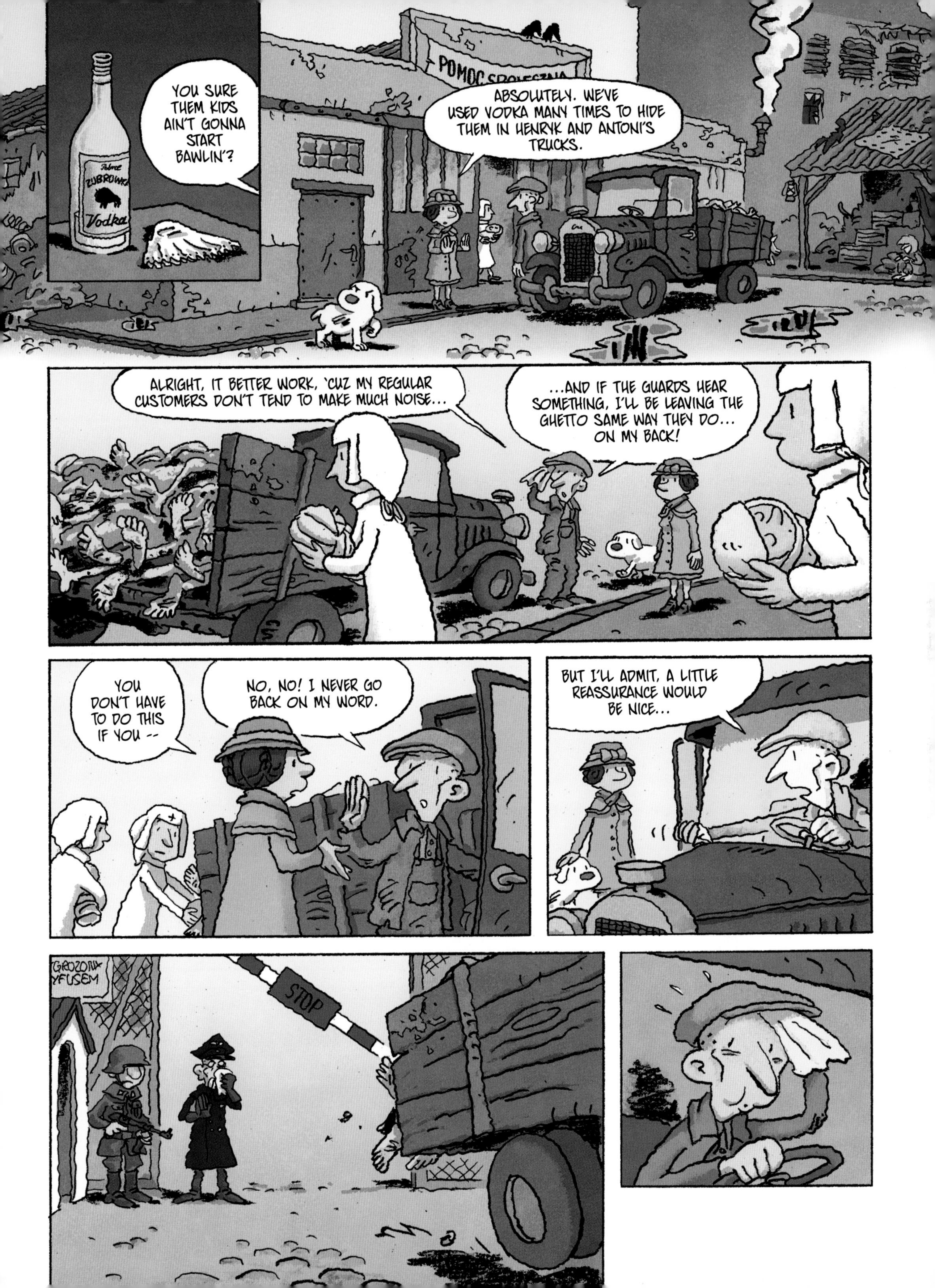
YOU SURE THEM KIDS AIN'T GONNA START BAWLIN'?
ABSOLUTELY. WE'VE USED VODKA MANY TIMES TO HIDE THEM IN HENRYK AND ANTONI'S TRUCKS.
ALRIGHT, IT BETTER WORK, 'CUZ MY REGULAR CUSTOMERS DON'T TEND TO MAKE MUCH NOISE...
...AND IF THE GUARDS HEAR SOMETHING, I'LL BE LEAVING THE GHETTO SAME WAY THEY DO... ON MY BACK!
YOU DON'T HAVE TO DO THIS IF YOU --
NO, NO! I NEVER GO BACK ON MY WORD.
BUT I'LL ADMIT, A LITTLE REASSURANCE WOULD BE NICE...
STOP

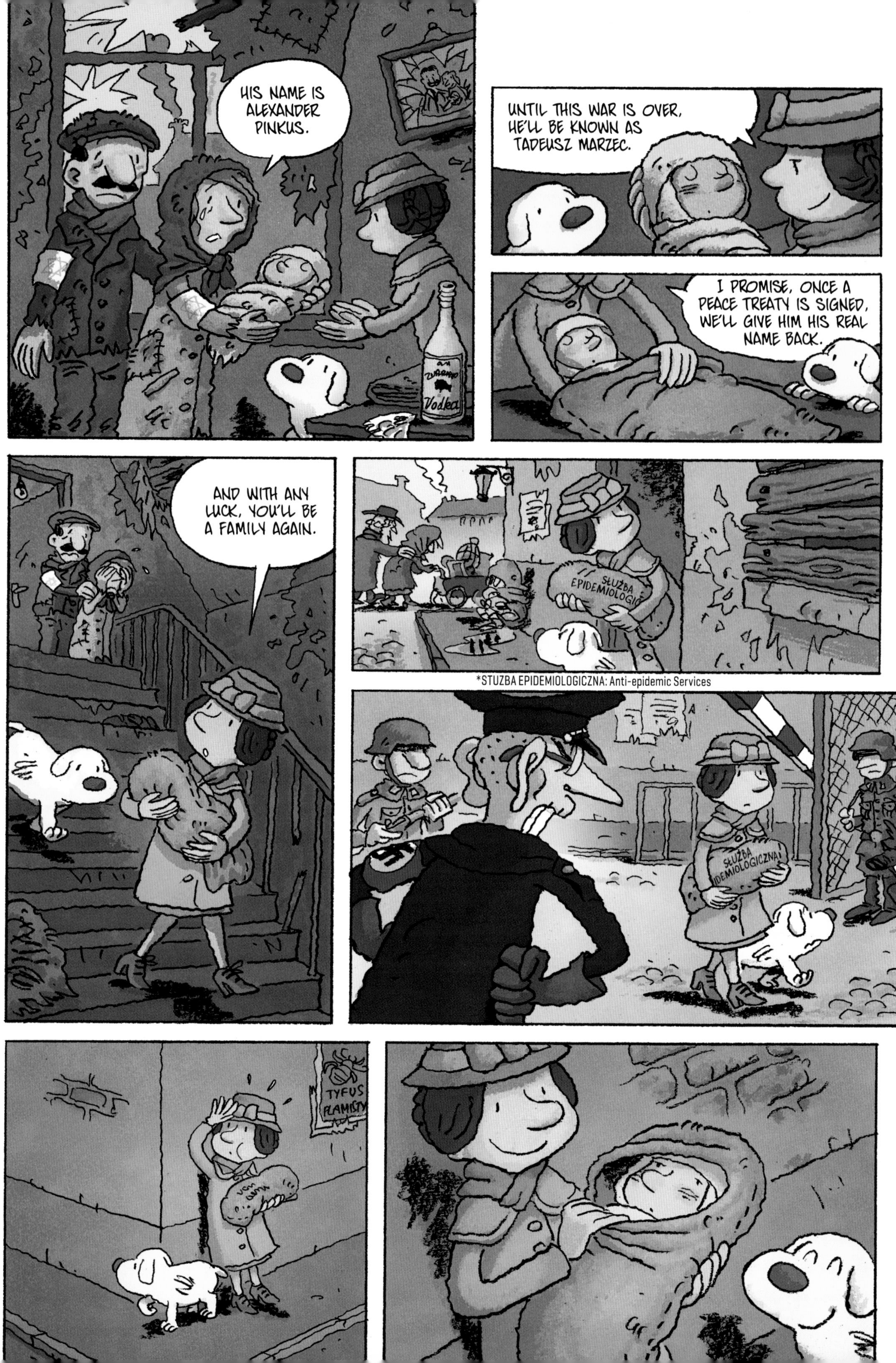
HIS NAME IS ALEXANDER PINKUS.
Vodka
UNTIL THIS WAR IS OVER, HE'LL BE KNOWN AS TADEUSZ MARZEC.
I PROMISE, ONCE A PEACE TREATY IS SIGNED, WE'LL GIVE HIM HIS REAL NAME BACK.
AND WITH ANY LUCK, YOU'LL BE A FAMILY AGAIN.
SŁUŻBA EPIDEMIOLOGIC
SŁUŻBA EPIDEMIOLOGICZNA
TYFUS PLAMISTY

*STUZBA EPIDEMIOLOGICZNA: Anti-epidemic Services

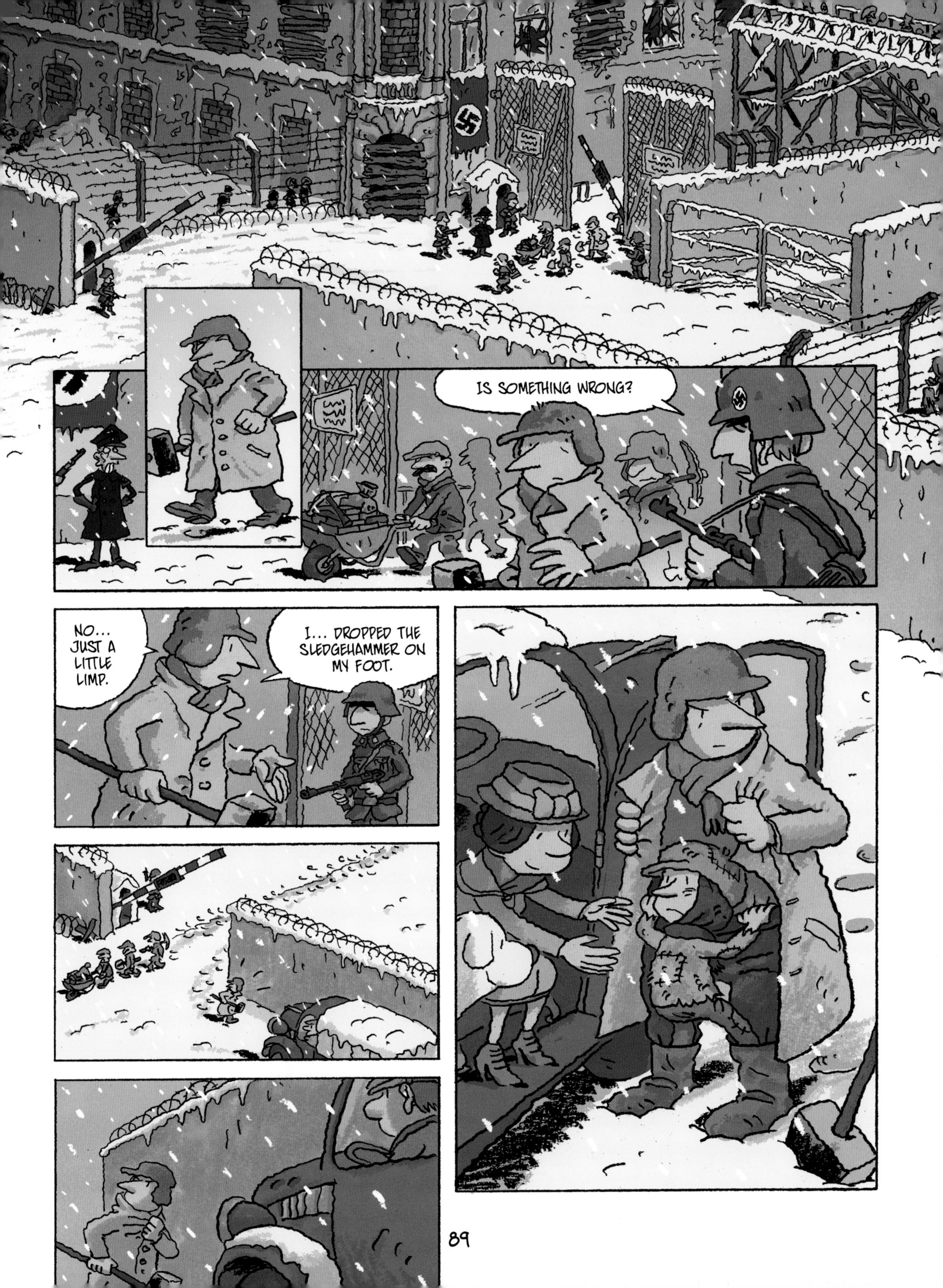
IS SOMETHING WRONG?
NO... JUST A LITTLE LIMP.
I... DROPPED THE SLEDGEHAMMER ON MY FOOT.

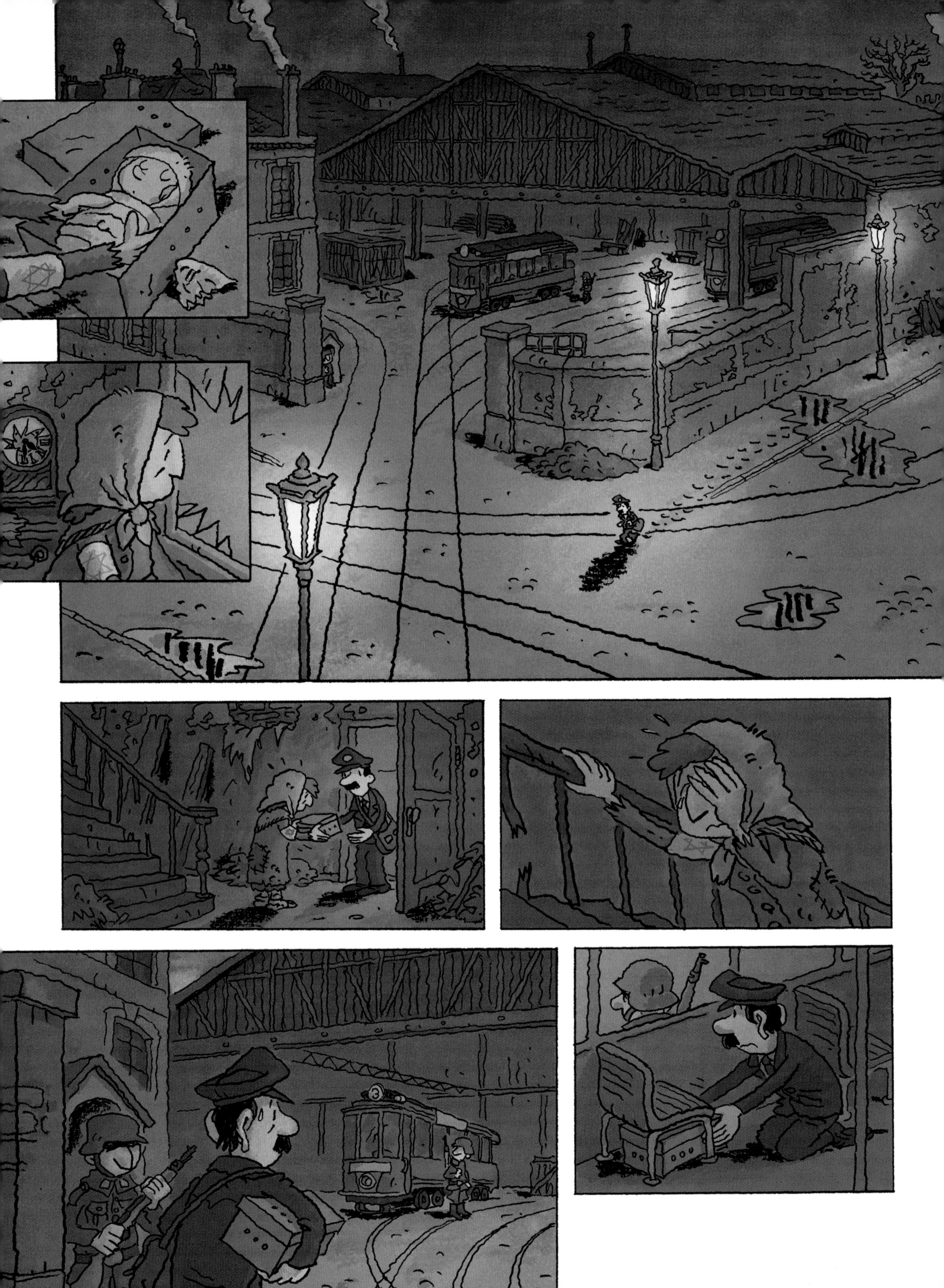

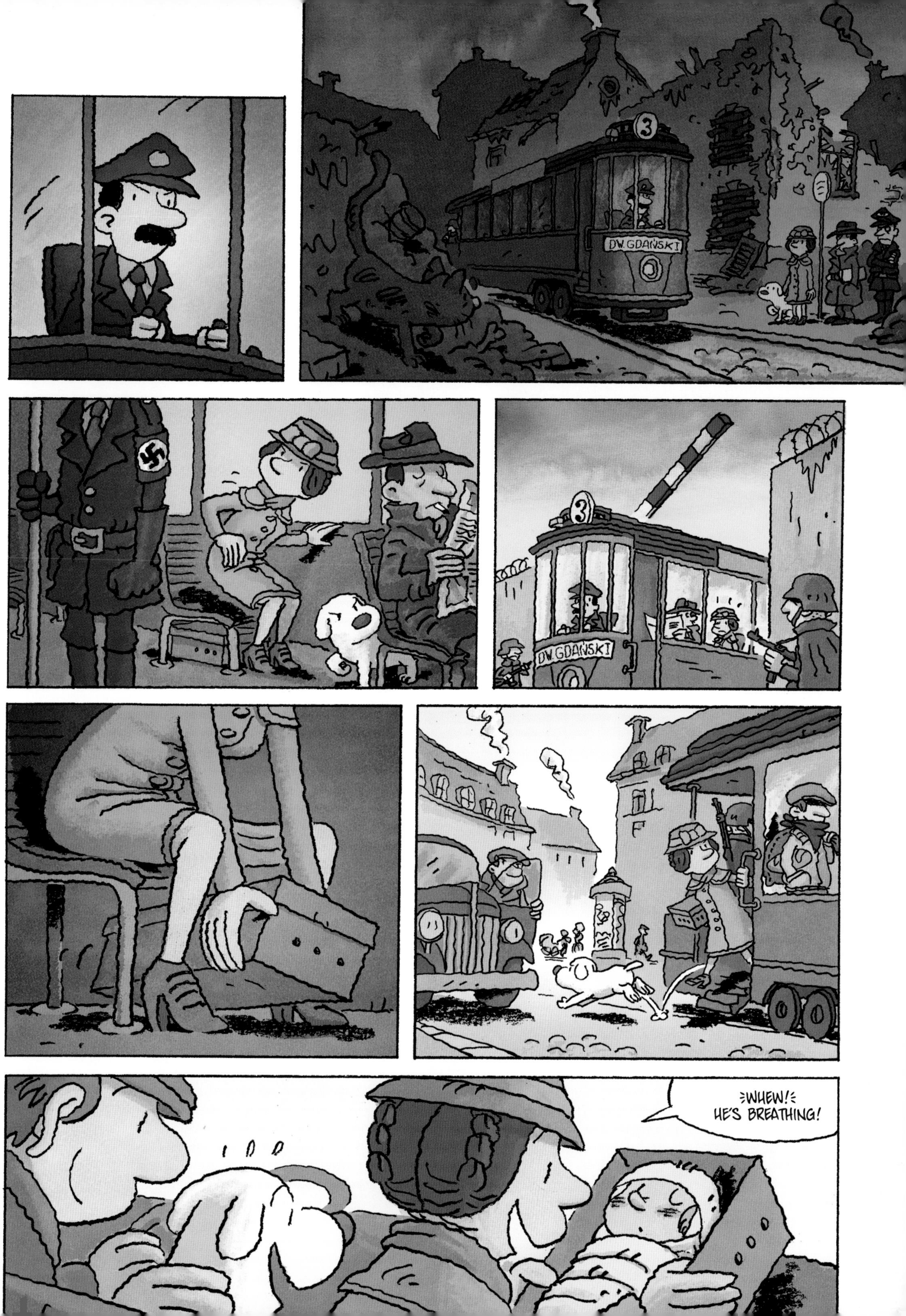
3
DW. GDAŃSKI
3
DW. GDAŃSKI
WHEW!
HE'S BREATHING!

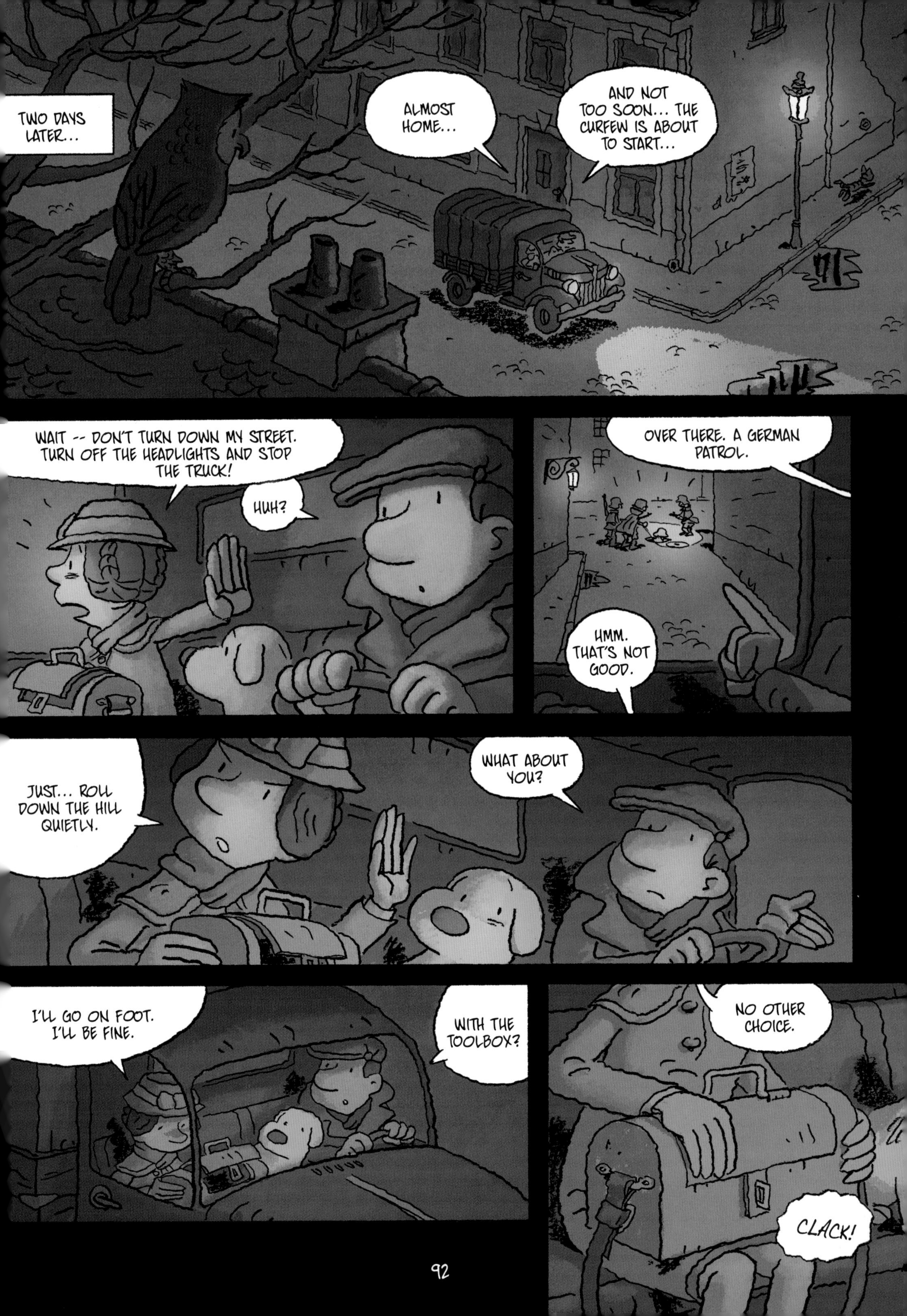
TWO DAYS LATER...
ALMOST HOME...
AND NOT TOO SOON... THE CURFEW IS ABOUT TO START...
WAIT -- DON'T TURN DOWN MY STREET. TURN OFF THE HEADLIGHTS AND STOP THE TRUCK!
HUH?
OVER THERE. A GERMAN PATROL.
HMM. THAT'S NOT GOOD.
JUST... ROLL DOWN THE HILL QUIETLY.
WHAT ABOUT YOU?
I'LL GO ON FOOT. I'LL BE FINE.
WITH THE TOOLBOX?
NO OTHER CHOICE.
CLACK!

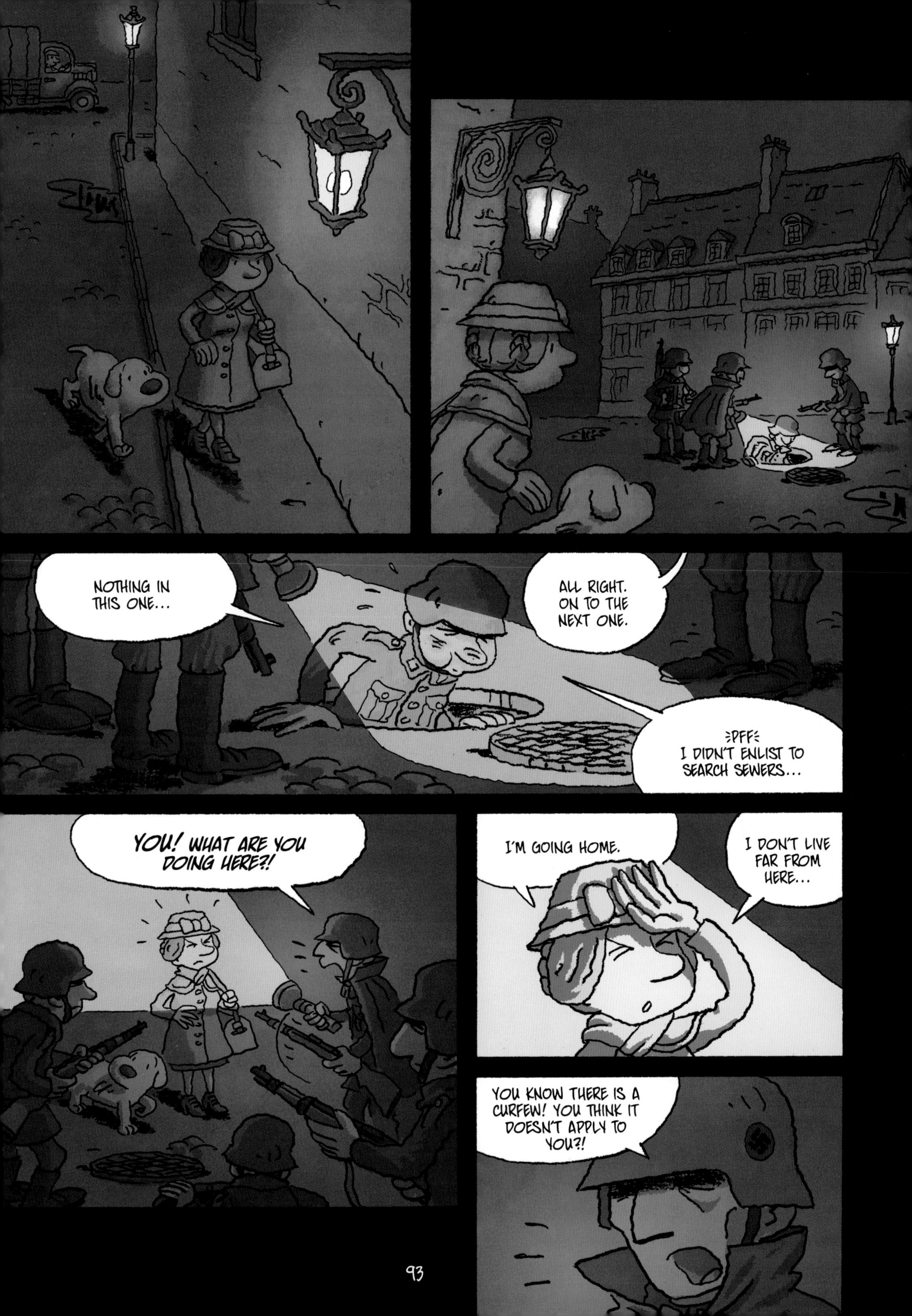
NOTHING IN THIS ONE...
ALL RIGHT. ON TO THE NEXT ONE.
PFF
I DIDN'T ENLIST TO SEARCH SEWERS...
YOU! WHAT ARE YOU DOING HERE?!
I'M GOING HOME.
I DON'T LIVE FAR FROM HERE...
YOU KNOW THERE IS A CURFEW! YOU THINK IT DOESN'T APPLY TO YOU?!

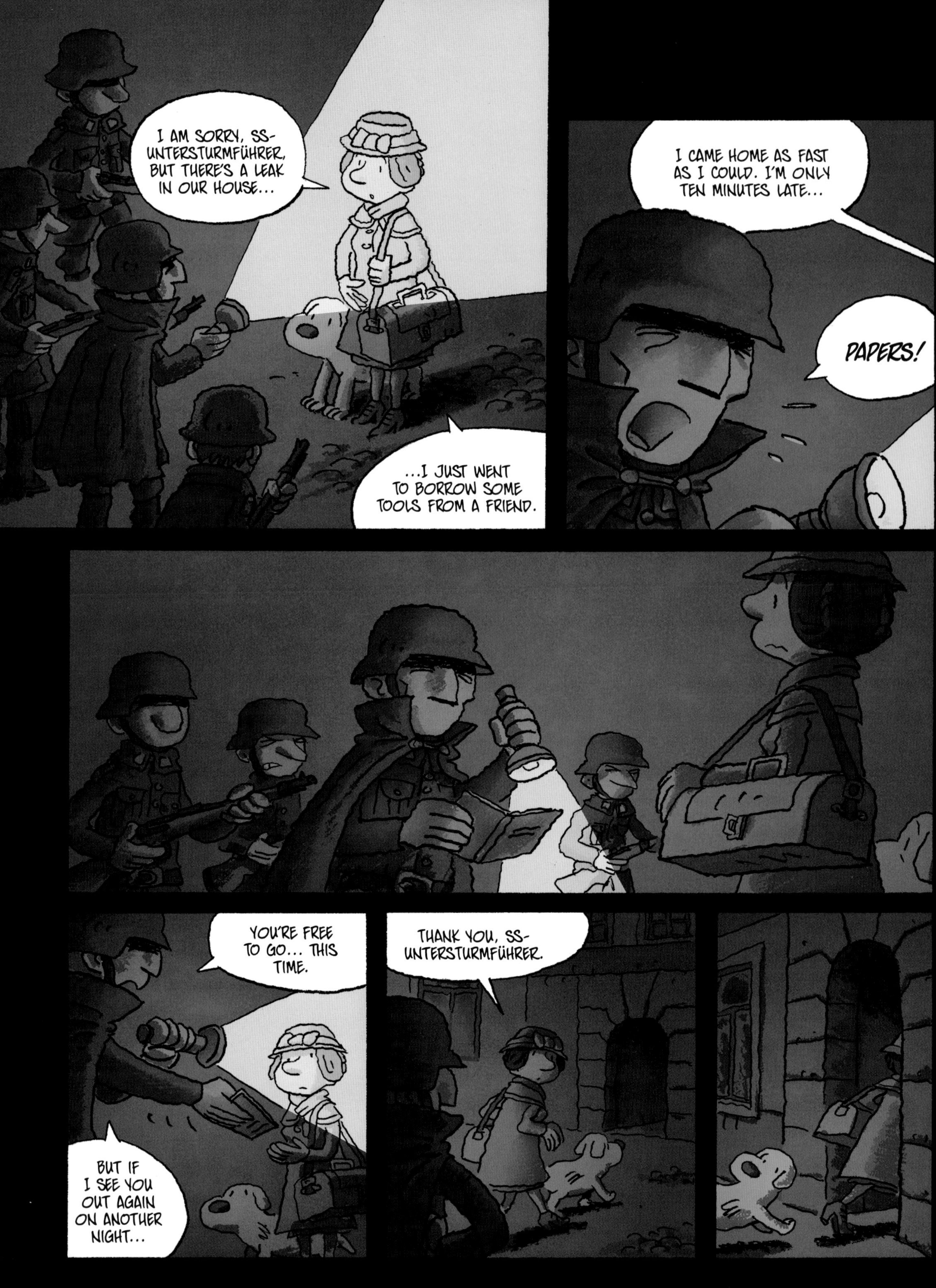

I AM SORRY, SS-UNTERSTURMFÜHRER, BUT THERE'S A LEAK IN OUR HOUSE...
...I JUST WENT TO BORROW SOME TOOLS FROM A FRIEND.
I CAME HOME AS FAST AS I COULD. I'M ONLY TEN MINUTES LATE...
PAPERS!
YOU'RE FREE TO GO... THIS TIME.
BUT IF I SEE YOU OUT AGAIN ON ANOTHER NIGHT...
THANK YOU, SS-UNTERSTURMFÜHRER.

HELLO, MOTHER.

YOU'RE HOME LATE, SWEETIE...

OH, YOU KNOW HOW BUSY WORK CAN GET...

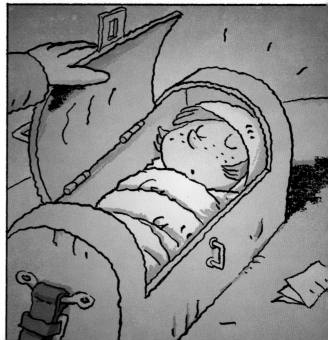

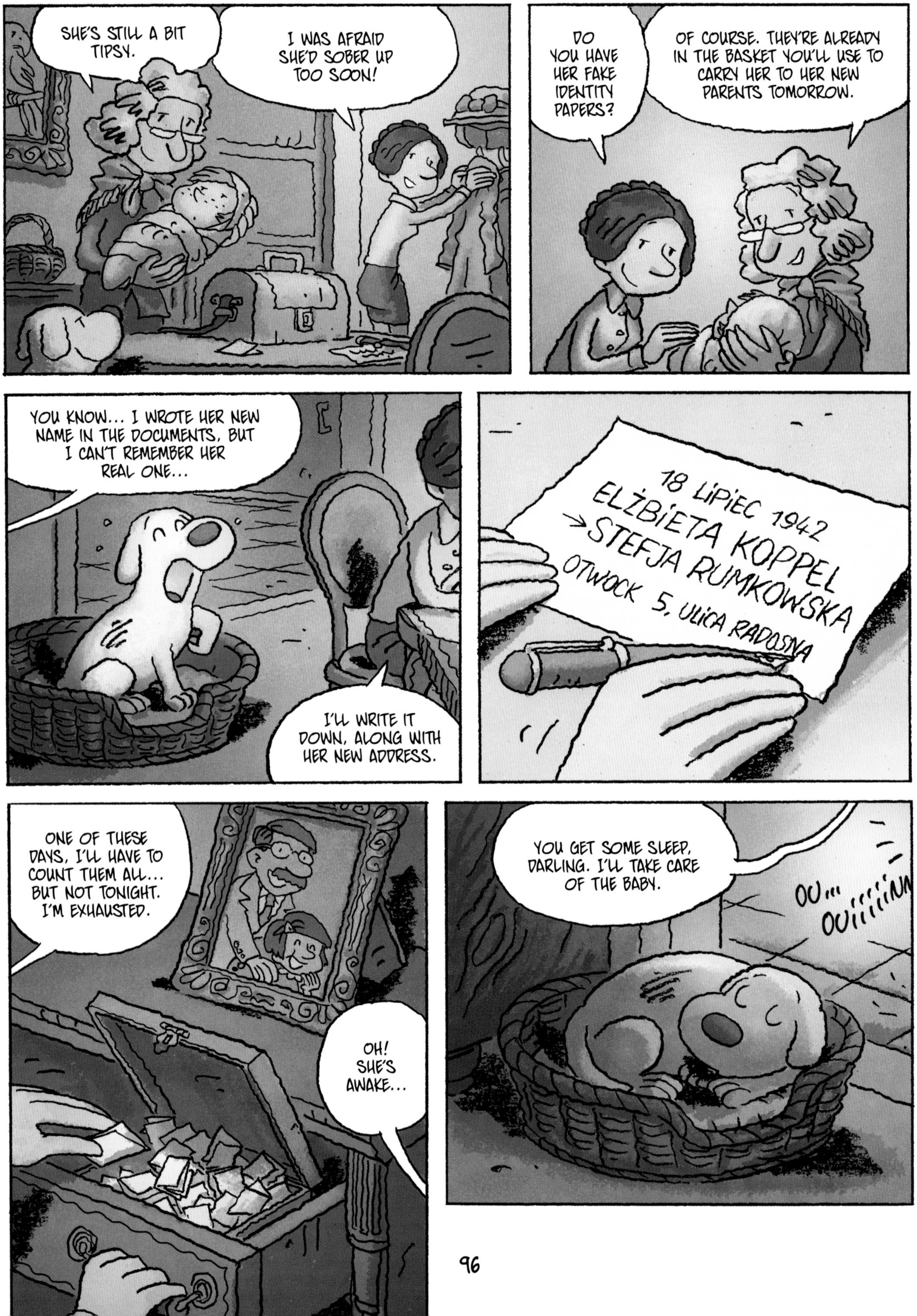
SHE'S STILL A BIT TIPSY.
I WAS AFRAID SHE'D SOBER UP TOO SOON!
DO YOU HAVE HER FAKE IDENTITY PAPERS?
OF COURSE. THEY'RE ALREADY IN THE BASKET YOU'LL USE TO CARRY HER TO HER NEW PARENTS TOMORROW.
YOU KNOW... I WROTE HER NEW NAME IN THE DOCUMENTS, BUT I CAN'T REMEMBER HER REAL ONE...
I'LL WRITE IT DOWN, ALONG WITH HER NEW ADDRESS.
18 LIPIEC 1942
ELŻBIETA KOPPEL
→STEFJA RUMKOWSKA
OTWOCK 5, ULICA RADOSNA
ONE OF THESE DAYS, I'LL HAVE TO COUNT THEM ALL... BUT NOT TONIGHT. I'M EXHAUSTED.
OH! SHE'S AWAKE...
YOU GET SOME SLEEP, DARLING. I'LL TAKE CARE OF THE BABY.
OU... OUiiiiiNN

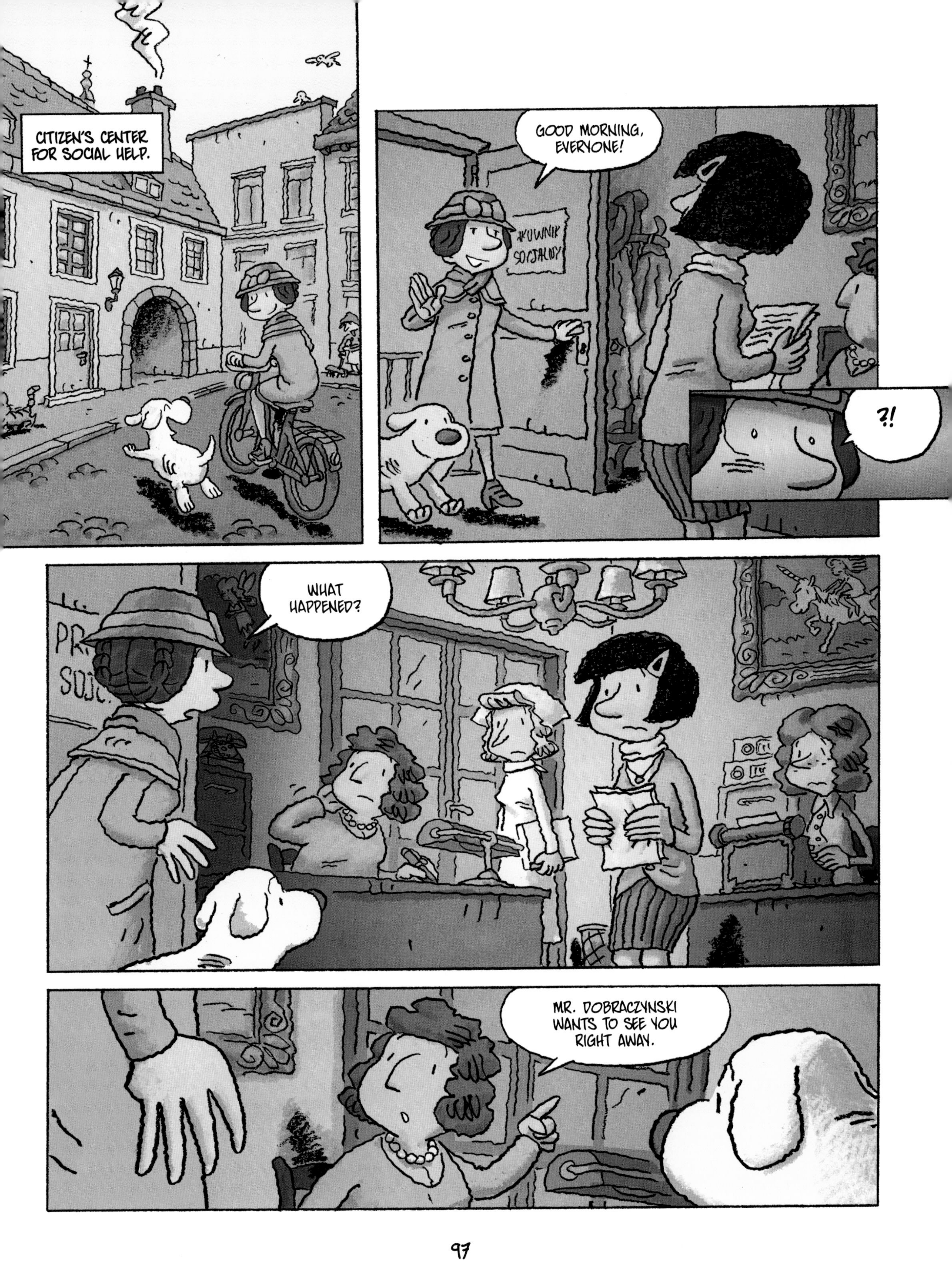
CITIZEN'S CENTER FOR SOCIAL HELP.
GOOD MORNING, EVERYONE!
?!
WHAT HAPPENED?
MR. DOBRACZYNSKI WANTS TO SEE YOU RIGHT AWAY.

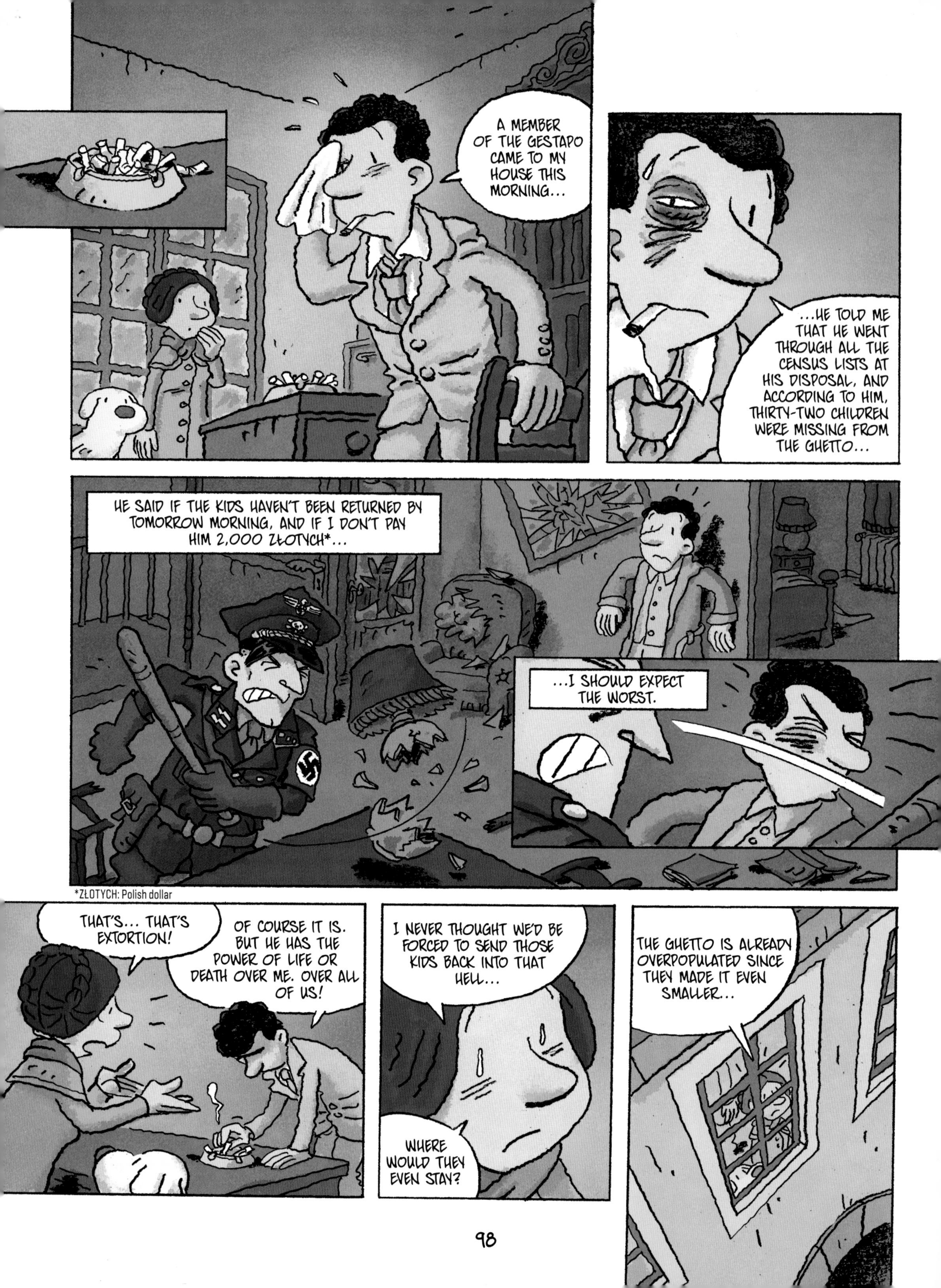
A MEMBER OF THE GESTAPO CAME TO MY HOUSE THIS MORNING...
...HE TOLD ME THAT HE WENT THROUGH ALL THE CENSUS LISTS AT HIS DISPOSAL, AND ACCORDING TO HIM, THIRTY-TWO CHILDREN WERE MISSING FROM THE GHETTO...
HE SAID IF THE KIDS HAVEN'T BEEN RETURNED BY TOMORROW MORNING, AND IF I DON'T PAY HIM 2,000 ZŁOTYCH*...
...I SHOULD EXPECT THE WORST.
THAT'S... THAT'S EXTORTION!
OF COURSE IT IS. BUT HE HAS THE POWER OF LIFE OR DEATH OVER ME. OVER ALL OF US!
I NEVER THOUGHT WE'D BE FORCED TO SEND THOSE KIDS BACK INTO THAT HELL...
WHERE WOULD THEY EVEN STAY?
THE GHETTO IS ALREADY OVERPOPULATED SINCE THEY MADE IT EVEN SMALLER...

*ZŁOTYCH: Polish dollar

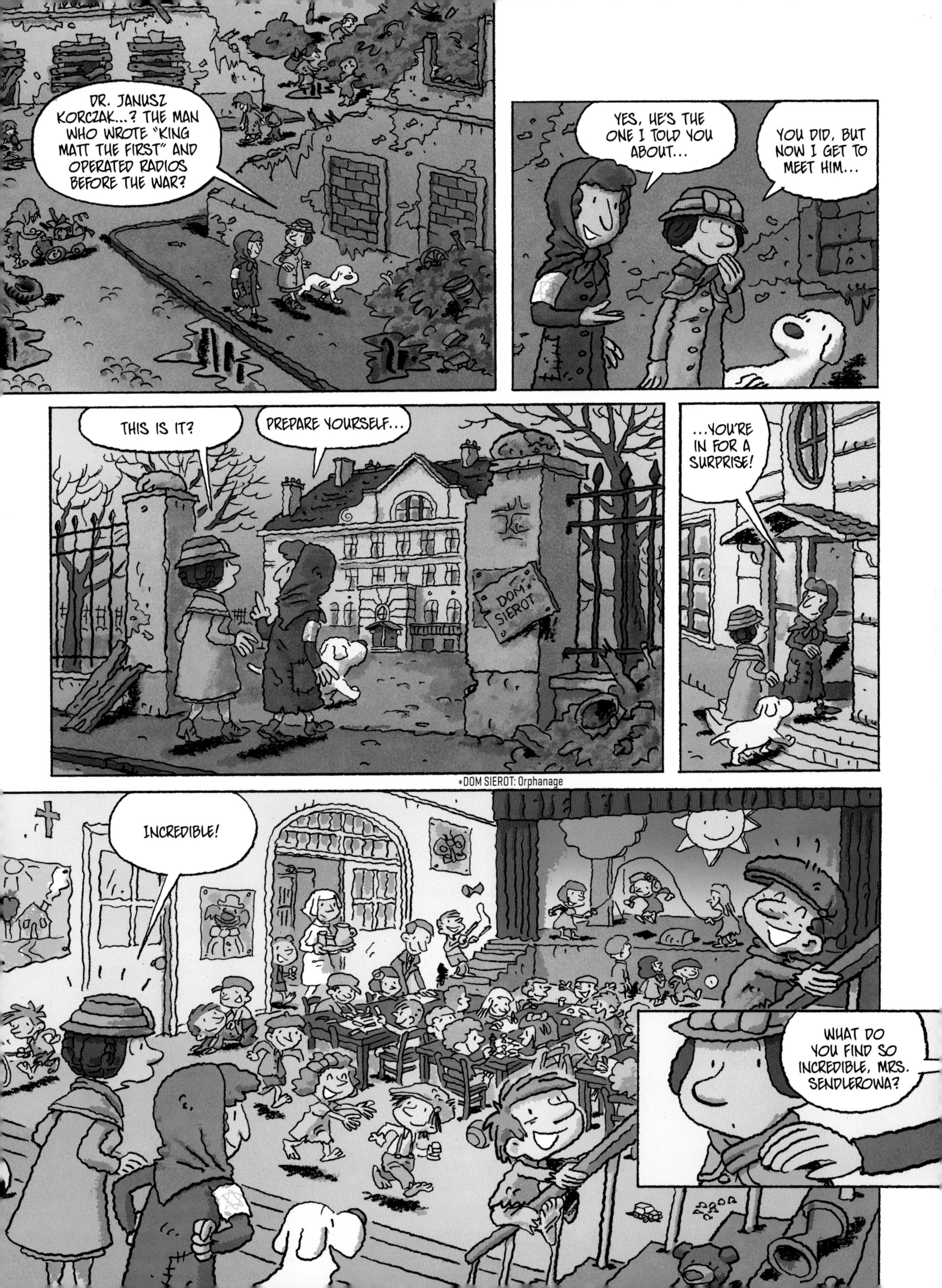
DR. JANUSZ KORCZAK...? THE MAN WHO WROTE "KING MATT THE FIRST" AND OPERATED RADIOS BEFORE THE WAR?
YES, HE'S THE ONE I TOLD YOU ABOUT...
YOU DID, BUT NOW I GET TO MEET HIM...
THIS IS IT?
PREPARE YOURSELF...
DOM SIEROT*
...YOU'RE IN FOR A SURPRISE!
INCREDIBLE!
WHAT DO YOU FIND SO INCREDIBLE, MRS. SENDLEROWA?

*DOM SIEROT: Orphanage

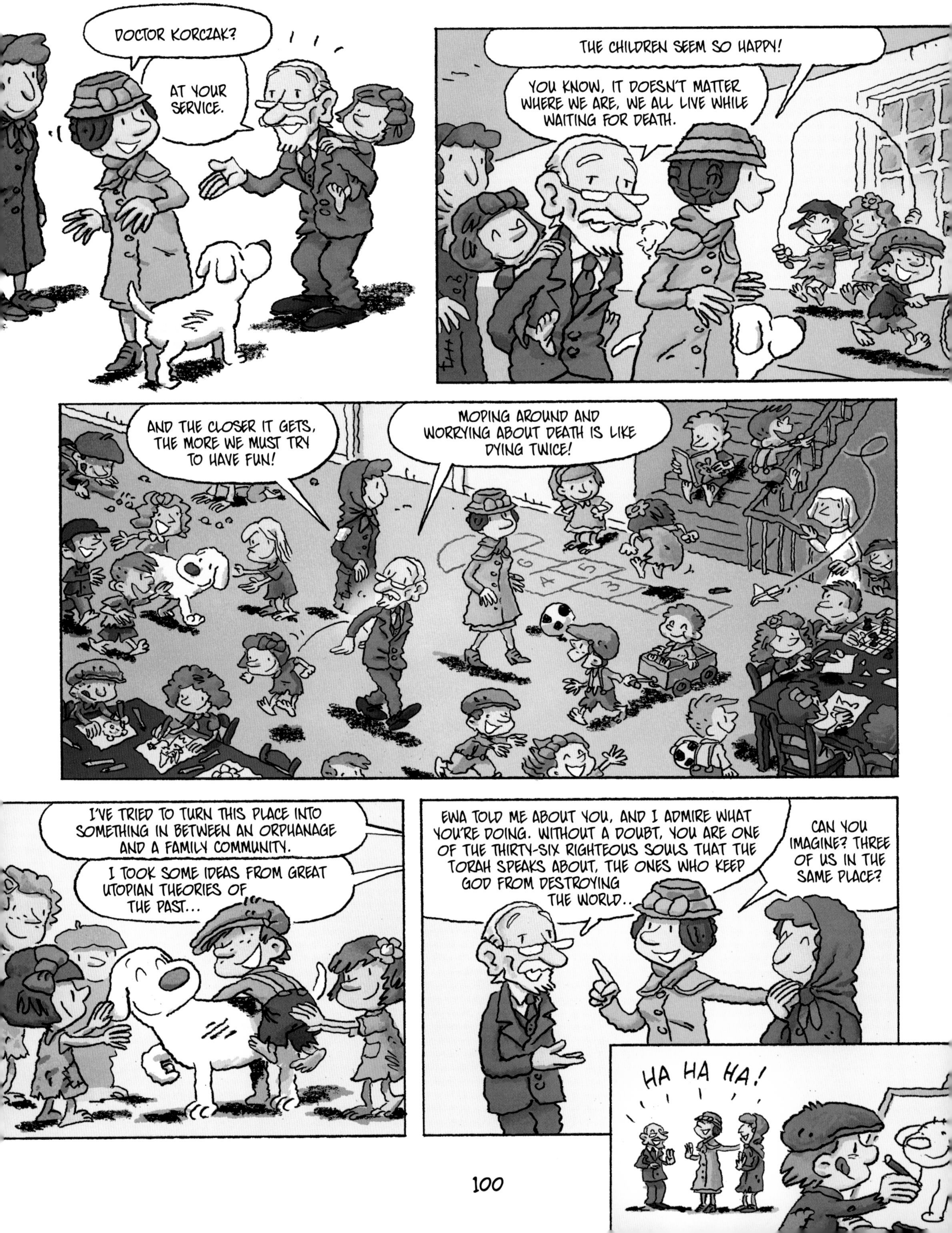

DOCTOR KORCZAK?
AT YOUR SERVICE.
THE CHILDREN SEEM SO HAPPY!
YOU KNOW, IT DOESN'T MATTER WHERE WE ARE, WE ALL LIVE WHILE WAITING FOR DEATH.
AND THE CLOSER IT GETS, THE MORE WE MUST TRY TO HAVE FUN!
MOPING AROUND AND WORRYING ABOUT DEATH IS LIKE DYING TWICE!
I'VE TRIED TO TURN THIS PLACE INTO SOMETHING IN BETWEEN AN ORPHANAGE AND A FAMILY COMMUNITY.
I TOOK SOME IDEAS FROM GREAT UTOPIAN THEORIES OF THE PAST...
EWA TOLD ME ABOUT YOU, AND I ADMIRE WHAT YOU'RE DOING. WITHOUT A DOUBT, YOU ARE ONE OF THE THIRTY-SIX RIGHTEOUS SOULS THAT THE TORAH SPEAKS ABOUT, THE ONES WHO KEEP GOD FROM DESTROYING THE WORLD...
CAN YOU IMAGINE? THREE OF US IN THE SAME PLACE?
HA HA HA!

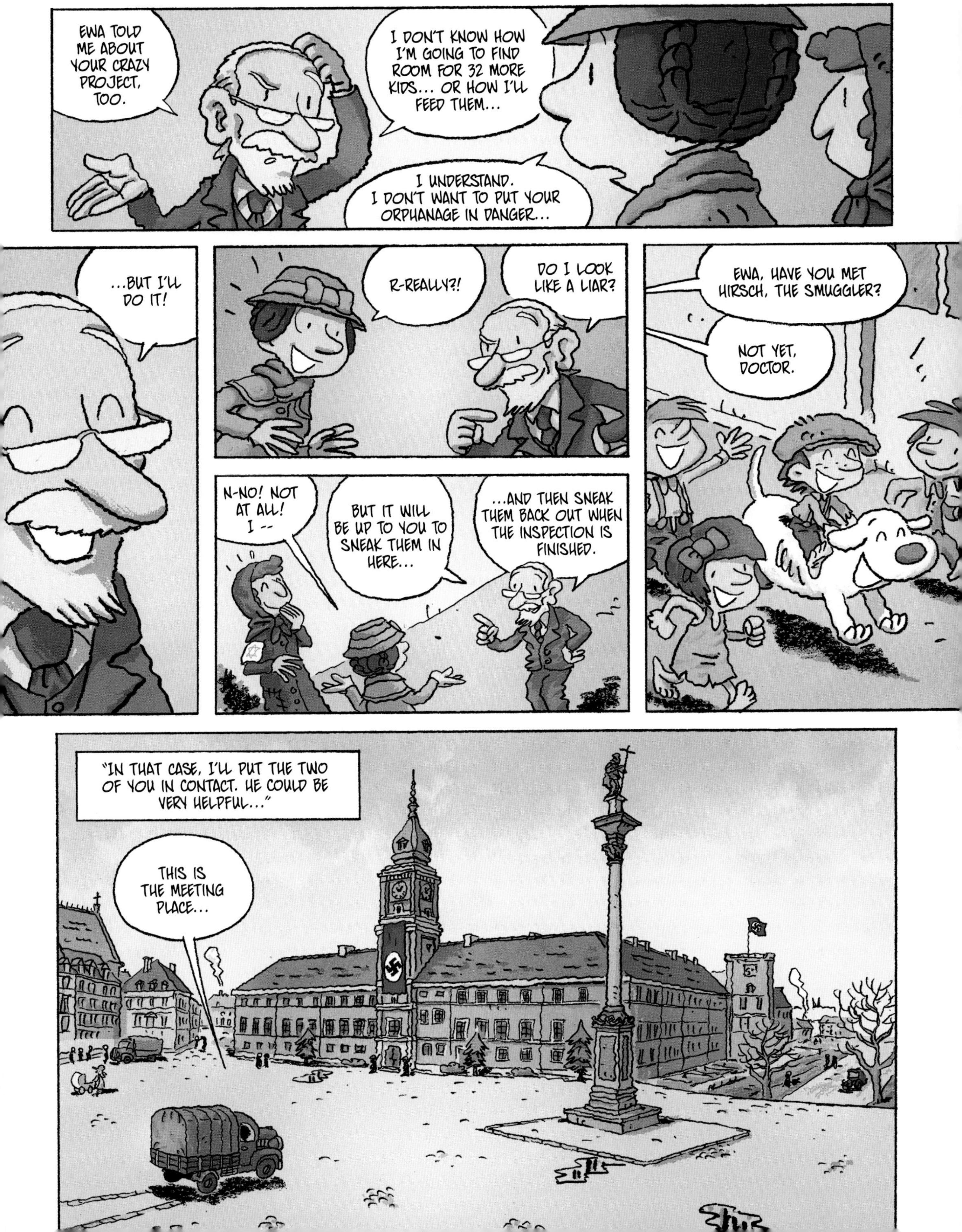
EWA TOLD ME ABOUT YOUR CRAZY PROJECT, TOO.
I DON'T KNOW HOW I'M GOING TO FIND ROOM FOR 32 MORE KIDS… OR HOW I'LL FEED THEM…
I UNDERSTAND. I DON'T WANT TO PUT YOUR ORPHANAGE IN DANGER…
…BUT I'LL DO IT!
R-REALLY?!
DO I LOOK LIKE A LIAR?
N-NO! NOT AT ALL! I --
BUT IT WILL BE UP TO YOU TO SNEAK THEM IN HERE…
…AND THEN SNEAK THEM BACK OUT WHEN THE INSPECTION IS FINISHED.
EWA, HAVE YOU MET HIRSCH, THE SMUGGLER?
NOT YET, DOCTOR.
"IN THAT CASE, I'LL PUT THE TWO OF YOU IN CONTACT. HE COULD BE VERY HELPFUL…"
THIS IS THE MEETING PLACE…

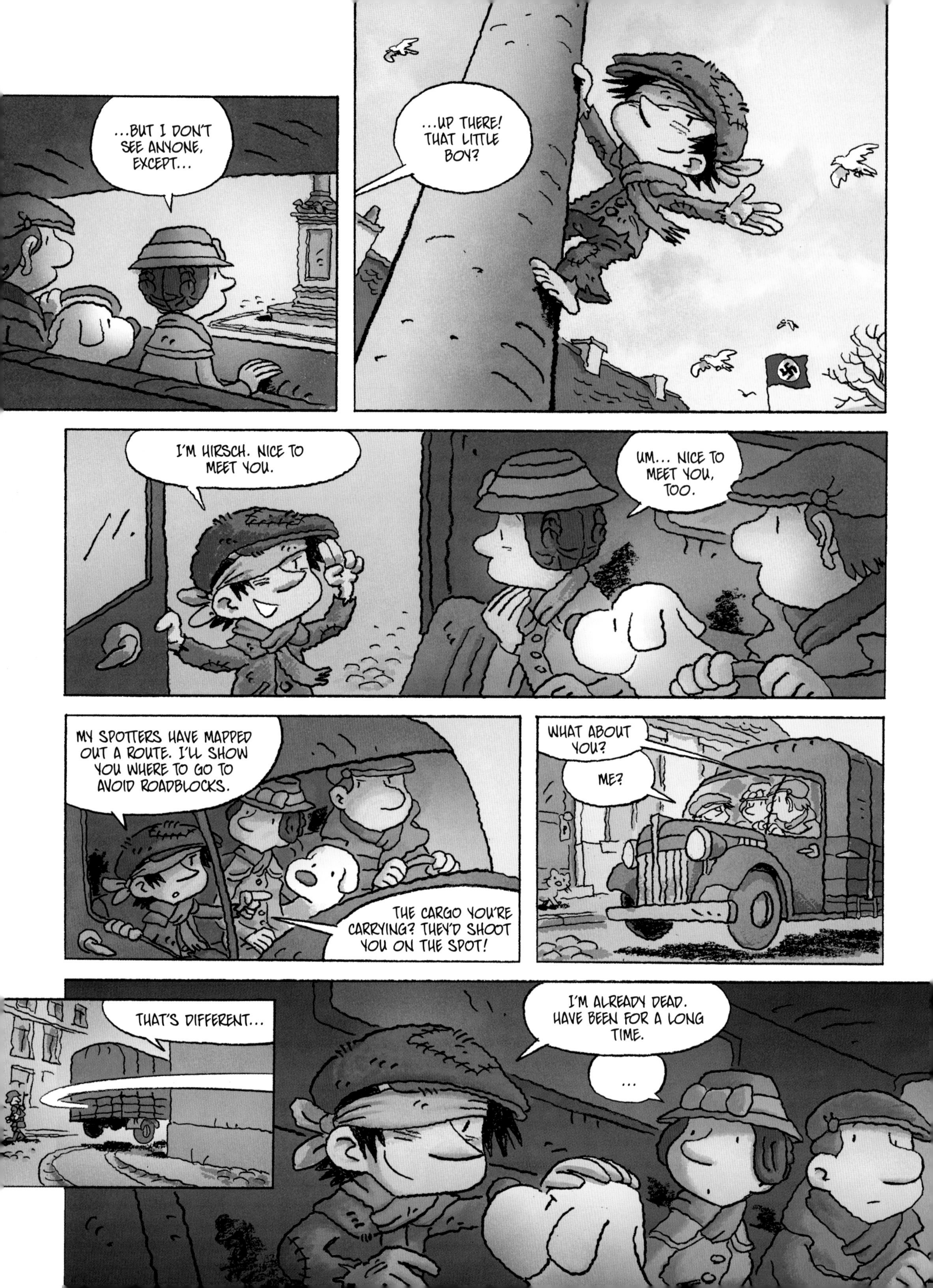
...BUT I DON'T SEE ANYONE, EXCEPT...
...UP THERE! THAT LITTLE BOY?
I'M HIRSCH. NICE TO MEET YOU.
UM... NICE TO MEET YOU, TOO.
MY SPOTTERS HAVE MAPPED OUT A ROUTE. I'LL SHOW YOU WHERE TO GO TO AVOID ROADBLOCKS.
THE CARGO YOU'RE CARRYING? THEY'D SHOOT YOU ON THE SPOT!
WHAT ABOUT YOU?
ME?
THAT'S DIFFERENT...
I'M ALREADY DEAD. HAVE BEEN FOR A LONG TIME.
...

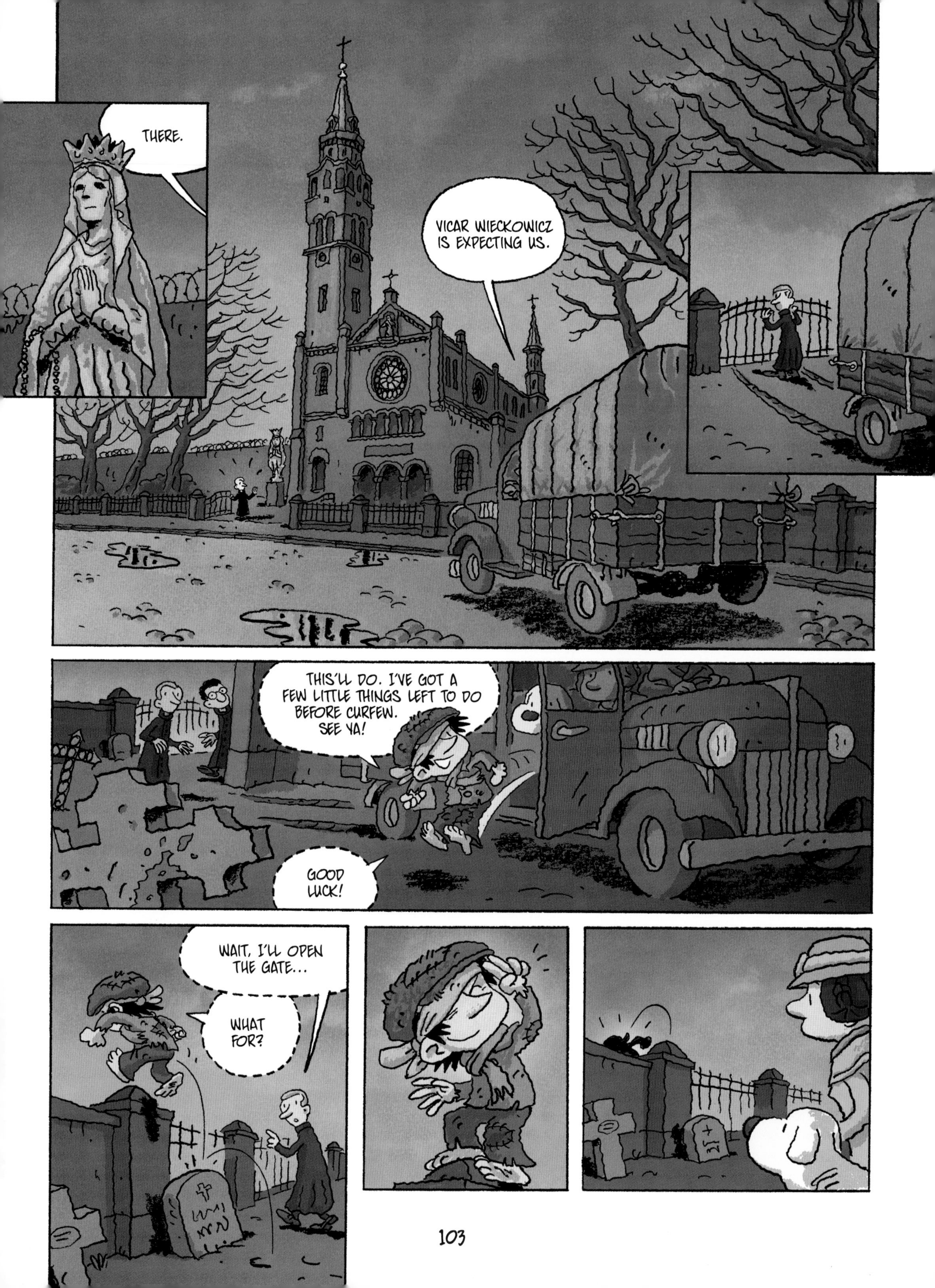
THERE.
VICAR WIECKOWICZ IS EXPECTING US.
THIS'LL DO. I'VE GOT A FEW LITTLE THINGS LEFT TO DO BEFORE CURFEW. SEE YA!
GOOD LUCK!
WAIT, I'LL OPEN THE GATE...
WHAT FOR?

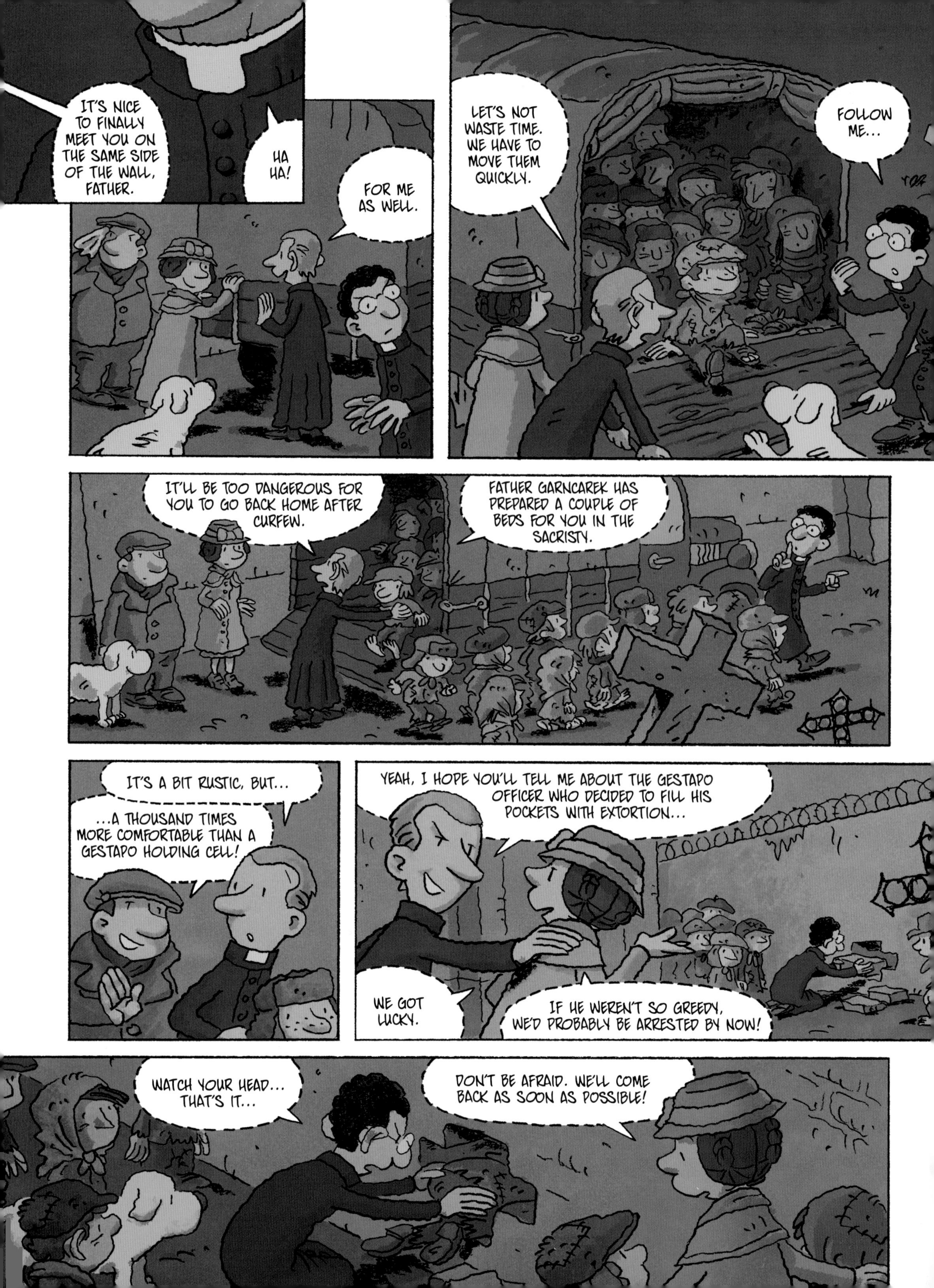
IT'S NICE TO FINALLY MEET YOU ON THE SAME SIDE OF THE WALL, FATHER.
HA HA!
FOR ME AS WELL.
LET'S NOT WASTE TIME. WE HAVE TO MOVE THEM QUICKLY.
FOLLOW ME...
IT'LL BE TOO DANGEROUS FOR YOU TO GO BACK HOME AFTER CURFEW.
FATHER GARNCAREK HAS PREPARED A COUPLE OF BEDS FOR YOU IN THE SACRISTY.
IT'S A BIT RUSTIC, BUT...
...A THOUSAND TIMES MORE COMFORTABLE THAN A GESTAPO HOLDING CELL!
YEAH, I HOPE YOU'LL TELL ME ABOUT THE GESTAPO OFFICER WHO DECIDED TO FILL HIS POCKETS WITH EXTORTION...
WE GOT LUCKY.
IF HE WEREN'T SO GREEDY, WE'D PROBABLY BE ARRESTED BY NOW!
WATCH YOUR HEAD... THAT'S IT...
DON'T BE AFRAID. WE'LL COME BACK AS SOON AS POSSIBLE!

COME ON, SON.

THIS WAY, PRINCESS.

THAT WAS THE LAST ONE.

YES, THAT'S THIRTY-TWO! THEY'RE ALL HERE.

DON'T WORRY, IRENA. THEY'LL BE HAPPY HERE.

I DON'T DOUBT IT, DOCTOR.

NOT FOR A SECOND.

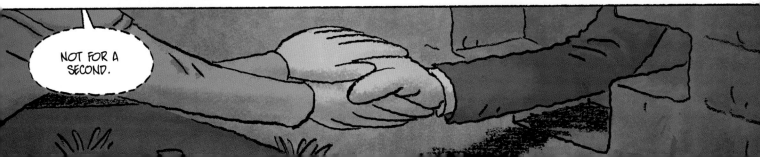

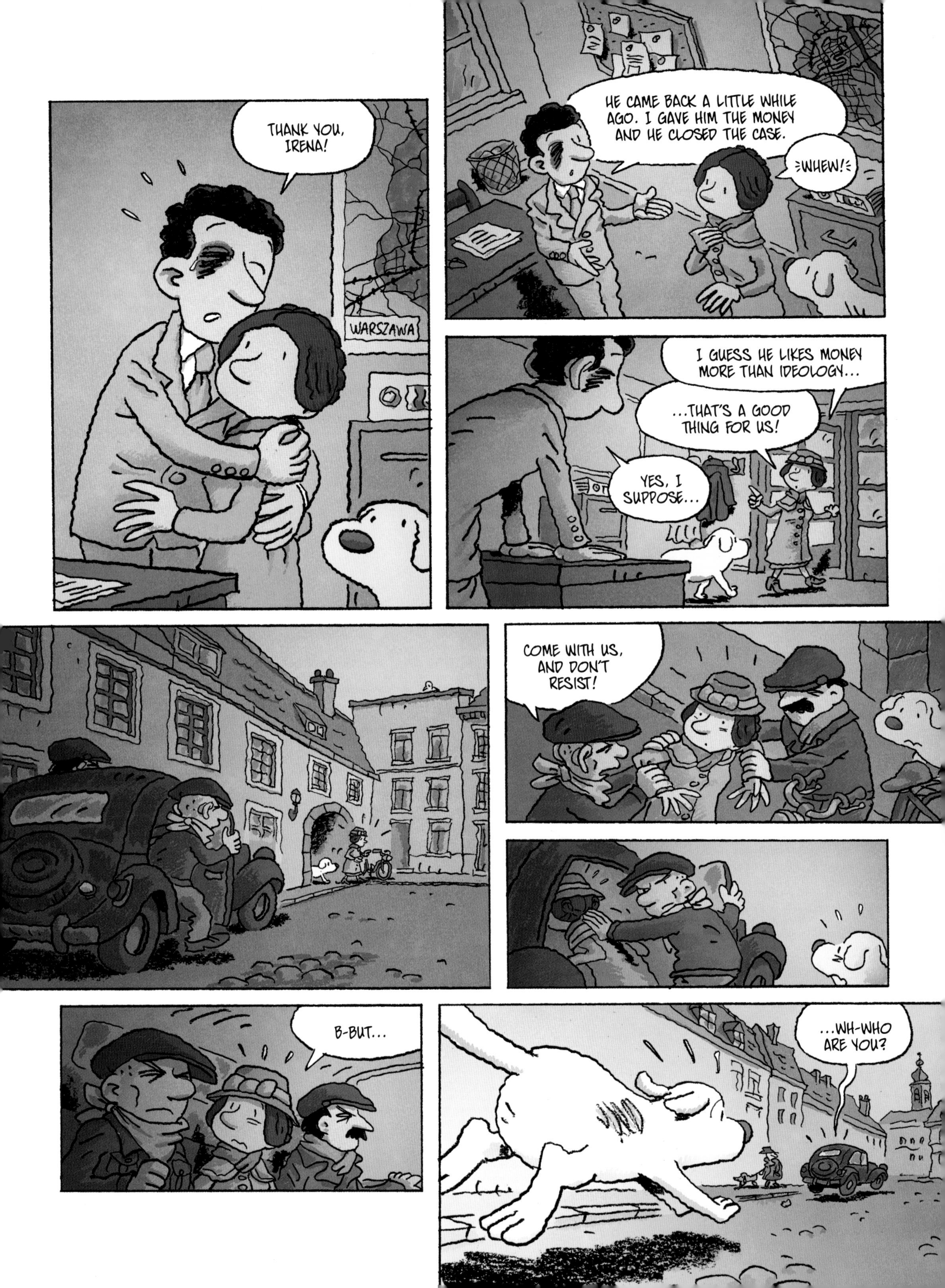

HE CAME BACK A LITTLE WHILE AGO. I GAVE HIM THE MONEY AND HE CLOSED THE CASE.
WHEW!
THANK YOU, IRENA!
WARSZAWA
I GUESS HE LIKES MONEY MORE THAN IDEOLOGY...
...THAT'S A GOOD THING FOR US!
YES, I SUPPOSE...
COME WITH US, AND DON'T RESIST!
B-BUT...
...WH-WHO ARE YOU?

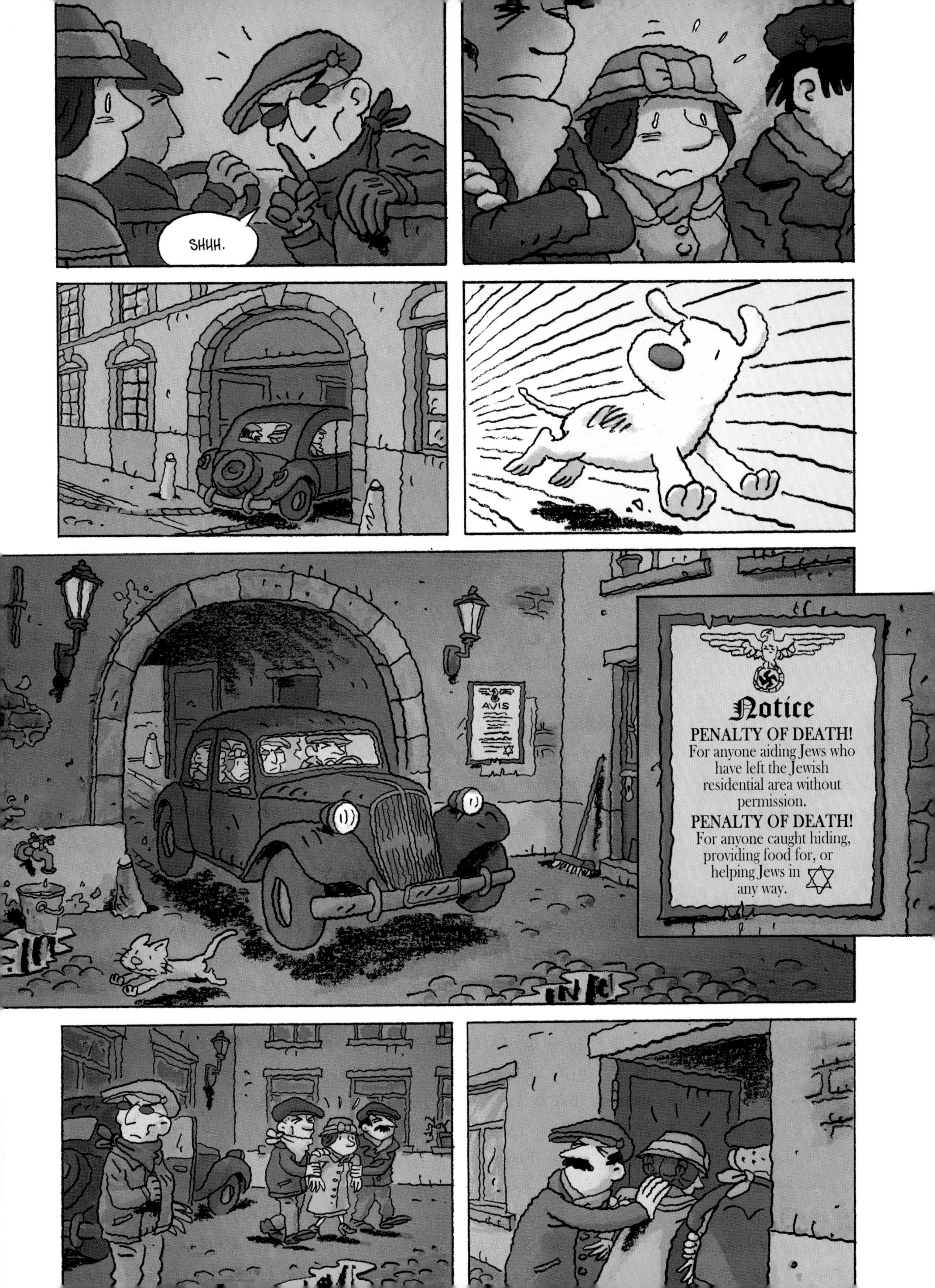
SHHH.
AVIS
Notice
PENALTY OF DEATH!
For anyone aiding Jews who have left the Jewish residential area without permission.
PENALTY OF DEATH!
For anyone caught hiding, providing food for, or helping Jews in any way.

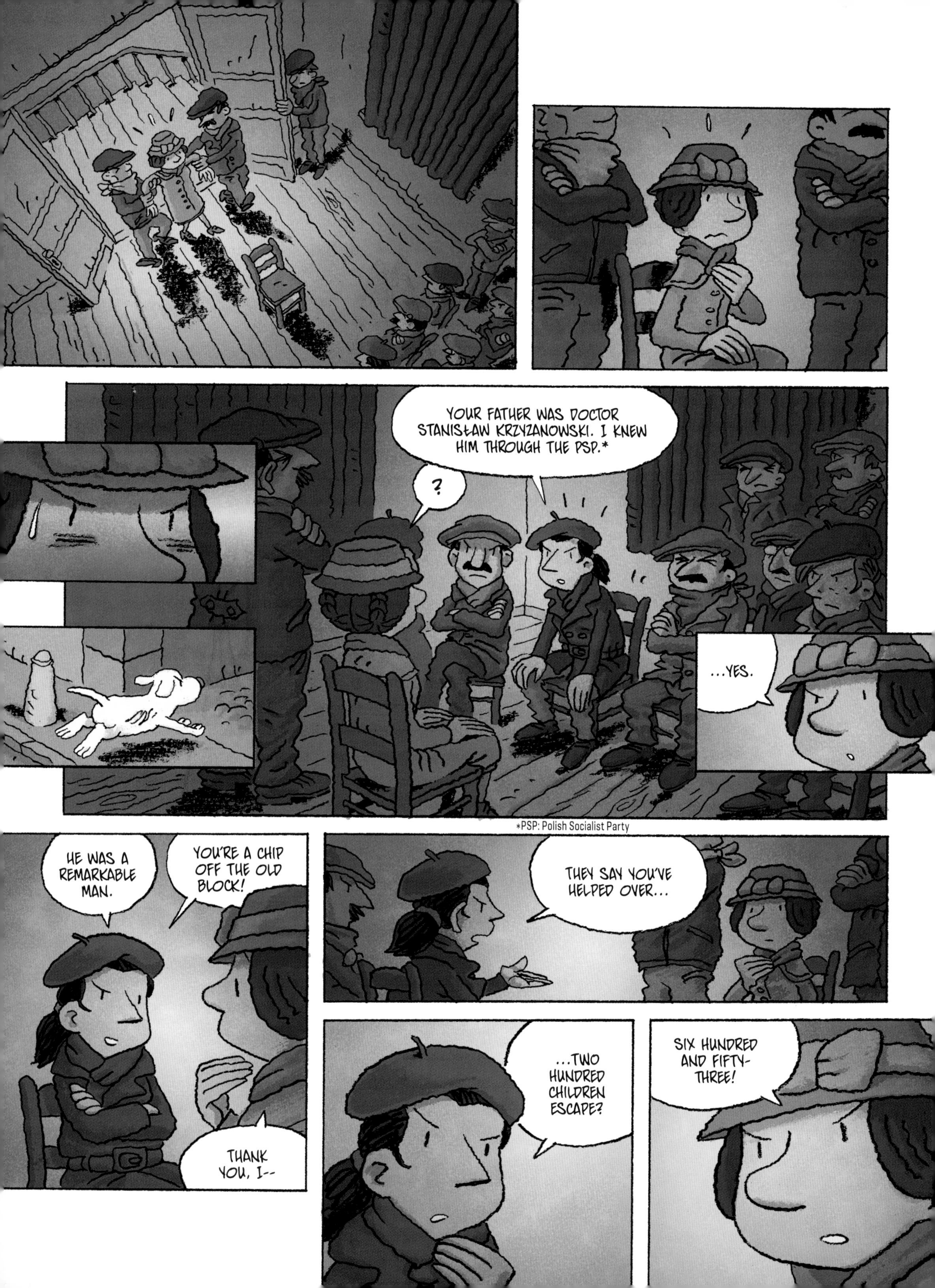
YOUR FATHER WAS DOCTOR STANISŁAW KRZYZANOWSKI. I KNEW HIM THROUGH THE PSP.*
?
...YES.
*PSP: Polish Socialist Party
HE WAS A REMARKABLE MAN.
YOU'RE A CHIP OFF THE OLD BLOCK!
THANK YOU, I--
THEY SAY YOU'VE HELPED OVER...
...TWO HUNDRED CHILDREN ESCAPE?
SIX HUNDRED AND FIFTY-THREE!

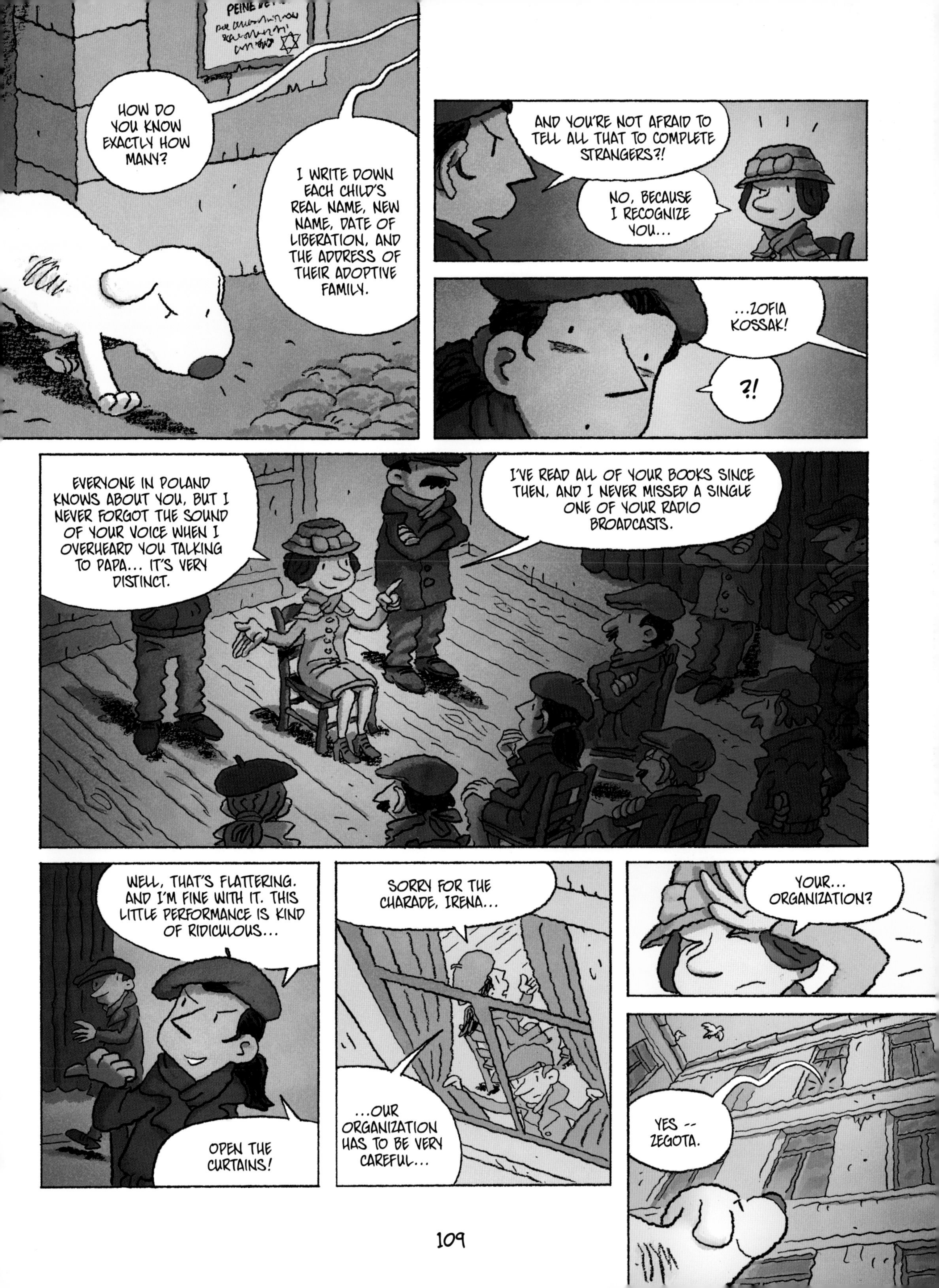

PEINE
HOW DO YOU KNOW EXACTLY HOW MANY?
I WRITE DOWN EACH CHILD'S REAL NAME, NEW NAME, DATE OF LIBERATION, AND THE ADDRESS OF THEIR ADOPTIVE FAMILY.
AND YOU'RE NOT AFRAID TO TELL ALL THAT TO COMPLETE STRANGERS?!
NO, BECAUSE I RECOGNIZE YOU...
...ZOFIA KOSSAK!
?!
EVERYONE IN POLAND KNOWS ABOUT YOU, BUT I NEVER FORGOT THE SOUND OF YOUR VOICE WHEN I OVERHEARD YOU TALKING TO PAPA... IT'S VERY DISTINCT.
I'VE READ ALL OF YOUR BOOKS SINCE THEN, AND I NEVER MISSED A SINGLE ONE OF YOUR RADIO BROADCASTS.
WELL, THAT'S FLATTERING. AND I'M FINE WITH IT. THIS LITTLE PERFORMANCE IS KIND OF RIDICULOUS...
OPEN THE CURTAINS!
SORRY FOR THE CHARADE, IRENA...
...OUR ORGANIZATION HAS TO BE VERY CAREFUL...
YOUR... ORGANIZATION?
YES -- ZEGOTA.

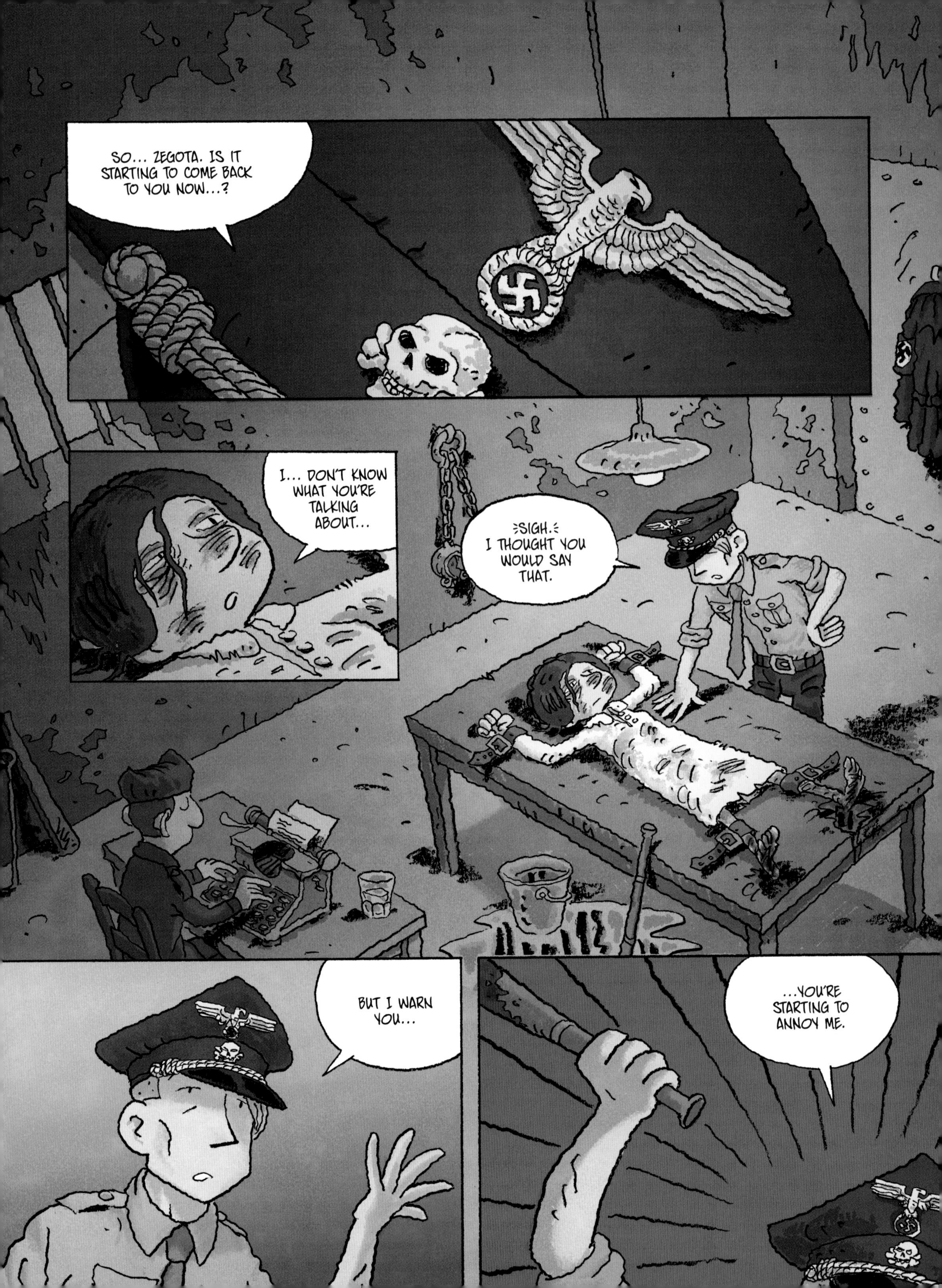
SO... ZEGOTA. IS IT STARTING TO COME BACK TO YOU NOW...?
I... DON'T KNOW WHAT YOU'RE TALKING ABOUT...
SIGH. I THOUGHT YOU WOULD SAY THAT.
BUT I WARN YOU...
...YOU'RE STARTING TO ANNOY ME.

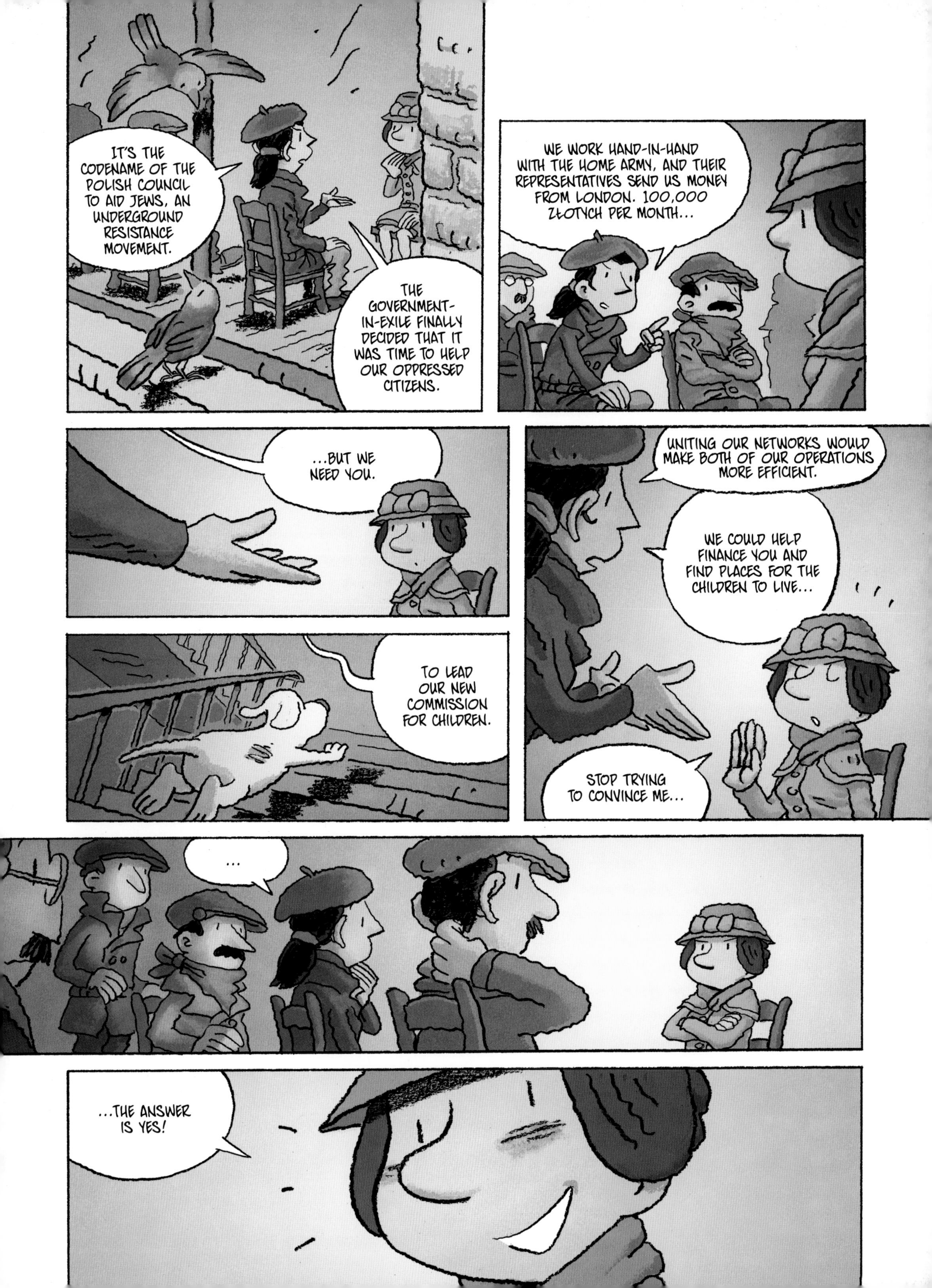
IT'S THE CODENAME OF THE POLISH COUNCIL TO AID JEWS, AN UNDERGROUND RESISTANCE MOVEMENT.
THE GOVERNMENT-IN-EXILE FINALLY DECIDED THAT IT WAS TIME TO HELP OUR OPPRESSED CITIZENS.
WE WORK HAND-IN-HAND WITH THE HOME ARMY, AND THEIR REPRESENTATIVES SEND US MONEY FROM LONDON. 100,000 ZŁOTYCH PER MONTH...
...BUT WE NEED YOU.
TO LEAD OUR NEW COMMISSION FOR CHILDREN.
UNITING OUR NETWORKS WOULD MAKE BOTH OF OUR OPERATIONS MORE EFFICIENT.
WE COULD HELP FINANCE YOU AND FIND PLACES FOR THE CHILDREN TO LIVE...
STOP TRYING TO CONVINCE ME...
...
...THE ANSWER IS YES!

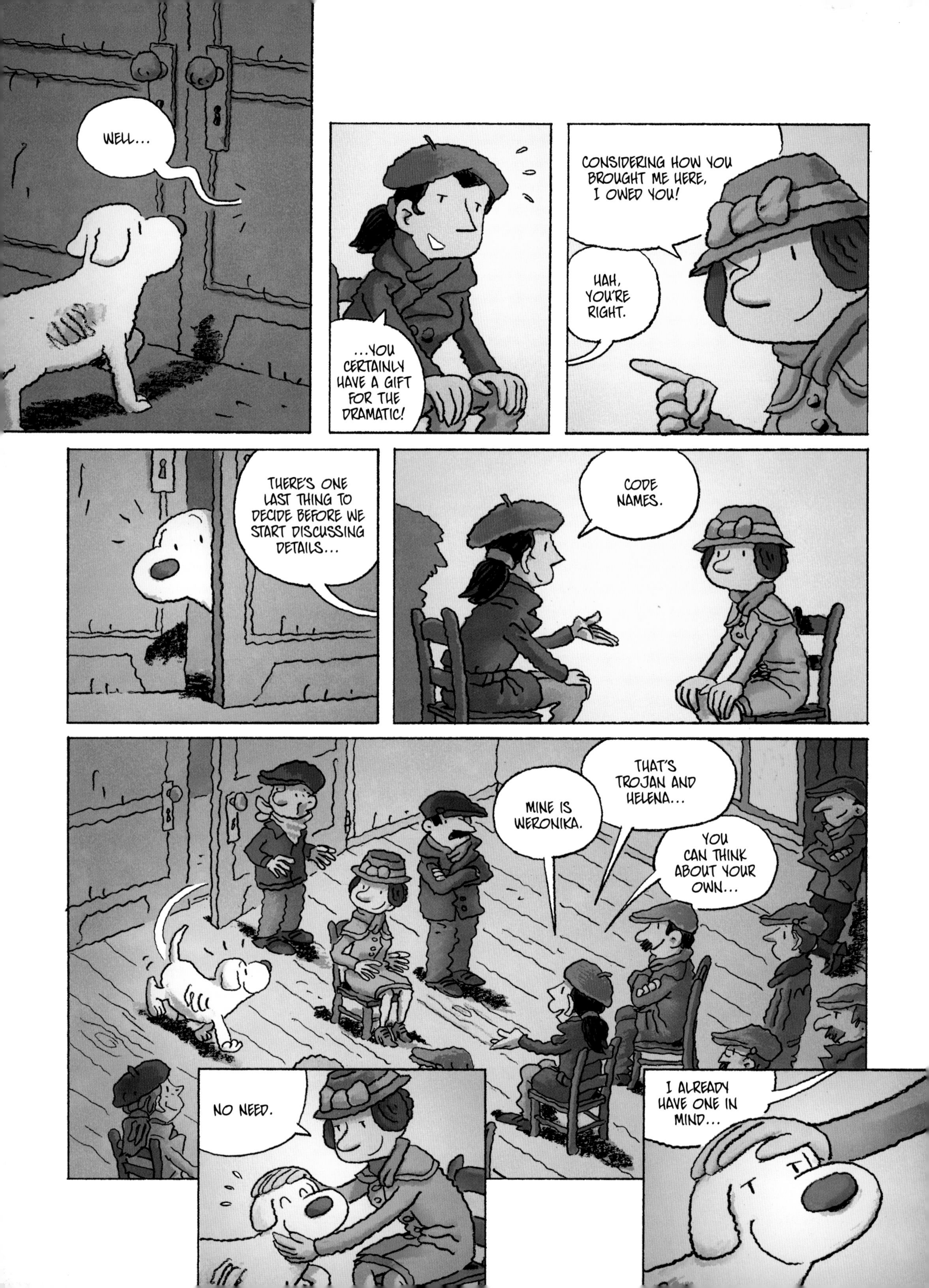
WELL...
...YOU CERTAINLY HAVE A GIFT FOR THE DRAMATIC!
CONSIDERING HOW YOU BROUGHT ME HERE, I OWED YOU!
HAH, YOU'RE RIGHT.
THERE'S ONE LAST THING TO DECIDE BEFORE WE START DISCUSSING DETAILS...
CODE NAMES.
MINE IS WERONIKA.
THAT'S TROJAN AND HELENA...
YOU CAN THINK ABOUT YOUR OWN...
NO NEED.
I ALREADY HAVE ONE IN MIND...

JOLANTA?

THAT DOESN'T RING A BELL EITHER?

NEVER MET HER.

AND YET, I'VE OBTAINED A NUMBER OF REPORTS ABOUT A TERRORIST WHO HAS HELPED JEWS ESCAPE FROM THE GHETTO... ONE WHO BEARS A CURIOUS RESEMBLANCE TO YOU...

EVERYONE HAS A LOOK-ALIKE SOMEWHERE...

ARGH... ENOUGH OF THIS!

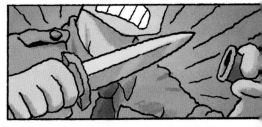

YOU HAVE ONE MINUTE TO REACH THE DOOR OR I'LL BLOW YOUR BRAINS OUT!

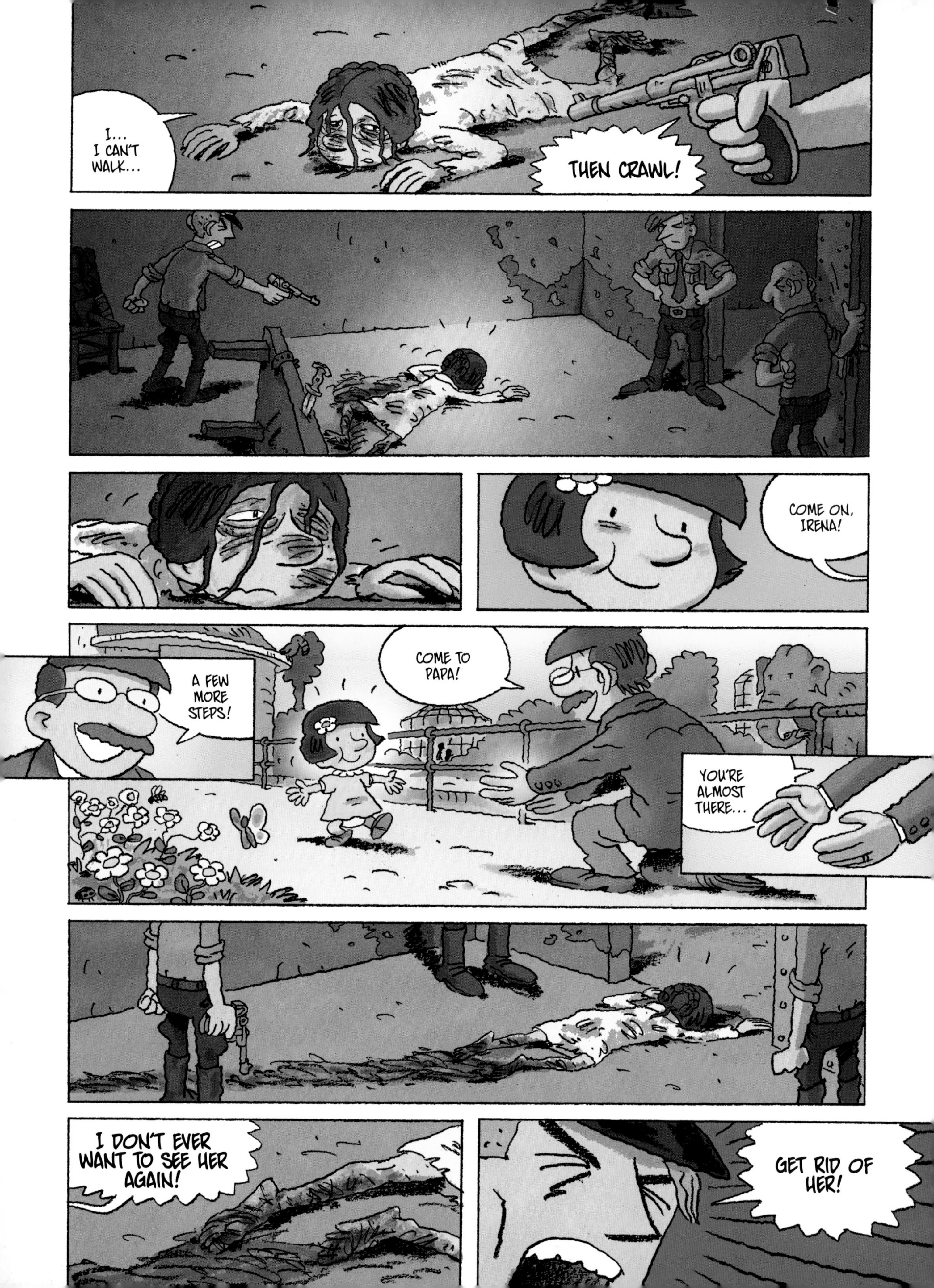
I...
I CAN'T
WALK...
THEN CRAWL!
COME ON,
IRENA!
A FEW
MORE
STEPS!
COME TO
PAPA!
YOU'RE
ALMOST
THERE...
I DON'T EVER
WANT TO SEE HER
AGAIN!
GET RID OF
HER!

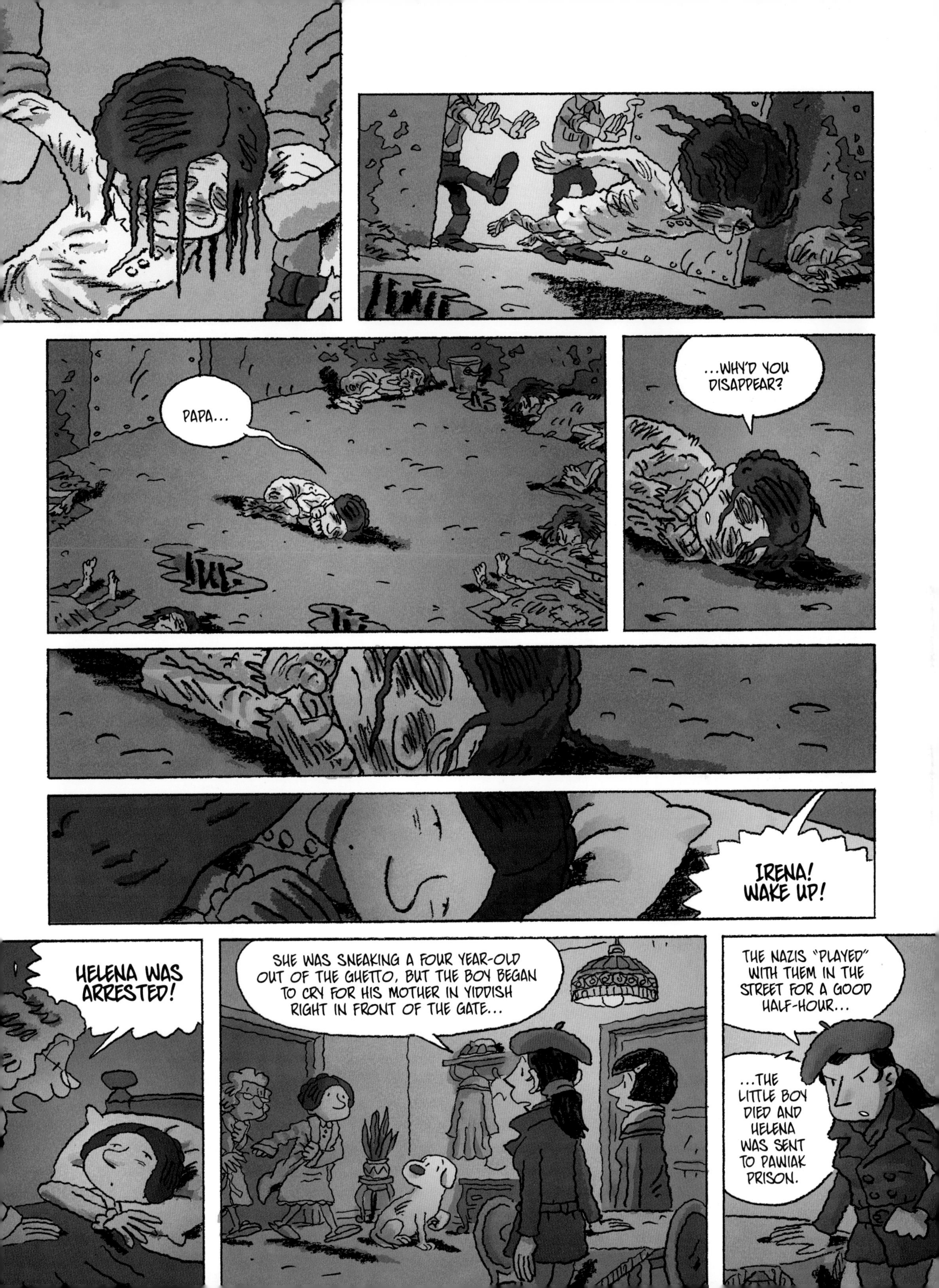
PAPA...
...WHY'D YOU DISAPPEAR?
IRENA! WAKE UP!
HELENA WAS ARRESTED!
SHE WAS SNEAKING A FOUR YEAR-OLD OUT OF THE GHETTO, BUT THE BOY BEGAN TO CRY FOR HIS MOTHER IN YIDDISH RIGHT IN FRONT OF THE GATE...
THE NAZIS "PLAYED" WITH THEM IN THE STREET FOR A GOOD HALF-HOUR...
...THE LITTLE BOY DIED AND HELENA WAS SENT TO PAWIAK PRISON.

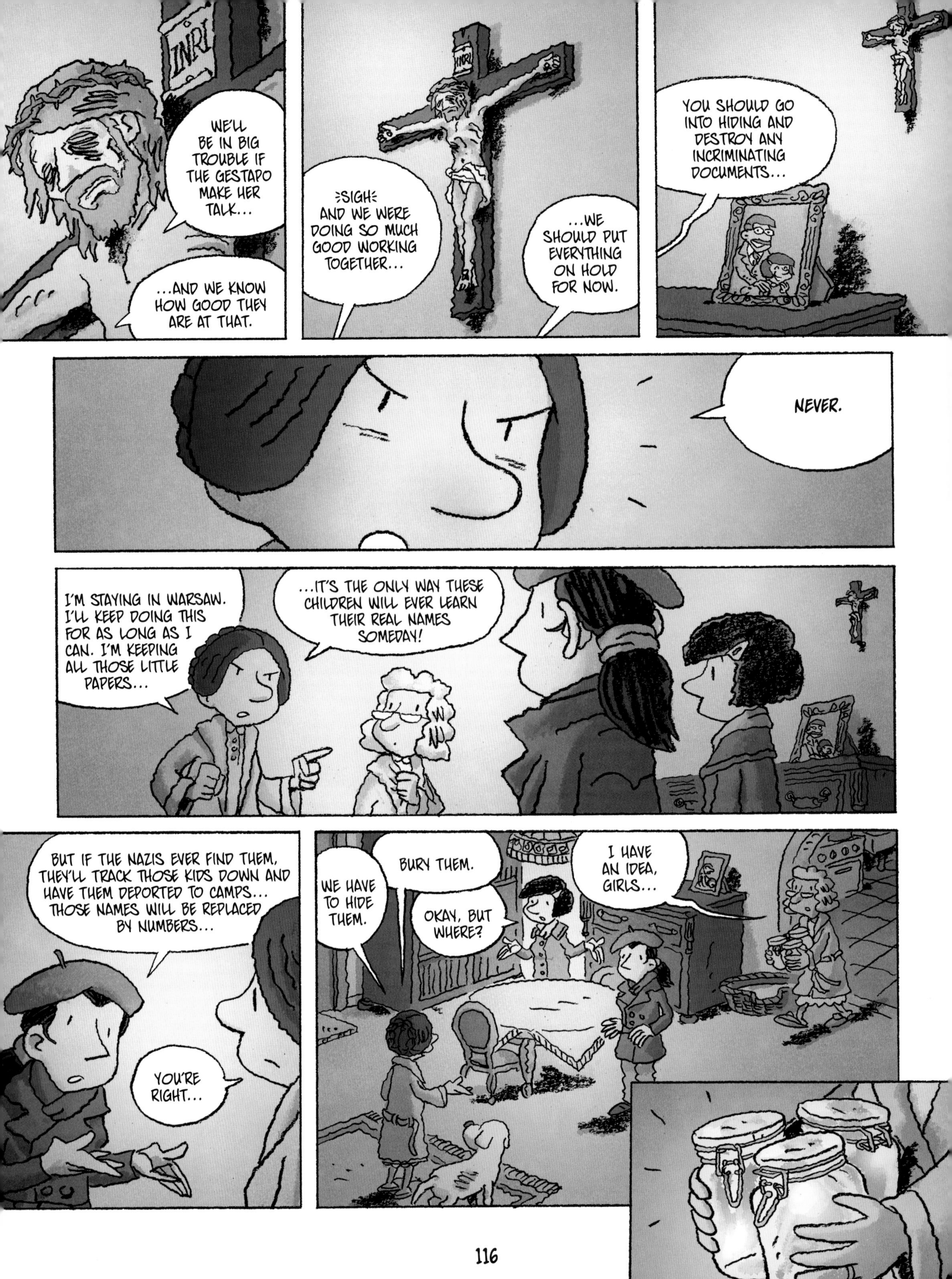
WE'LL BE IN BIG TROUBLE IF THE GESTAPO MAKE HER TALK...
...AND WE KNOW HOW GOOD THEY ARE AT THAT.
SIGH AND WE WERE DOING SO MUCH GOOD WORKING TOGETHER...
...WE SHOULD PUT EVERYTHING ON HOLD FOR NOW.
YOU SHOULD GO INTO HIDING AND DESTROY ANY INCRIMINATING DOCUMENTS...
NEVER.
I'M STAYING IN WARSAW. I'LL KEEP DOING THIS FOR AS LONG AS I CAN. I'M KEEPING ALL THOSE LITTLE PAPERS...
...IT'S THE ONLY WAY THESE CHILDREN WILL EVER LEARN THEIR REAL NAMES SOMEDAY!
BUT IF THE NAZIS EVER FIND THEM, THEY'LL TRACK THOSE KIDS DOWN AND HAVE THEM DEPORTED TO CAMPS... THOSE NAMES WILL BE REPLACED BY NUMBERS...
YOU'RE RIGHT...
WE HAVE TO HIDE THEM.
BURY THEM.
OKAY, BUT WHERE?
I HAVE AN IDEA, GIRLS...

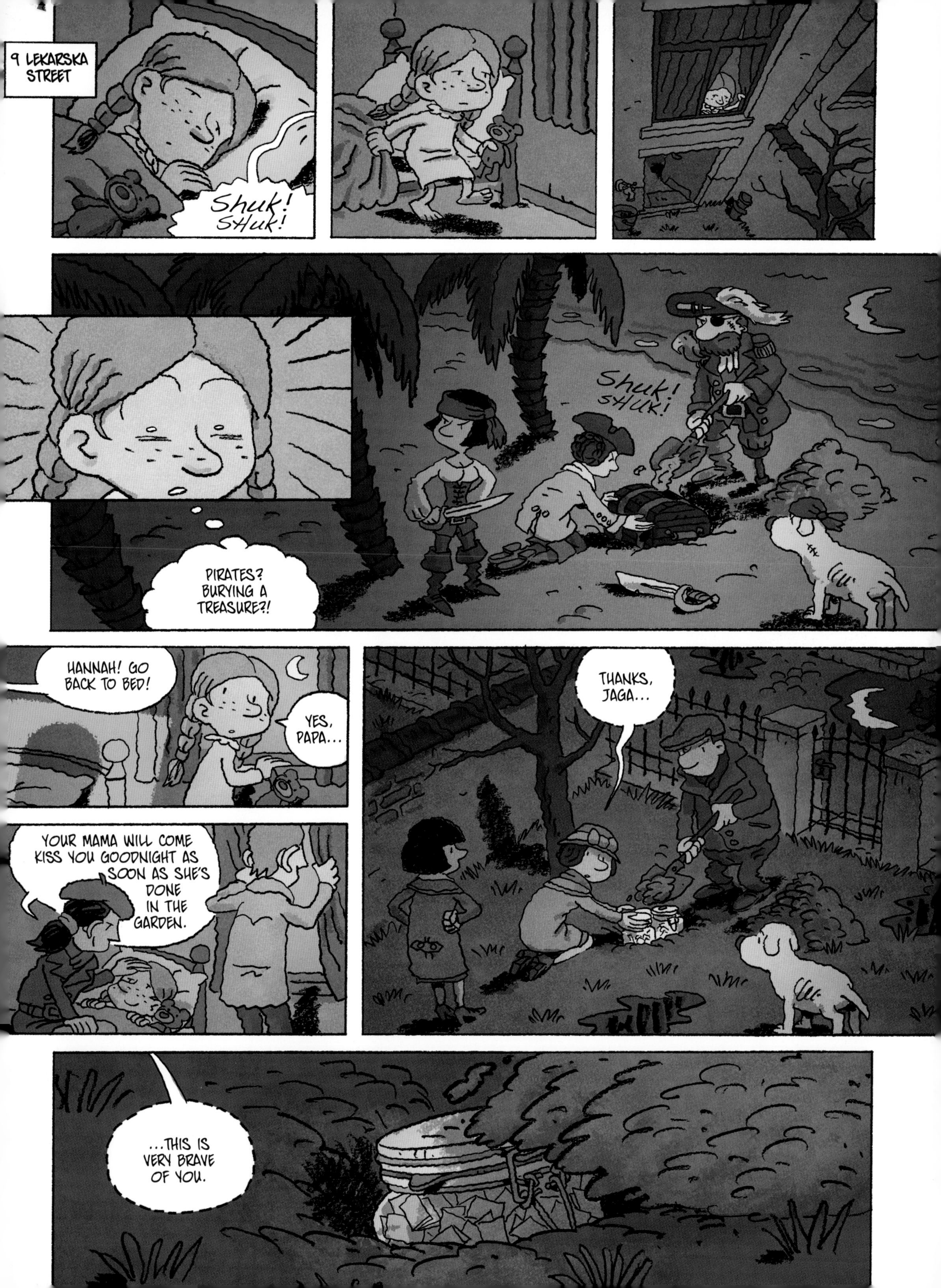
9 LEKARSKA STREET
Shuk! SHUK!
Shuk! SHUK!
PIRATES? BURYING A TREASURE?!
HANNAH! GO BACK TO BED!
YES, PAPA...
YOUR MAMA WILL COME KISS YOU GOODNIGHT AS SOON AS SHE'S DONE IN THE GARDEN.
THANKS, JAGA...
...THIS IS VERY BRAVE OF YOU.

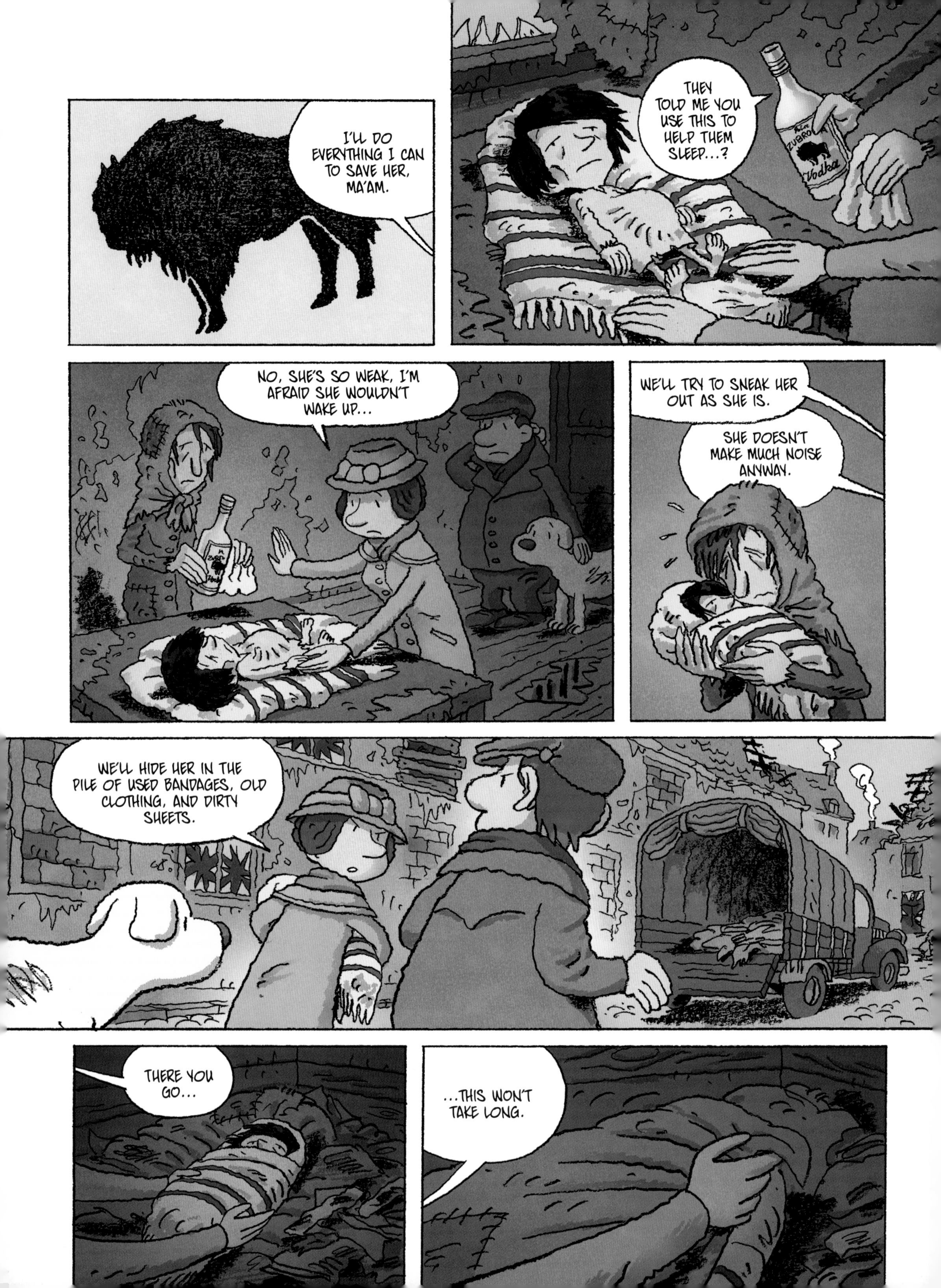
I'LL DO EVERYTHING I CAN TO SAVE HER, MA'AM.
THEY TOLD ME YOU USE THIS TO HELP THEM SLEEP...?
ZUBROWKA
Vodka
NO, SHE'S SO WEAK, I'M AFRAID SHE WOULDN'T WAKE UP...
WE'LL TRY TO SNEAK HER OUT AS SHE IS.
SHE DOESN'T MAKE MUCH NOISE ANYWAY.
WE'LL HIDE HER IN THE PILE OF USED BANDAGES, OLD CLOTHING, AND DIRTY SHEETS.
THERE YOU GO...
...THIS WON'T TAKE LONG.

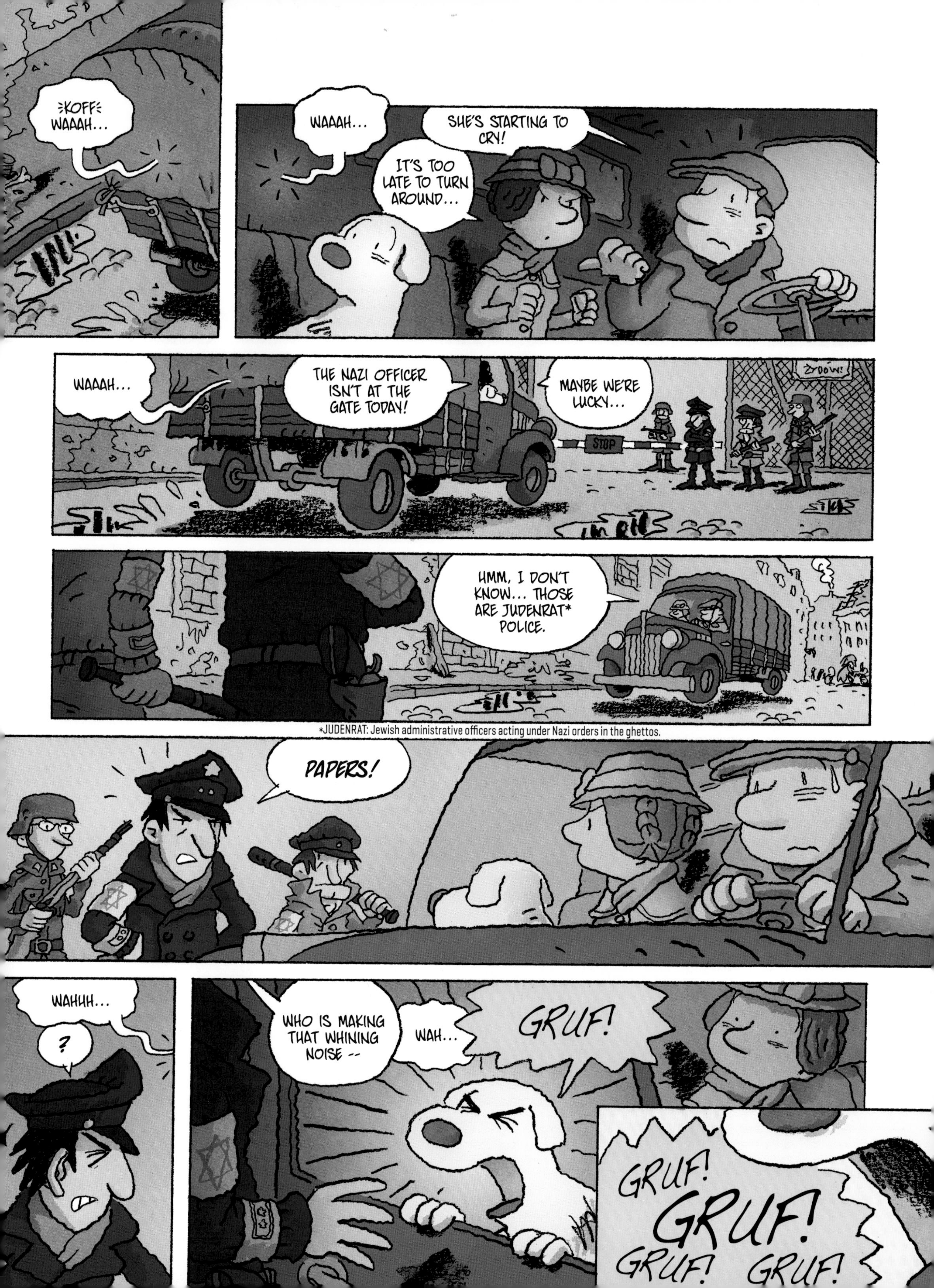
≈KOFF≈
WAAAH...
WAAAH...
SHE'S STARTING TO CRY!
IT'S TOO LATE TO TURN AROUND...
WAAAH...
THE NAZI OFFICER ISN'T AT THE GATE TODAY!
MAYBE WE'RE LUCKY...
STOP
HMM, I DON'T KNOW... THOSE ARE JUDENRAT* POLICE.
PAPERS!
WAHHH...
?
WHO IS MAKING THAT WHINING NOISE --
WAH...
GRUF!
GRUF!
GRUF!
GRUF! GRUF!

*JUDENRAT: Jewish administrative officers acting under Nazi orders in the ghettos.

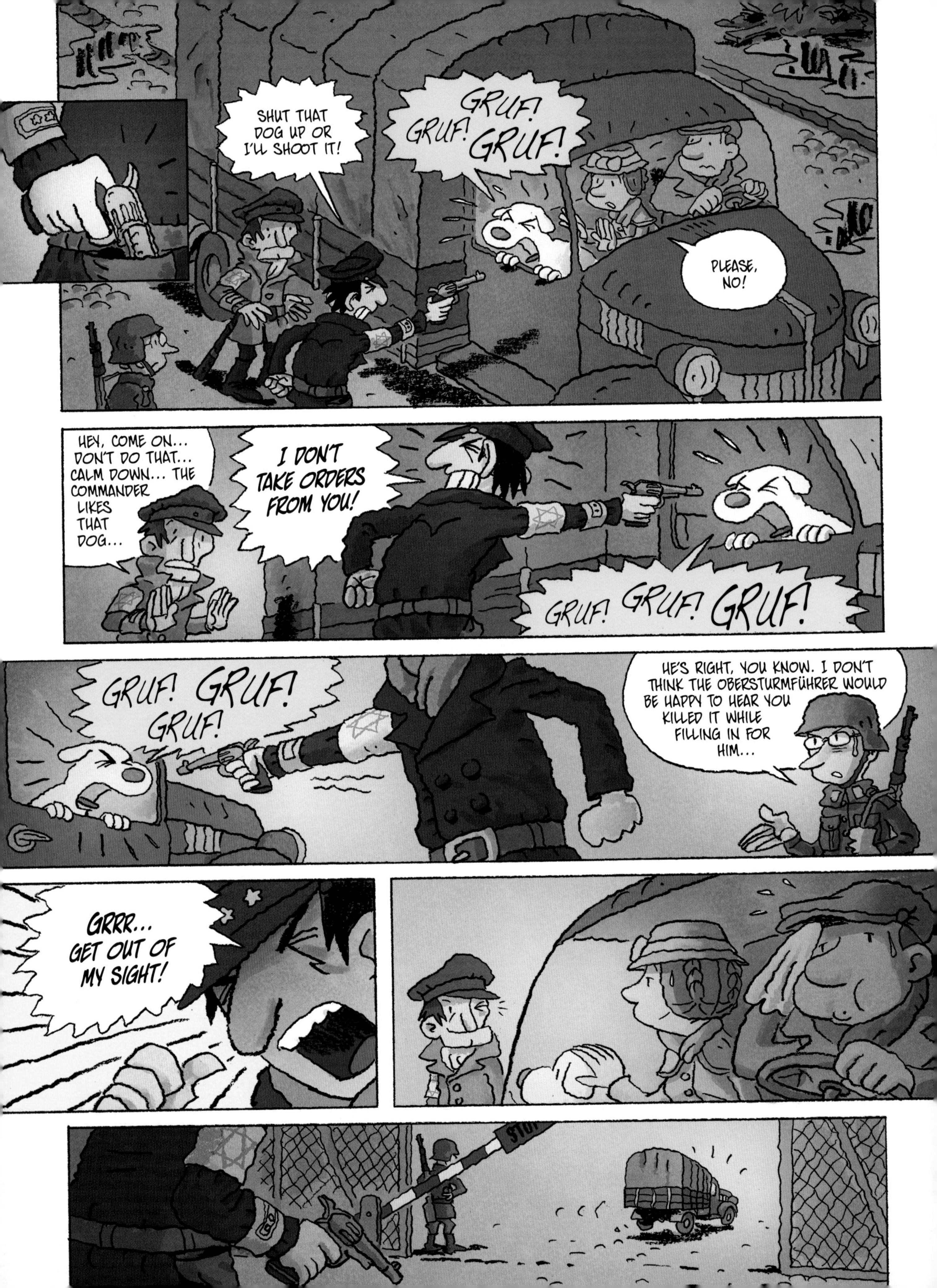
SHUT THAT DOG UP OR I'LL SHOOT IT!
GRUF! GRUF! GRUF!
PLEASE, NO!
HEY, COME ON... DON'T DO THAT... CALM DOWN... THE COMMANDER LIKES THAT DOG...
I DON'T TAKE ORDERS FROM YOU!
GRUF! GRUF! GRUF!
GRUF! GRUF! GRUF!
HE'S RIGHT, YOU KNOW. I DON'T THINK THE OBERSTURMFÜHRER WOULD BE HAPPY TO HEAR YOU KILLED IT WHILE FILLING IN FOR HIM...
GRRR... GET OUT OF MY SIGHT!
STOP

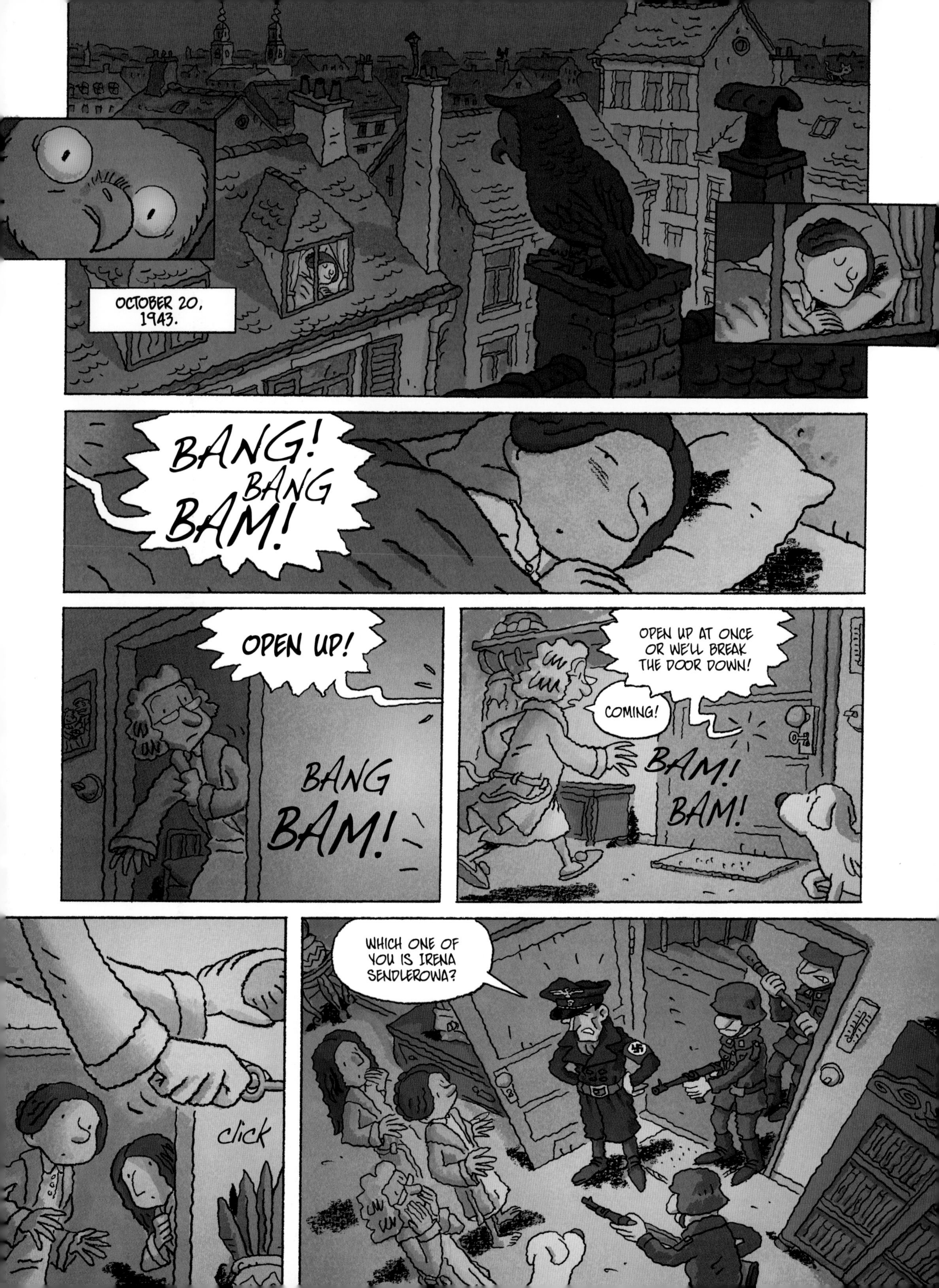

OCTOBER 20, 1943.
BANG! BANG BAM!
OPEN UP!
BANG BAM!
OPEN UP AT ONCE OR WE'LL BREAK THE DOOR DOWN!
COMING!
BAM! BAM!
click
WHICH ONE OF YOU IS IRENA SENDLEROWA?

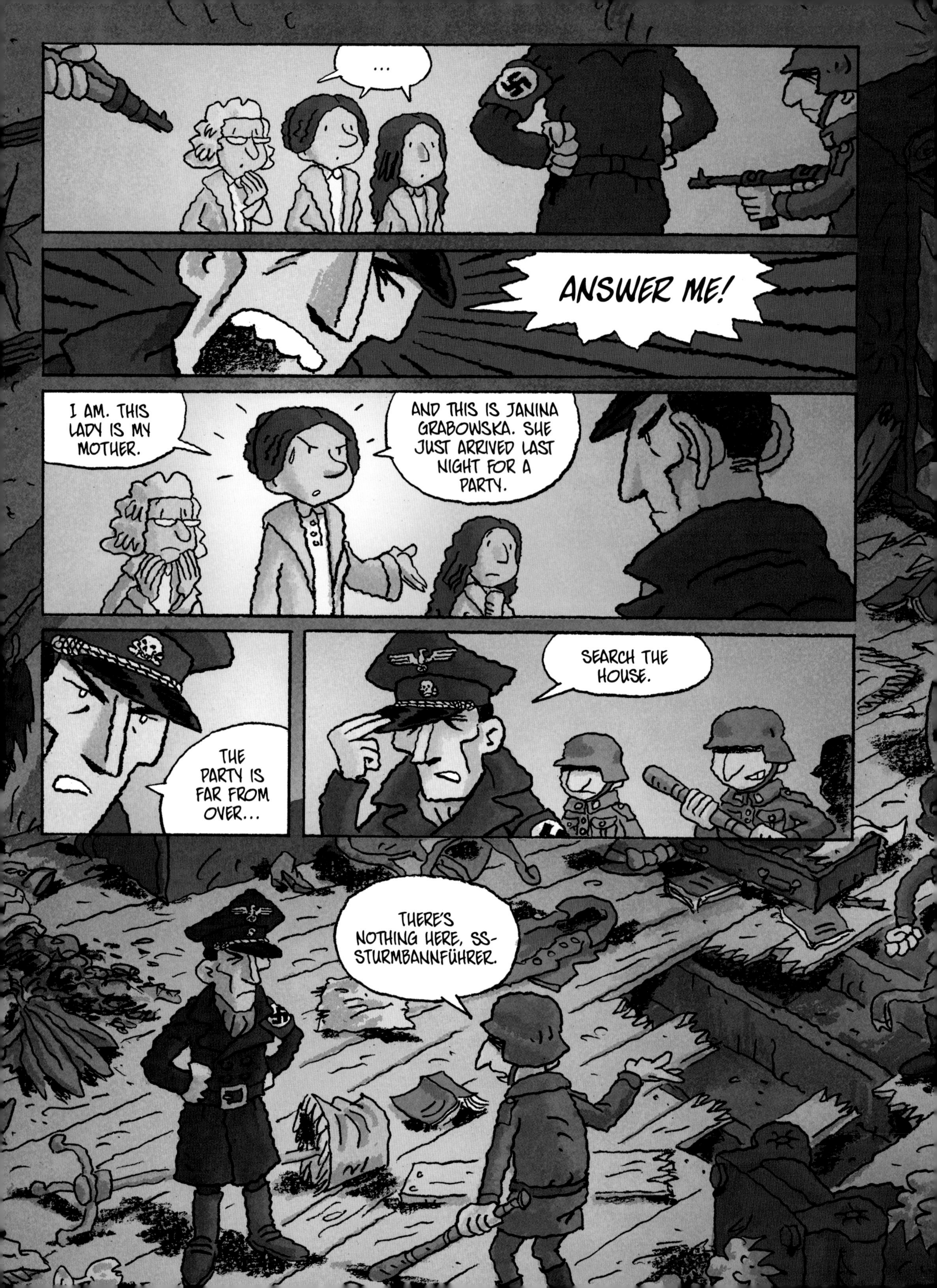
...
ANSWER ME!
I AM. THIS LADY IS MY MOTHER.
AND THIS IS JANINA GRABOWSKA. SHE JUST ARRIVED LAST NIGHT FOR A PARTY.
THE PARTY IS FAR FROM OVER...
SEARCH THE HOUSE.
THERE'S NOTHING HERE, SS-STURMBANNFÜHRER.

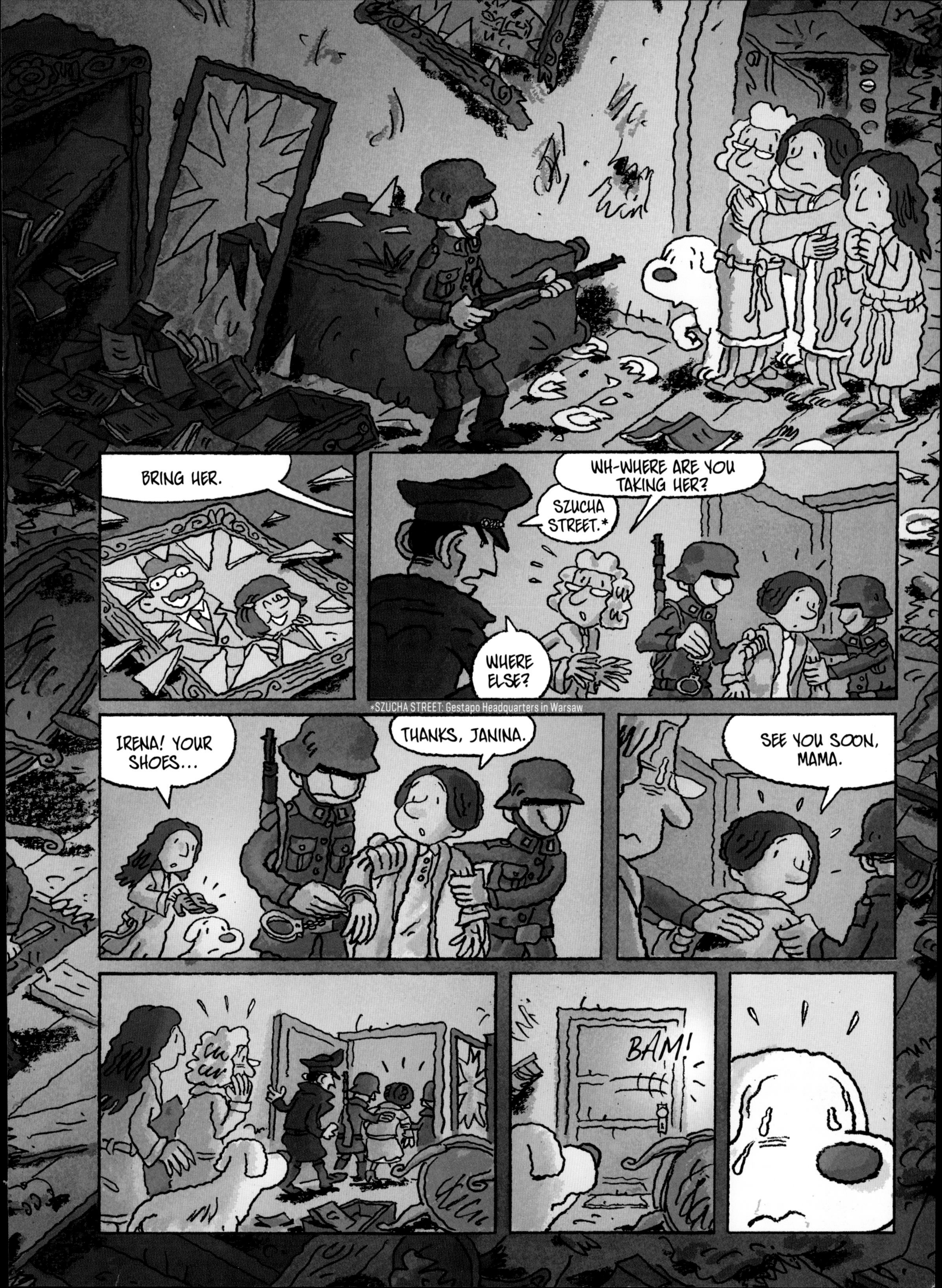
BRING HER.
WH-WHERE ARE YOU TAKING HER?
SZUCHA STREET.*
WHERE ELSE?
*SZUCHA STREET: Gestapo Headquarters in Warsaw
IRENA! YOUR SHOES...
THANKS, JANINA.
SEE YOU SOON, MAMA.
BAM!

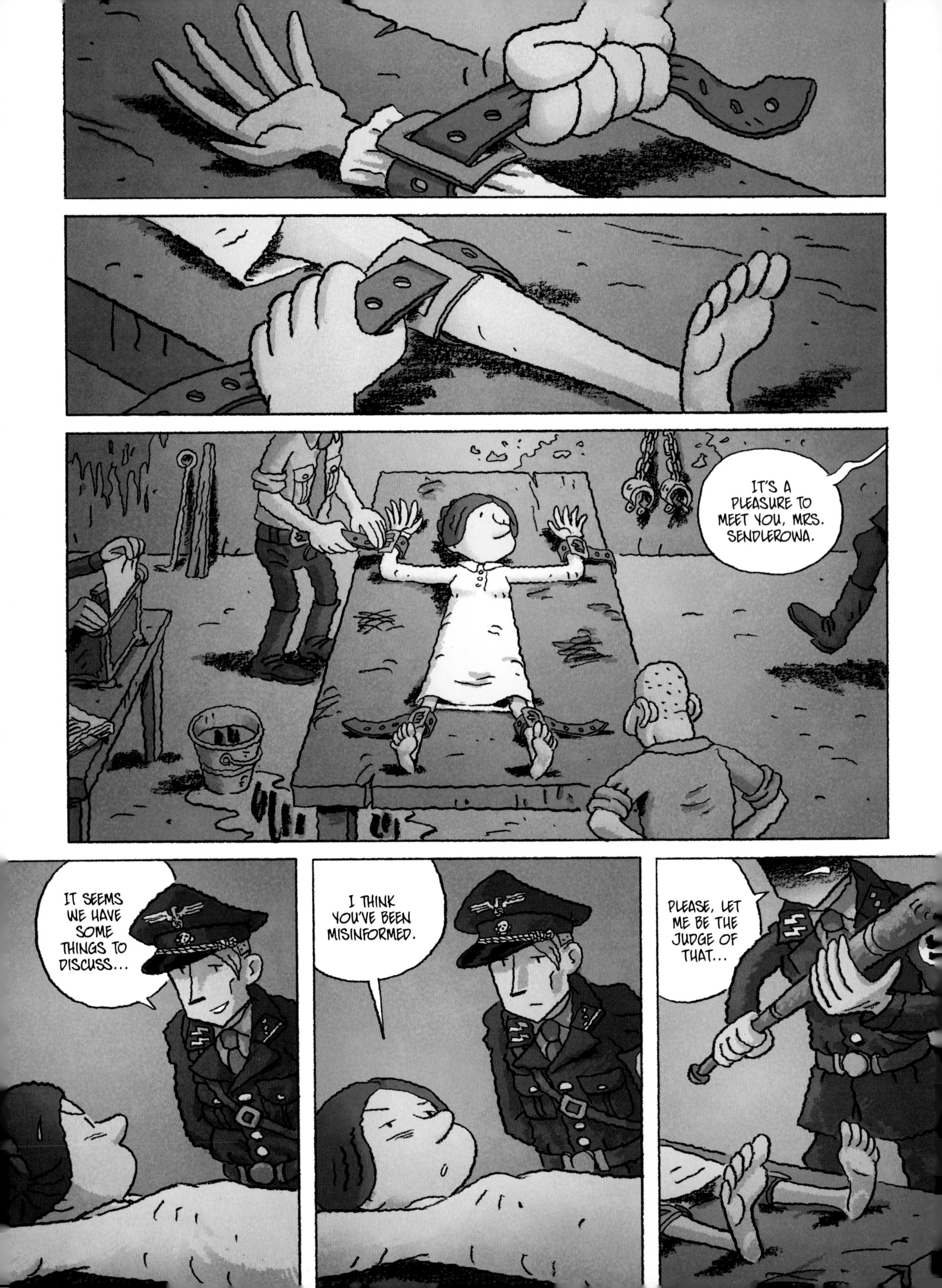
IT'S A PLEASURE TO MEET YOU, MRS. SENDLEROWA.
IT SEEMS WE HAVE SOME THINGS TO DISCUSS...
I THINK YOU'VE BEEN MISINFORMED.
PLEASE, LET ME BE THE JUDGE OF THAT...

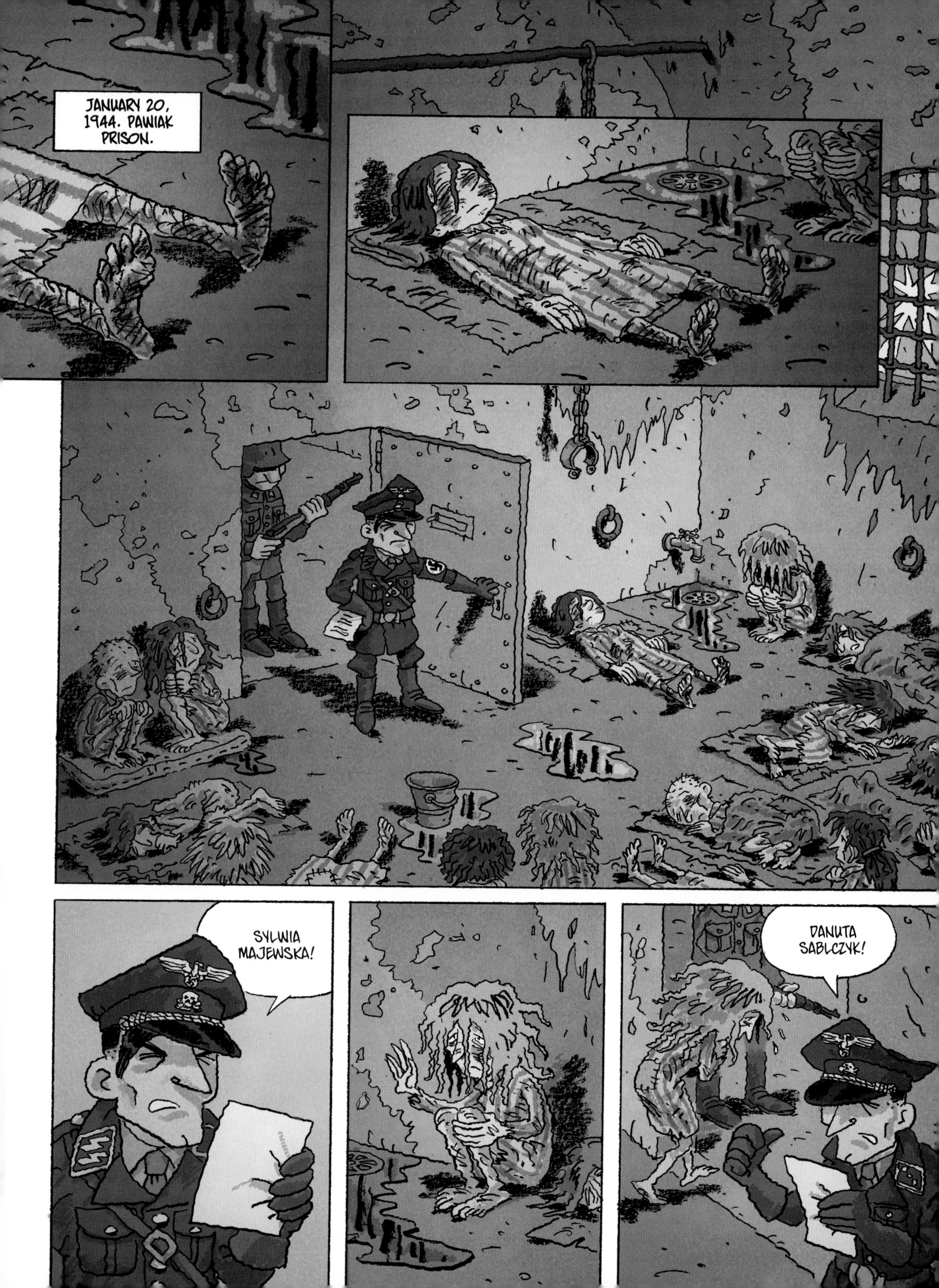
JANUARY 20, 1944. PAWIAK PRISON.
SYLWIA MAJEWSKA!
DANUTA SABLCZYK!

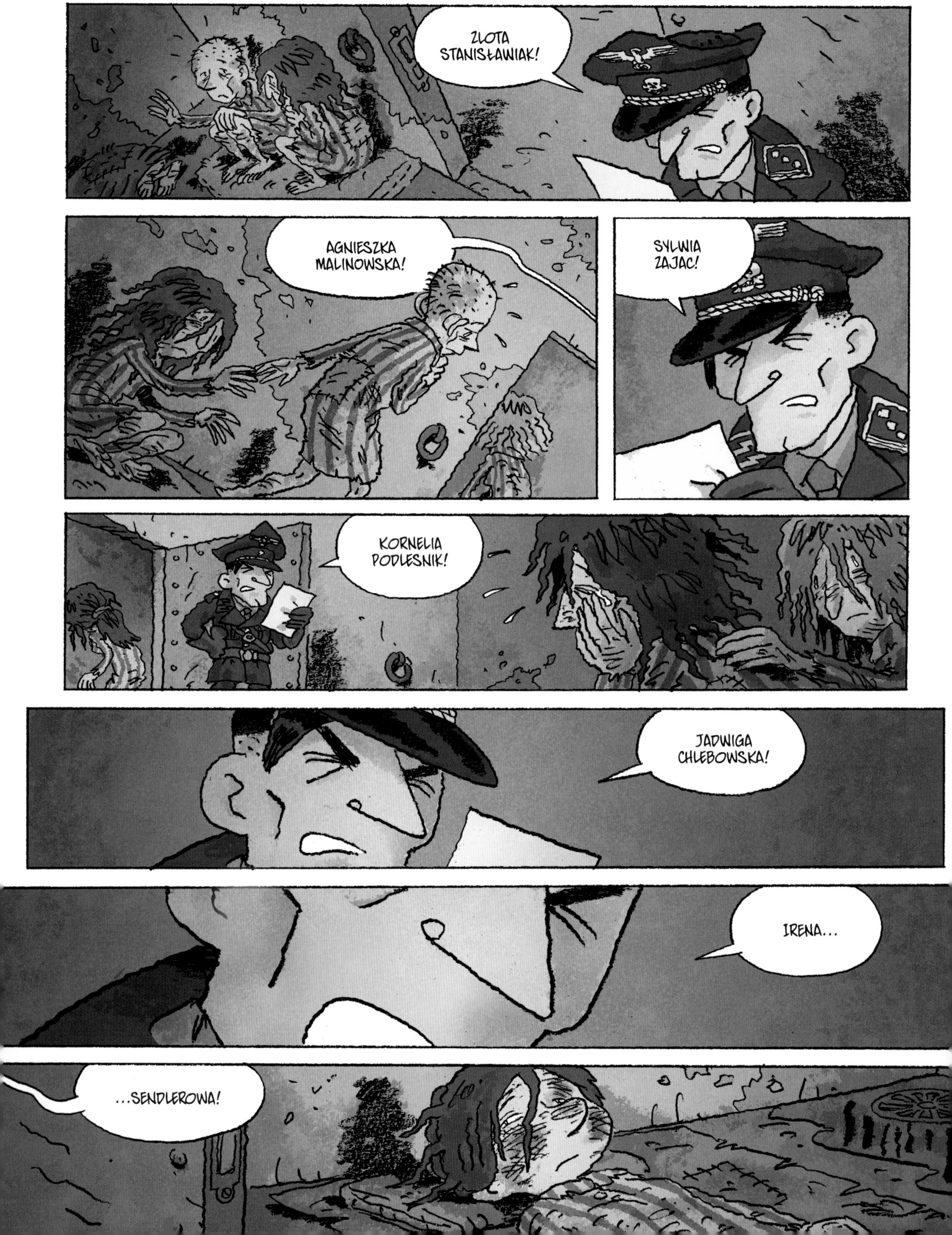
ZLOTA STANISŁAWIAK!
AGNIESZKA MALINOWSKA!
SYLWIA ZAJAC!
KORNELIA PODLESNIK!
JADWIGA CHLEBOWSKA!
IRENA...
...SENDLEROWA!

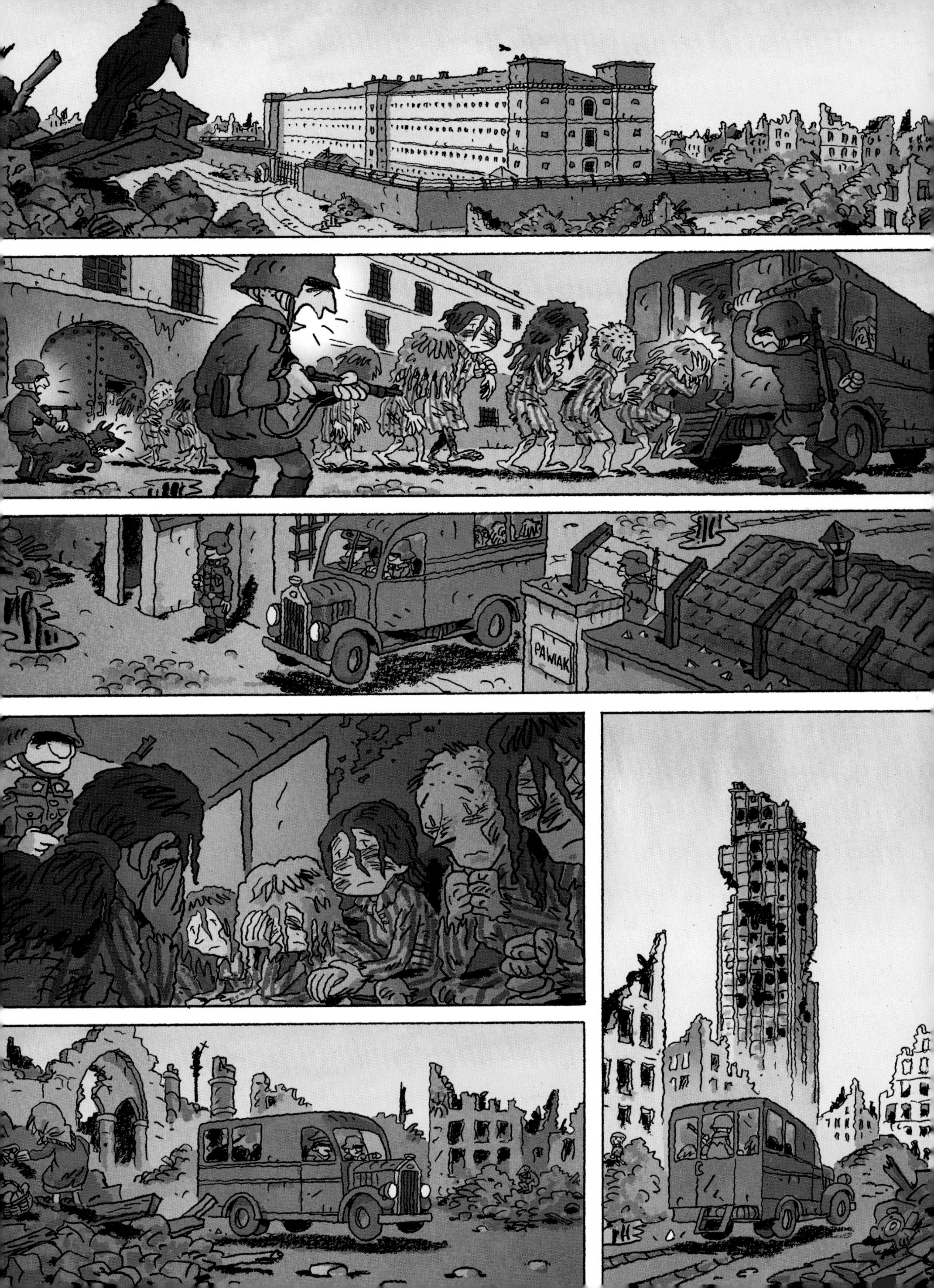
PAWIAK

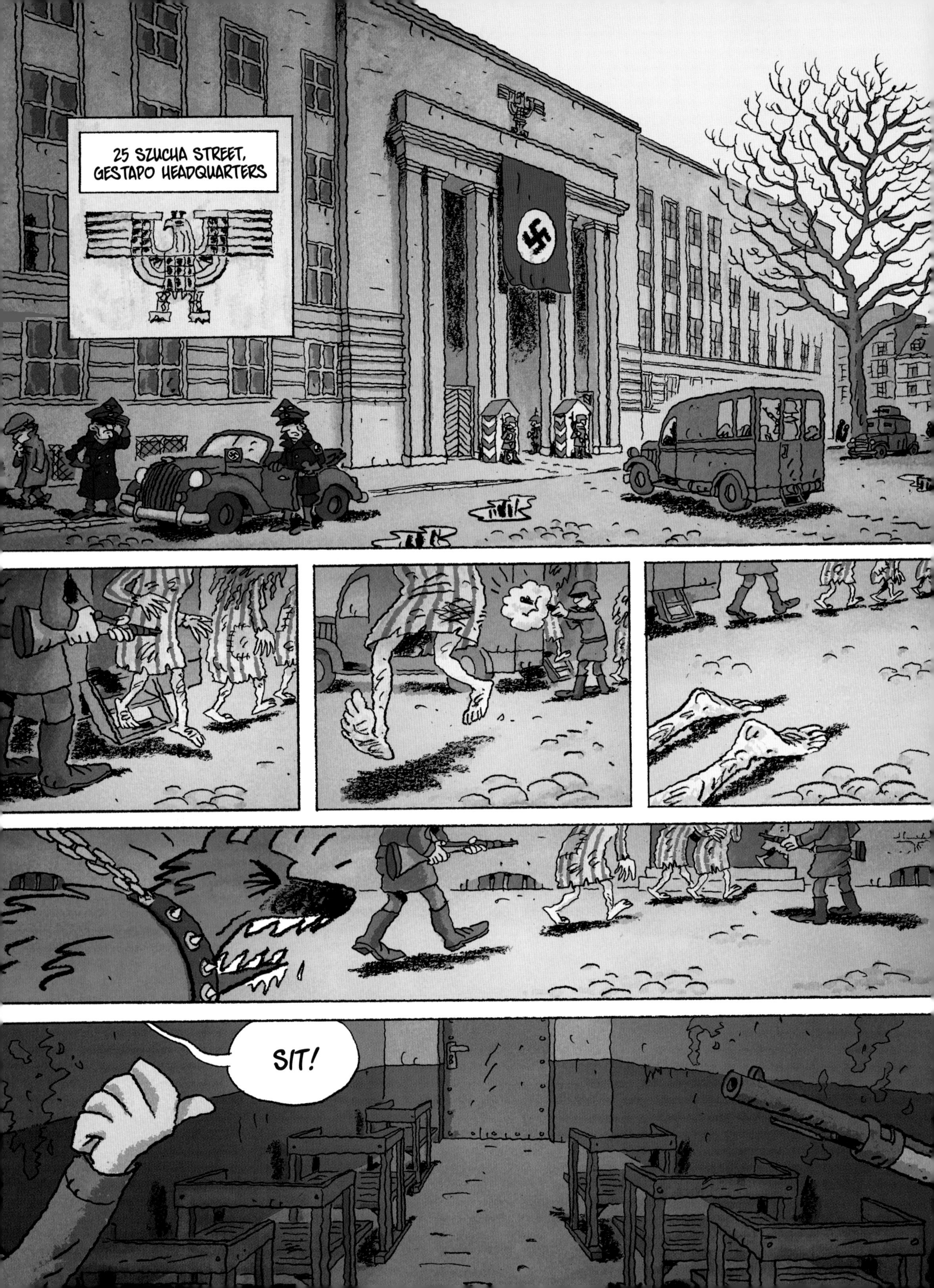
25 SZUCHA STREET, GESTAPO HEADQUARTERS
SIT!

YOU!
BANG!
MOVE UP ONE SEAT AS THIS ONE BECOMES EMPTY.
I'M NOT GOING TO COME FETCH YOU...
BANG!
BANG!

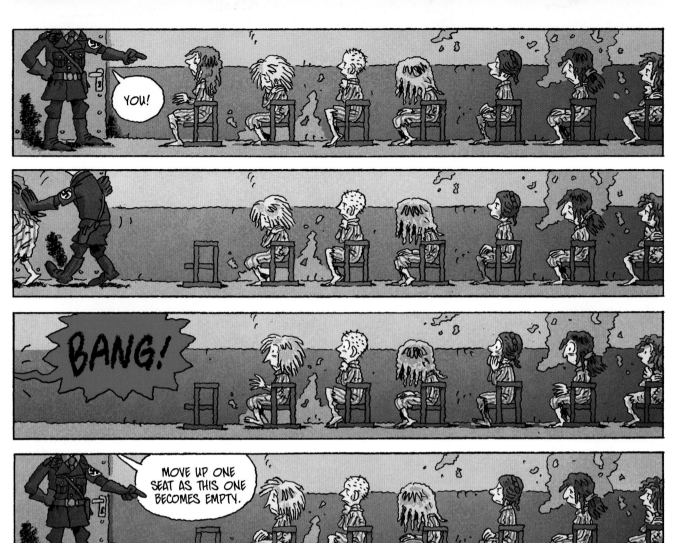

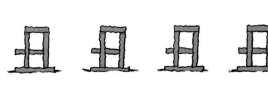

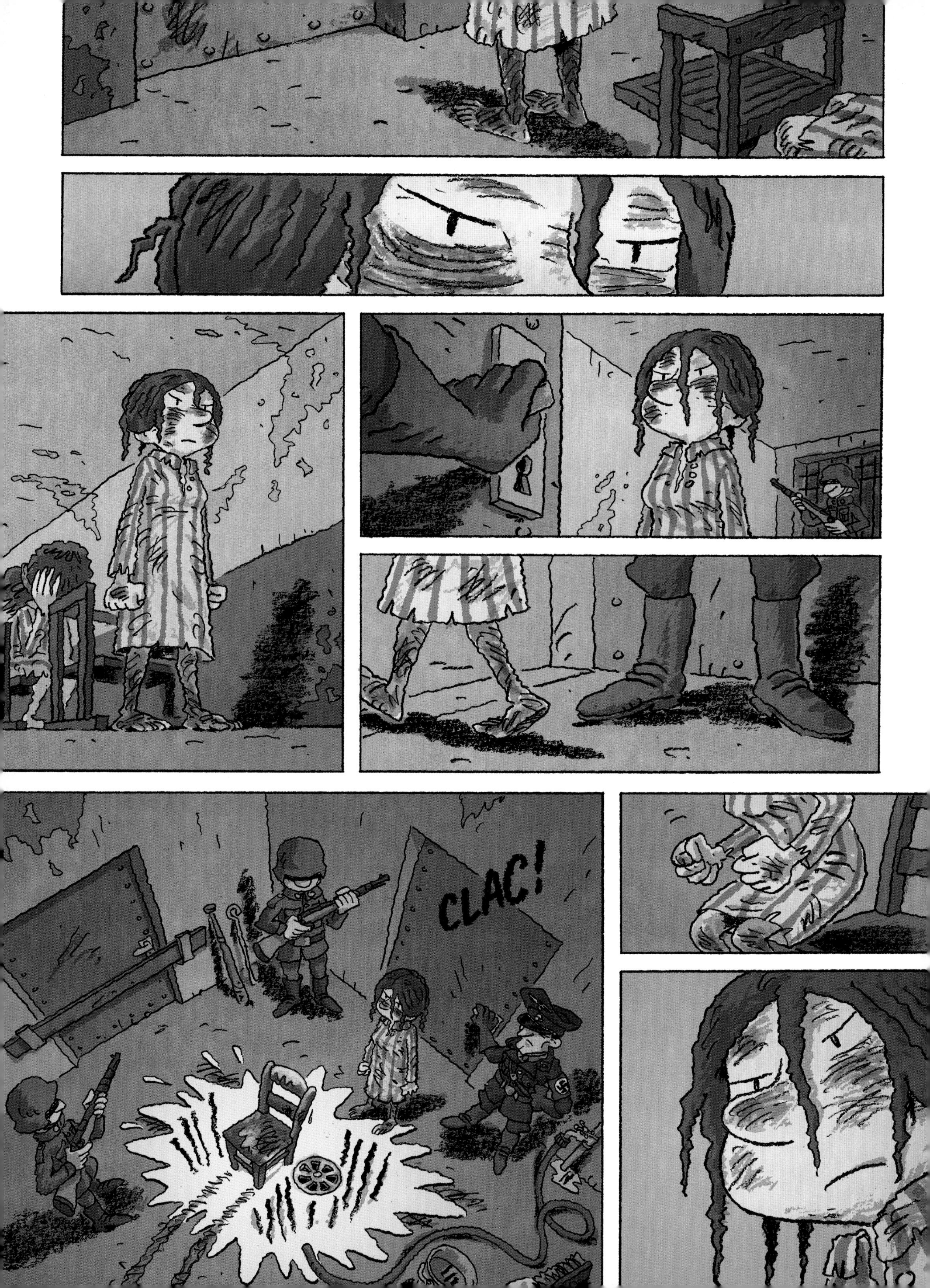
CLAC!

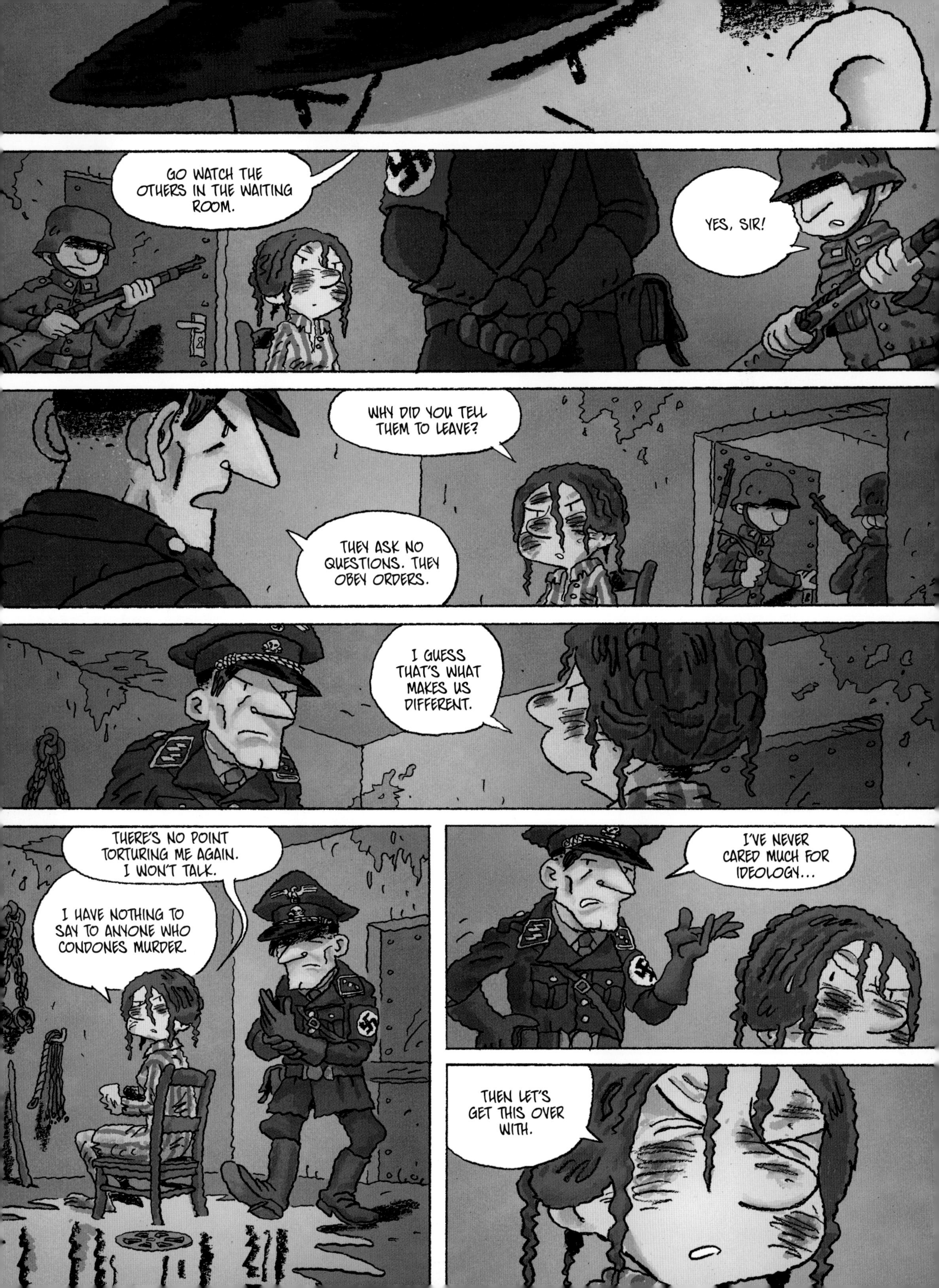
GO WATCH THE OTHERS IN THE WAITING ROOM.
YES, SIR!
WHY DID YOU TELL THEM TO LEAVE?
THEY ASK NO QUESTIONS. THEY OBEY ORDERS.
I GUESS THAT'S WHAT MAKES US DIFFERENT.
THERE'S NO POINT TORTURING ME AGAIN. I WON'T TALK.
I HAVE NOTHING TO SAY TO ANYONE WHO CONDONES MURDER.
I'VE NEVER CARED MUCH FOR IDEOLOGY...
THEN LET'S GET THIS OVER WITH.

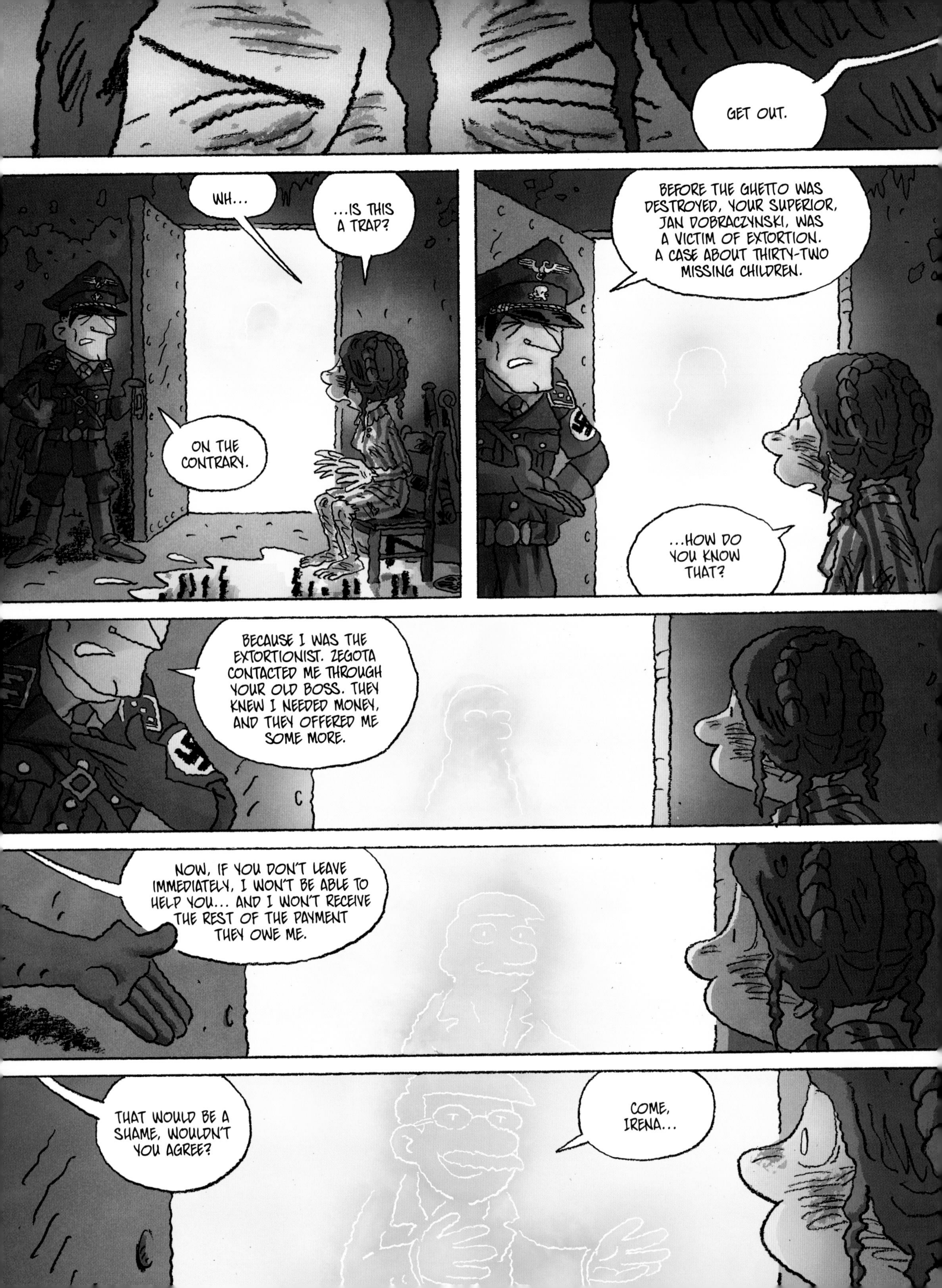
GET OUT.
WH...
...IS THIS A TRAP?
ON THE CONTRARY.
BEFORE THE GHETTO WAS DESTROYED, YOUR SUPERIOR, JAN DOBRACZYNSKI, WAS A VICTIM OF EXTORTION. A CASE ABOUT THIRTY-TWO MISSING CHILDREN.
...HOW DO YOU KNOW THAT?
BECAUSE I WAS THE EXTORTIONIST. ZEGOTA CONTACTED ME THROUGH YOUR OLD BOSS. THEY KNEW I NEEDED MONEY, AND THEY OFFERED ME SOME MORE.
NOW, IF YOU DON'T LEAVE IMMEDIATELY, I WON'T BE ABLE TO HELP YOU... AND I WON'T RECEIVE THE REST OF THE PAYMENT THEY OWE ME.
THAT WOULD BE A SHAME, WOULDN'T YOU AGREE?
COME, IRENA...

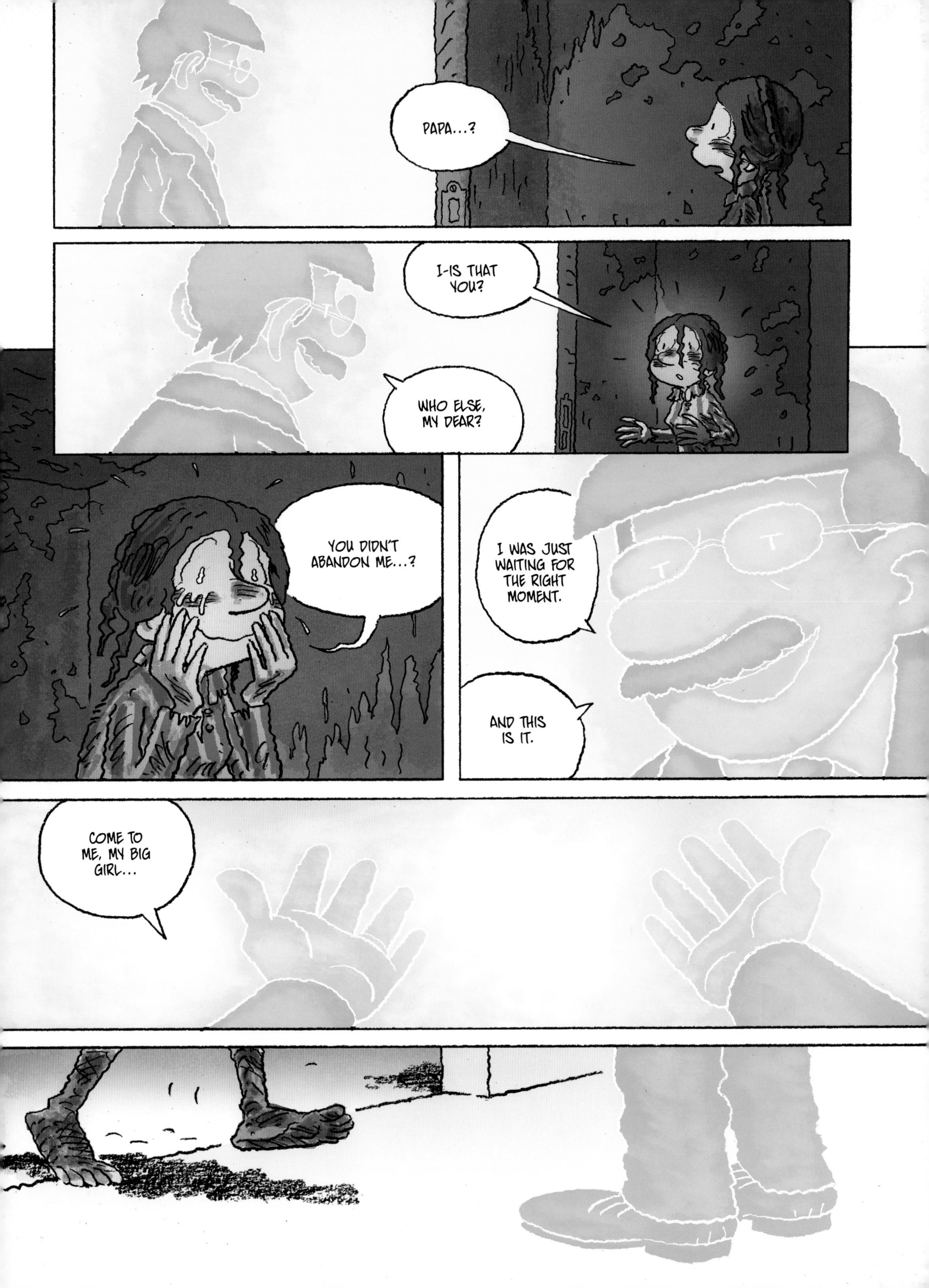
PAPA...?
I-IS THAT YOU?
WHO ELSE, MY DEAR?
YOU DIDN'T ABANDON ME...?
I WAS JUST WAITING FOR THE RIGHT MOMENT.
AND THIS IS IT.
COME TO ME, MY BIG GIRL...

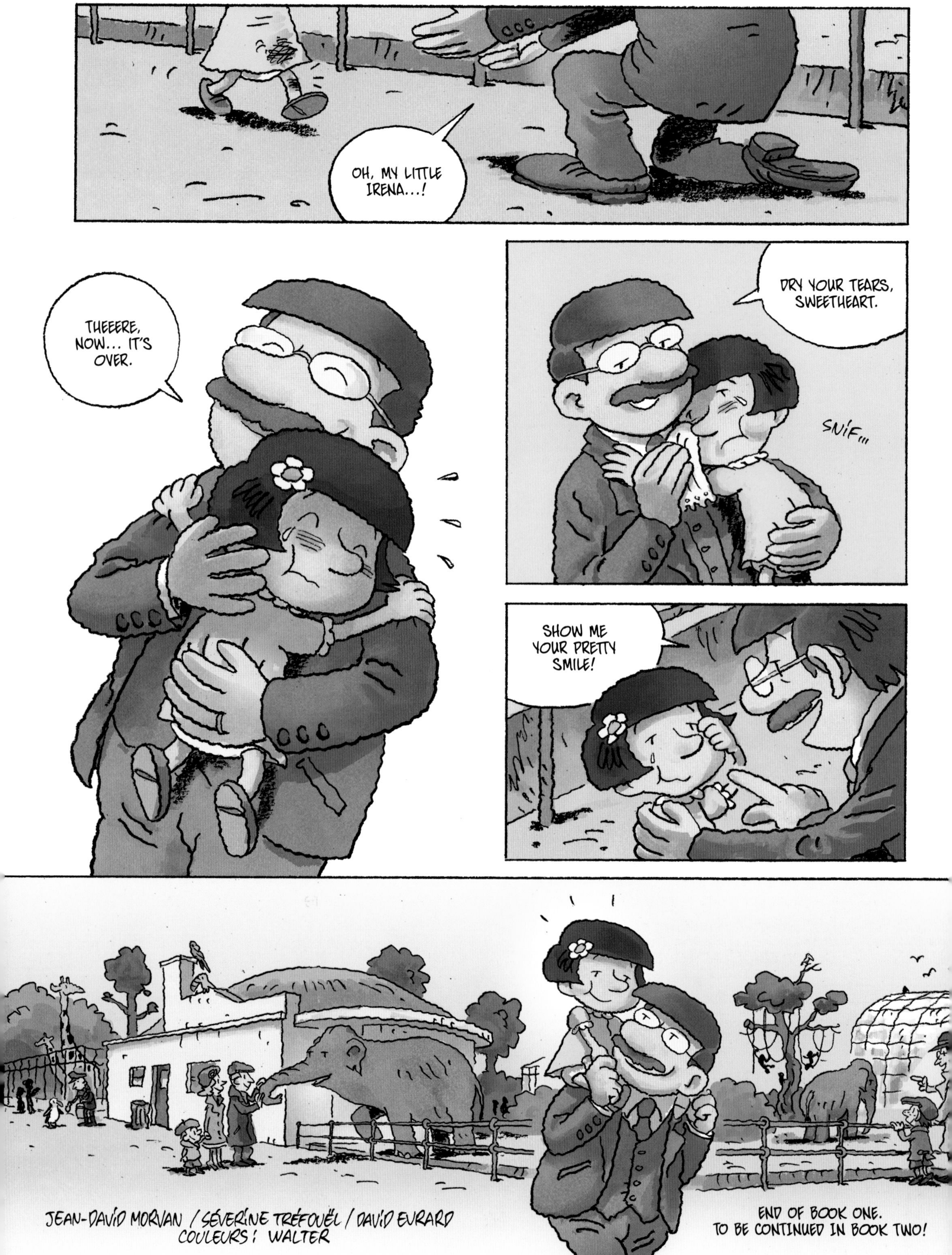
OH, MY LITTLE IRENA...!
THEEERE, NOW... IT'S OVER.
DRY YOUR TEARS, SWEETHEART.
SNIF...
SHOW ME YOUR PRETTY SMILE!
JEAN-DAVID MORVAN / SÉVERINE TRÉFOUËL / DAVID EVRARD
COULEURS : WALTER
END OF BOOK ONE.
TO BE CONTINUED IN BOOK TWO!

THE REAL Irena

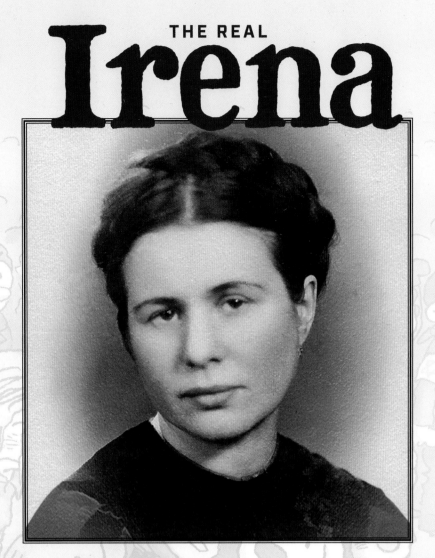

Irena Sendlerowa was born Irena Krzyzanowska in 1910 in Otwock, a small town in central Poland just a few miles southeast of the capital city of Warsaw. It was a very vibrant and friendly community of Jewish people, even though her family was Roman Catholic. Irena's father was a doctor and a humanitarian who offered free medical treatment to the poorest members of the population, regardless of their religion. He was a beloved member of the community, and he spread his sense of goodness to everyone he knew, including his daughter. But his selflessness soon got the best of him, and he contracted typhus from some of his patients during an outbreak. He died in 1917, when Irena was only seven years old. He had been so well respected, however, that the Jewish community offered to help Irena and her mother with financial assistance after his passing. They graciously refused, however, and went to live with family out in the country.

When Irena finished school at the age of 17, she went to the University of Warsaw. She studied law for two years before switching to Polish studies for another three years. She was very active in a variety of political and social clubs, including the Polish Democratic Youth Union and the Polish Socialist Party. She met an assistant professor named Mieczyslaw Sendlerowa, and they started dating. In 1931, the two were married.

Soon, the German army began to march across Europe, and Irena's husband was recruited into the Polish army. He was captured by the Germans during the Invasion of Poland in 1939, and soon the Germans had taken over most of the country, including Warsaw. But despite the presence of German soldiers everywhere, Irena continued to help people through her work with the Social Welfare Department.

In November 1940, the Germans gathered all the Jews in Warsaw – nearly 400,000 people – into a small portion of the city that became known as the Warsaw Ghetto. They locked the gates and patrolled the area like a large prison – no Jews were allowed to leave, and only authorized people were allowed to enter. Thousands died every month from starvation and disease. As a non-Jewish social worker, however, Irena was one of a few outsiders allowed inside. She was granted a special permit to check the grounds for typhus and to help contain the disease from spreading outside the ghetto. But she soon decided to use that special access to secretly help the people by smuggling out the innocent children trapped inside.

Slowly and carefully, she and a group of friends began sneaking children out of the ghetto, setting them up with new identities and temporary families. She wrote down each child's original name, new name, and new address on small slips of paper, so that she could one day reunite the children with their parents once the German Occupation had ended. To keep the children's new identity safe, she buried these pieces of paper inside of glass jars, which she would dig up once things were safe again.

Things became more dangerous in 1942, when the Germans began the gradual process of closing down the Ghetto as part of their "Great Action." That didn't mean letting the Jews free; it meant sending them in large groups to death camps. So in 1943, Irena joined a secret group called "Zegota," an underground resistance organization dedicated to helping the Jews in their time of crisis. It included Jewish- and non-Jewish members from many different political parties. Some of them were quite wealthy and influential, and soon they were helping Irena smuggle more and more children out of the Ghetto. But in October of that year, she was arrested by the Gestapo.

The Gestapo brutally interrogated her for information about Zegota, but she refused to betray her comrades or give up any of the children they had rescued. She was sent to Pawiak Prison and interrogated for several more months before eventually being scheduled for execution. Her life was saved, however, when the German guards escorting her let her go, thanks to bribes paid for by Zegota.

Irena refused to give up her mission. She returned to work as a nurse using the name Klara Dabrowska. In August of 1944, the Polish underground resistance led the Warsaw Uprising, fighting the German forces in hopes of driving them out of the city. Irena helped a number of Jews escape, hidden among other patients. Even though she was wounded by a German deserter searching for food, she continued her work until the Germans were driven out of Warsaw by Soviet troops in 1945.

After the war, Irena returned to social work and became head of the Department of Social Welfare in Warsaw. She and her colleagues dug up all of the jars with the names and locations of the hidden Jewish children and started looking for the parents. Unfortunately, almost all of them had been killed in one of the German death camps, or had simply gone missing. Since most of the children had been taken out of Poland by their new families, there wasn't much more she could do.

She spent the rest of her life working for various social groups, political parties, and health commissions. Her deeds were recognized by the Polish government, but not many others heard her story outside of her own country until 1983, when she was presented with a tree planted in her honor at the Garden of the Righteous Among the Nations in Jerusalem. Then, in 1991, she was made an honorary citizen of Israel, and received the Commander's Cross of the Order of Polonia Restituta, one of Poland's highest honors, in 1996. Her story was embraced worldwide in 1999 with a celebrated play and television movie helping bring global awareness of her bravery. She was nominated for the Nobel Peace Prize in both 2007 and 2008, among countless other commendations and praise.

She passed away on May 12th, 2008 at the age of 98.

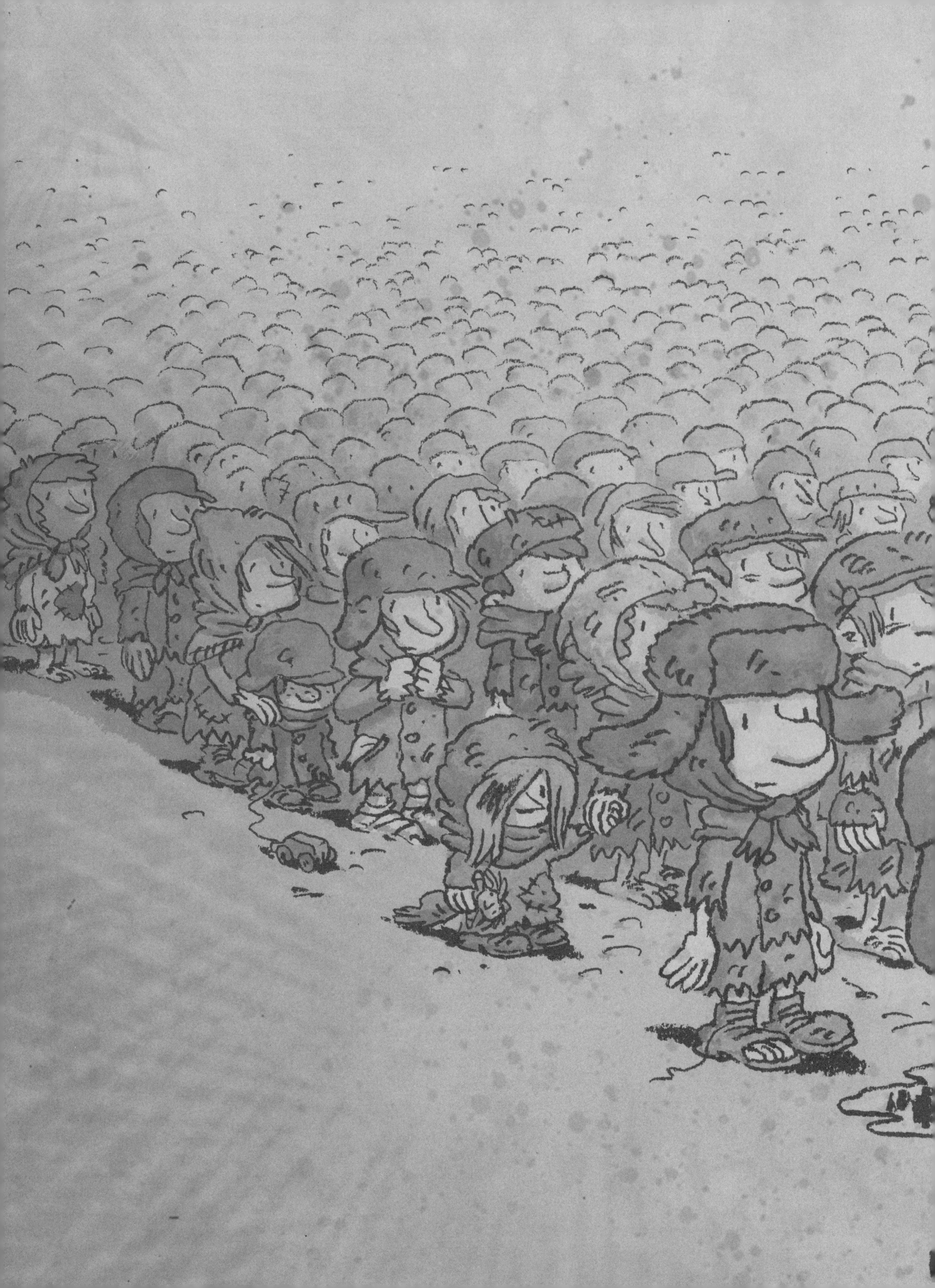